P9-CRG-264

Everything I Need to Know I Learned from a Children's Book

Everything Know I Lea a Childre

I Need to
rned from
n's Book

Life Lessons from Notable
People from All Walks of Life

Edited by Anita Silvey

Roaring Brook Press
New York

For my colleagues: the women and men who have created, published, taught about, promoted, and championed children's books over the years. They have made it possible for our children to find the right book at the right time.

Compilation copyright © 2009 by Anita Silvey

Published by Roaring Brook Press

Roaring Brook Press is a division of Holtzbrinck Publishing Holdings Limited Partnership

175 Fifth Avenue, New York, New York 10010

All rights reserved

Distributed in Canada by H. B. Fenn and Company Ltd.

Cataloging-in-Publication Data is available at the Library of Congress

ISBN: 978-1-59643-395-3

Roaring Brook Press books are available for special promotions and premiums.

For details contact: Director of Special Markets, Holtzbrinck Publishers.

First Edition October 2009

Book design by Edward Miller

Printed in October 2009 in the United States of America by Worzalla, Stevens Point, Wisconsin

10 9 8 7 6 5 4 3 2

Contents

Introduction

For almost forty years, I have been engaged in evaluating, lecturing about, and publishing children's books. In the process I have talked to thousands of people about books they remember from childhood; I've also read thousands of testimonies about the books that continue to resonate in people's lives. In *Everything I Need to Know I Learned from a Children's Book*, some of those accounts have been brought together. In this book 110 society leaders from various areas—science, politics, sports, and the arts—talk about a children's book that they loved and its impact on their lives. Funny, insightful, and inspiring, these stories testify to the amazing power of the right book for the right child—at the right time.

A single illustration from *Treasure Island* created by N.C. Wyeth made his son Andrew want to become a painter and inspired Robert Montgomery to become an actor. Sometimes a specific book sent an individual on a career path: Steve Wozniak of Apple Inc. read the Tom Swift books, knew he wanted to be an inventor, and eventually created Apple I and Apple II. Characters became role models; Jo March of *Little Women* inspired actress Julianne Moore, television commentator Judy Woodruff, and writer Bobbie Ann Mason. A book revealed a truth about the person's character, as *Mike Mulligan and His Steam Shovel* did for Jay Leno. At times single lines from a book have resonated for a lifetime: William DeVries, the cardiothoracic surgeon who implanted the first artificial heart, has thought about a statement from *The Wizard of* Oz all of his career— "I will bear all the unhappiness without a murmur, if you will give me a heart."

Some of these essays were written for the book, some adapted from statements already in print, and others came from interviews. They have been organized into six different sections: Inspiration, Understanding, Principles & Precepts, Vocation, Motivation, and Storytelling. Along with my notes about each book selected, an excerpt and often artwork from each title has been included. Although *Everything I Need to Know I Learned from a Children's Book* can be read straight through, it is also ideal for browsing. For the families it inspires, I have included at the end of the book a reading list, divided by age, and information on some books written by the contributors. Because the Children's Book Council has always provided important support for those creating new books for children, proceeds from this book will benefit the Children's Book Council Foundation, which supports Children's Book Week activities and the National Ambassador for Young People's Literature.

All of the essays reveal interesting details about the person who wrote them. Many of the people in this volume remember the name of their librarian or teacher, the bookstore they frequented, or the person who handed them a beloved book. When we give children books, we become part of their future, part of their most cherished memories, and part of their entire lives.

Children's books change lives. *Everything I Need to Know I Learned from a Children's Book* provides insight into how they do this. I hope the essays in this book will inspire you to find great books for the children in your life and move you to read to them. The act of reading to a child is the most important contribution to the future of our society that adults can make.

Anita Silvey
Westwood, Massachusetts

Inspiration

Today the challenge of political courage looms larger than ever before. For our everyday life is becoming so saturated with the tremendous power of mass communications that any unpopular or unorthodox course arouses a storm of protests such as John Quincy Adams—under attack in 1807—could never have envisioned. Our political life is becoming so expensive, so mechanized and so dominated by professional politicians and public relations men that the idealist who dreams of independent statesmanship is rudely awakened by the necessities of election and accomplishment.

And thus, in the days ahead, only the very courageous will be able to take the hard and unpopular decisions necessary for our survival in the struggle with a powerful enemy—an enemy with leaders who need give little thought to the popularity of their course, who need pay little tribute to the public opinion they themselves manipulate, and who may force, without fear of retaliation at the polls, their citizens to sacrifice present laughter for future glory. And only the very courageous will be able to keep alive the spirit of individualism and dissent which gave birth to this nation, nourished it as an infant and carried it through its severest tests upon the attainment of its maturity.

We shall need compromises in the days ahead, to be sure. But these will be, or should be, compromises of issues, not of principles. Compromises need not mean cowardice. Indeed it is frequently the compromisers and conciliators who are faced with the severest tests of political courage as they oppose the extremist views of their constituents. It was because Daniel Webster conscientiously favored compromise in 1850 that he earned a condemnation unsurpassed in the annals of political history.

His is a story worth remembering today. So, I believe, are the stories of the other Senators of courage—men whose abiding loyalty to their nations triumphed over all personal and political considerations, men who showed the real meaning of courage and a real faith in democracy, men who made the Senate of the United States something more than a mere collection of robots dutifully recording the views of their constituents, or a gathering of time-servers skilled only in predicting and following the tides of public sentiment. Whatever their differences, the American politicians whose stories are here retold shared that one heroic quality—courage. In the pages that follow, I have attempted to set forth their lives—the ideals they lived for and the principles they fought for, their virtues and their sins, their dreams and their disillusionments, the praise they earned and the abuse they endured. All this may be set down on the printed page. It is ours to write about, it is ours to read about. But there was in the lives of each of these men something that it is difficult for the printed page to capture—and yet something that has reached the homes and enriched the heritage of every citizen in every part of the land.

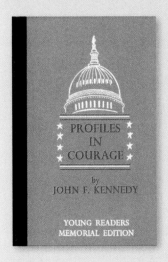

PROFILES IN COURAGE, YOUNG READERS MEMORIAL EDITION

by John F. Kennedy

Over the years many popular works of adult nonfiction have been successfully adapted for a younger readership and issued in a young people's version. Recently both James Bradley's *Flags of Our Fathers* and Nathaniel Philbrick's *In the Heart of the Sea* (called *Revenge of the Whale*) were streamlined to create compelling narratives for a younger audience. John F. Kennedy's Pulitzer Prize–winning *Profiles in Courage* was released in a Young Readers Edition, which contained illustrations by Emil Weiss. Kennedy himself wrote an introduction to the volume, describing his book as one "about politicians who were failures." But, of course, the book also shows the principles and ideals of the historical figures Kennedy brings so vividly to life—John Quincy Adams, Thomas Hart Benton, Daniel Webster, Sam Houston, Edmund G. Ross, Lucius Quintus Cincinnatus Lamar, George Norris, and Robert A. Taft.

Profiles in Courage, either in the original or the Young Readers Edition, shaped a generation in the 1960s who were becoming adults. Just as Kennedy attracted young voters to his side in his race for the presidency, he delivered a message in this book that fit into the moral vision and idealism of teenagers. Critic and children's book historian Leonard S. Marcus found this book in 1961.

Leonard Marcus
The courage to stand up for my beliefs and the courage to write

The first book I recall asking my parents for was the Young Readers Edition of John F. Kennedy's *Profiles in Courage*. Harper & Brothers released the illustrated, abridged edition of the Pulitzer Prize winner in January of 1961, in time for the presidential inauguration, and I wanted a copy as soon as I heard about it. I was ten, and a history buff, and I had campaigned for Kennedy by distributing leaflets in my neighborhood. I had done so not at my parents' urging but because after studying the saucy caricatures of all the candidates on the cover of *Mad*, I had simply decided—as though it were the most obvious thing in the world to do—to get involved in the election and to throw my support behind JFK.

Profiles in Courage's idealistic message of sticking to principle regardless of the consequences appealed greatly to my ten-year-old sense of idealism and high purpose. Even more powerful for me than the theme of Kennedy's book, however, was the mere fact that the president of the United States had written it. The only other president I knew anything about from firsthand observation, Dwight Eisenhower, had been little more to me than a kindly, balding television grandfather figure. I now saw that a president could also be a vibrant young man, and (even better) that he could be a writer, too—just as I dreamed of being one day. When in his inaugural address President Kennedy declared that the "torch" had been "passed to a new generation," I was sure that he was talking about my generation as well as his own. As I grew older, the courage I continued to draw from his treasured book was equally the courage to stand up for my beliefs and the courage to write.

"The greater part of these dishes are unknown to you," he said to me. "However, you may partake of them without fear. They are wholesome and nourishing. For a long time I have renounced the food of the earth, and I am never ill now. My crew, who are healthy, are fed on the same food."

"So," said I, "all these eatables are the produce of the sea?"

"Yes, Professor, the sea supplies all my wants. Sometimes I cast my nets in tow, and I draw them in ready to break. Sometimes I hunt in the midst of this element, which appears to be inaccessible to man, and quarry the game which dwells in my submarine forests. My flocks, like those of Neptune's old shepherds, graze fearlessly in the immense prairies of the ocean. I have a vast property there, which I cultivate myself, and which is always sown by the hand of the Creator of all things."

"I can understand perfectly, sir, that your nets furnish excellent fish for your table; I can understand also that you hunt aquatic game in your submarine forests; but I cannot understand at all how a particle of meat, no matter how small, can figure in your bill of fare."

"This, which you believe to be meat, Professor, is nothing else than fillet of turtle. Here are also some dolphins' livers, which you take to be ragout of pork. My cook is a clever fellow, who excels in dressing these various products of the ocean. Taste all these dishes. Here is a preserve of sea-cucumber, which a Malay would declare to be unrivalled in the world; here is a cream, of which the milk has been furnished by the cetacea, and the sugar by the great fucus of the North Sea; and, lastly, permit me to offer you some preserve of anemones, which is equal to that of the most delicious fruits."

I tasted, more from curiosity than as a connoisseur, whilst Captain Nemo enchanted me with his extraordinary stories.

"You like the sea, Captain?"

"Yes; I love it! The sea is everything. It covers seven tenths of the terrestrial globe. Its breath is pure and healthy. It is an immense desert, where man is never lonely, for he feels life stirring on all sides. The sea is only the embodiment of a supernatural and wonderful existence. It is nothing but love and emotion; it is the `Living Infinite,' as one of your poets has said. In fact, Professor, Nature manifests herself in it by her three kingdoms—mineral, vegetable, and animal. The sea is the vast reservoir of Nature. The globe began with sea, so to speak; and who knows if it will not end with it? In it is supreme tranquillity. The sea does not belong to despots. Upon its surface men can still exercise unjust laws, fight, tear one another to pieces, and be carried away with terrestrial horrors. But at thirty feet below its level, their reign ceases, their influence is quenched, and their power disappears. Ah! sir, live—live in the bosom of the waters! There only is independence! There I recognize no masters! There I am free!"

Captain Nemo suddenly became silent in the midst of this enthusiasm, by which he was quite carried away. For a few moments he paced up and down, much agitated. Then he became more calm, regained his accustomed coldness of expression, and turning towards me: "Now, Professor," said he, "if you wish to go over the *Nautilus*, I am at your service."

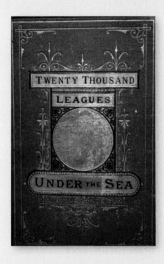

TWENTY THOUSAND LEAGUES UNDER THE SEA

by Jules Verne

Published in 1870, Jules Verne's science-fiction masterpiece *Twenty Thousand Leagues Under the Sea* reads like one of the page-turning, plot-driven novels for children of the twenty-first century. If living, Verne might compare writing notes with J. K. Rowling.

Professor Aronnax of the Paris Museum of Natural History presents a first-person narrative of an amazing ten-month period in which he traveled twenty thousand leagues in the oceans of Earth. Setting out with an American crew to find a mythical narwhal that has been damaging ships, the professor discovers an entirely different universe. The monster is the *Nautilus*, the submarine of the enigmatic Captain Nemo. Taken on board with two other prisoners, the professor delights in living on this completely self-sustaining vessel. They observe sunken ships, retrieve treasures from the sea floor, walk on the bottom of the sea, battle giant squids, and even examine the lost continent of Atlantis. Part science, part thriller, the story revolves around the mounting tension as the prisoners seek to escape their captor.

Dr. Robert Ballard, who located the wreck of the *Titanic*, discovered Jules Verne, Captain Nemo, and his own obsession at the age of ten.

Robert Ballard

All of us have dreams; all of us should try to live those dreams.

When I was about ten years old, my favorite book was Jules Verne's *Twenty Thousand Leagues Under the Sea*. My hero was Captain Nemo. I wanted to be inside his ship, the *Nautilus*. He built his own submarine, using advanced technology. He was a technologist but also an adventurer. Through a giant window, he examined the sea.

I wanted to be an undersea explorer. Fortunately, when I told my parents, they didn't laugh at me. They actually encouraged me. They said, "Maybe you need to become an oceanographer, if you want to become a Captain Nemo." So I became an oceanographer. Then my parents said, "Maybe you need to become a naval officer," and I did.

What am I today? A high-tech, modern-day Captain Nemo. Absolutely no doubt about it. I'm doing now exactly what he was doing, what I wanted to do, after I read *Twenty Thousand Leagues Under the Sea*. All kids have marvelous images of what they want to do. But then society often tells them they can't do it. I believe all of us have dreams; all of us should try to live those dreams.

The Time Traveller (for so it will be convenient to speak of him) was expounding a recondite matter to us. His grey eyes shone and twinkled, and his unusually pale face was flushed and animated. The fire burned brightly, and the soft radiance of the incandescent lights in the lilies of silver caught the bubbles that flashed and passed in our glasses. Our chairs, being his patents, embraced and caressed us rather than submitted to be sat upon, and there was that luxurious after-dinner atmosphere when thought runs gracefully free of the trammels of precision. And he put it to us in this way—marking the points with a lean forefinger—as we sat and lazily admired his earnestness over this new paradox (as we thought it:) and his fecundity.

"You must follow me carefully. I shall have to controvert one or two ideas that are almost universally accepted. The geometry, for instance, they taught you at school is founded on a misconception."

"Is not that rather a large thing to expect us to begin upon?" said Filby, an argumentative person with red hair.

"I do not mean to ask you to accept anything without reasonable ground for it. You will soon admit as much as I need from you. You know of course that a mathematical line, a line of thickness nil, has no real existence. They taught you that? Neither has a mathematical plane. These things are mere abstractions."

"That is all right," said the Psychologist.

"Nor, having only length, breadth, and thickness, can a cube have a real existence."

"There I object," said Filby. "Of course a solid body may exist. All real things—"

"So most people think. But wait a moment. Can an instantaneous cube exist?"

"Don't follow you," said Filby.

"Can a cube that does not last for any time at all, have a real existence?"

Filby became pensive. "Clearly," the Time Traveller proceeded, "any real body must have extension in four directions: it must have Length, Breadth, Thickness, and—Duration. But through a natural infirmity of the flesh, which I will explain to you in a moment, we incline to overlook this fact. There are really four dimensions, three which we call the three planes of Space, and a fourth, Time. There is, however, a tendency to draw an unreal distinction between the former three dimensions and the latter, because it happens that our consciousness moves intermittently in one direction along the latter from the beginning to the end of our lives."

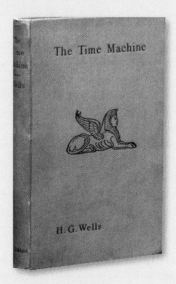

THE TIME MACHINE

by H. G. Wells

In 1895, with the publication of *The Time Machine*, a heretofore unknown journalist, Herbert George Wells, leapt into fame and fortune. After seven years of writing, he produced a short, novella-length manuscript, initially serialized in *The New Review*. For a public fascinated with the possibilities of science and mathematics, Wells's view of the future shocked their sensibilities. Influenced by Darwin, Hawthorne, Edgar Allen Poe, and contemporary scientific inquiry, Wells crafted a story that initially makes the reader believe they are witnessing a utopian society—only to discover that it is actually a dystopian world.

In *The Time Machine* an unnamed scientist invents the means to travel in time. At the beginning, he alerts a group of gentlemen about his experiments; then placing himself in his time machine, he travels to the year 802,701. Here he finds a peaceful, pastoral community of the Eloi—lovely, childlike, and without aggression. But eventually, to his horror, he realizes they can live without working because toiling underground are the cannibal Morlocks that control the planet. Barely escaping the Morlocks, the time traveler catapults himself thirty million years into the future, only to witness the end of the Earth.

Adapted for movies, documentaries, even classic comics, *The Time Machine*, not intentionally written for children, has continued to intrigue adults and children alike. Currently several theoretical physicists believe time travel to be possible. The journey of one of these scientists, Dr. Ronald L. Mallett, Professor at the University of Connecticut, began when he read *The Time Machine* as a child.

Ronald Mallett
Inspiration that shaped my life

When I was ten years old, my father died of a heart attack at the age of thirty-three. Mourning the loss of him, I became increasingly isolated. Not interested in games, sports, or socializing, I escaped into magazines, books, and movies, many of them fantasy and science fiction.

Just about a year after my father died, I came across *The Time Machine*, first as Illustrated Comics Edition #133. Since I wanted to read more about the time traveler, I went to the public library and took out Wells's original book. I needed a dictionary for even the first sentence: "The Time Traveller (for so it will be convenient to speak of him) was expounding a recondite matter to us." But I was mesmerized by Wells's vision of time: "If Time is really only a fourth dimension of Space, why is it, and why has it always been, regarded as something different? And why cannot we move in Time as we move about in the other dimensions of Space?"

I decided that if I could build a time machine, I could go back and see my father and warn him about the dangers to his health. So building a time machine became an obsession for me, and I read that book again and again to get clues about how to do this. That obsession kept me from going into a total depression—because I had an inspiration.

My life then became shaped by books, one after another. Today as someone in physics, I am working on the possibilities of time travel. I now know that the right book at the right time saved me—and it gave me direction for the rest of my life.

One of the nice little gusts of wind rushed down the walk, and it was a stronger one than the rest. It was strong enough to wave the branches of the trees, and it was more than strong enough to sway the trailing sprays of untrimmed ivy hanging from the wall. Mary had stepped close to the robin, and suddenly the gust of wind swung aside some loose ivy trails, and more suddenly still she jumped toward it and caught it in her hand. This she did because she had seen something under it—a round knob which had been covered by the leaves hanging over it. It was the knob of a door.

She put her hands under the leaves and began to pull and push them aside. Thick as the ivy hung, it nearly all was a loose and swinging curtain, though some had crept over wood and iron. Mary's heart began to thump and her hands to shake a little in her delight and excitement. The robin kept singing and twittering away and tilting his head on one side, as if he were as excited as she was. What was this under her hands which was square and made of iron and which her fingers found a hole in?

It was the lock of the door which had been closed ten years and she put her hand in her pocket, drew out the key and found it fitted the keyhole. She put the key in and turned it. It took two hands to do it, but it did turn.

And then she took a long breath and looked behind her up the long walk to see if any one was coming. No one was coming. No one ever did come, it seemed, and she took another long breath, because she could not help it, and she held back the swinging curtain of ivy and pushed back the door which opened, slowly—slowly.

Then she slipped through it, and shut it behind her, and stood with her back against it, looking about her and breathing quite fast with excitement, and wonder, and delight.

She was standing inside the secret garden.

THE SECRET GARDEN by Frances Hodgson Burnett, illustrated by Tasha Tudor

By FRANCES HODGSON BURNETT
Illustrated by TASHA TUDOR

THE SECRET GARDEN

by Frances Hodgson Burnett

Frances Hodgson Burnett, the J. K. Rowling of her day, enjoyed an audience of both adults and children for all of her best-selling books. In her lifetime everyone believed she had written a masterpiece in *Little Lord Fauntleroy*, a book that caused a fashion craze—young boys wearing suits patterned after the Little Lord. But *The Secret Garden*, a quieter book of Burnett's, unmentioned in her *New York Times* obituary, grew in importance after she died and has become her contemporary legacy.

When Mary Lennox becomes an orphan because of a cholera epidemic, she is sent to Misselthwaite Manor, an isolated country estate in Yorkshire, England. Left mostly alone, she explores her environment and becomes curious about a walled garden, now locked away. Eventually, Mary finds the key, opens the garden, and brings Dickon, a servant's brother, and Colin, her uncle's sickly child, into the mysterious place. Published in 1911 and considered the first modern children's novel, the book features two initially unattractive protagonists, Colin and Mary, who become better human beings as they transform the garden into a beautiful place. Mary's cry in this book, "Might I have a bit of earth?" continues to speak to anyone who wants to dig in the ground and bring forth life.

Newbery Award winner Katherine Paterson found *The Secret Garden* as a child and continues to reinterpret its meaning as she moves through the stages of her life. Librarian Pat Scales discovered a reason to read when she picked up the book at age eight.

Katherine Paterson
A sense of wonder

In trying to say what reading *The Secret Garden* meant to me as a child, I find myself awash in feelings that do not easily translate into words. *What was the gift of this magical book?* I ask myself. Then I realize that it was wonder—not the kind of wonder that fantasy evokes, but the wonder of the natural world when I take the time to look. Frances Hodgson Burnett taught me to marvel that a shriveled brown bulb can produce a tulip, that dead sticks can give birth to roses, and that even people, shriveled by illness and deadened by grief, can still blossom. Her book helped me to see the miracle of new life bursting forth from apparent death.

In *The Sense of Wonder*, Rachel Carson says: "If I had influence with the good fairy who is supposed to preside over the christening of all children, I should ask that her gift to each child in the world be a sense of wonder so indestructible that it would last throughout life, as an unfailing antidote against the boredom and disenchantments of later years, the sterile preoccupation with things that are artificial, the alienation from the sources of our strength." This was surely the gift *The Secret Garden* gave to me as a child, and although I'm no good fairy, it is a gift I seek to share.

Pat Scales
A sense of courage

When I was six years old and in first grade, my parents promised me a bicycle if I would learn to read. I don't know if I was rebelling against Dick, Jane, and Sally, or why my parents thought that I needed to be bribed to read. I got the bicycle, and by the end of my first-grade year nothing could stop me from reading. There was no bookstore in my small Alabama town, and the library had a limited collection of books for children—the Bobbsey Twins, Nancy Drew, and Childhood of Famous Americans series. But the book that had the greatest impact on me was *The Secret Garden* by Frances Hodgson Burnett. I loved the idea of Mary Lennox being a stranger in a rambling estate like Misselthwaite Manor in Yorkshire, England. I even thought that it would be exciting to be an orphan like her, a lonely child who was an outsider in a bizarre and mysterious household. I pretended that the hedge in my backyard was the entrance to an overgrown garden that had possibilities of becoming something beautiful.

There was no Colin in my life. But there was a girl in my class who had polio. She was the only handicapped person in my school, and we were fascinated with her circumstances. For a while, everyone wanted a turn at pushing her wheelchair or carrying her books. But she was a bit sour and disagreeable like Colin, and she learned at a very young age to use her handicap to get sympathy. As we grew older, no one in my class wanted to deal with her anymore. She was simply too demanding. I remember thinking that she needed someone like Mary to give her something beautiful. She needed a garden filled with sweet-smelling roses and a variety of fragrant flowers. She needed a Mary to show her courage.

I have committed to memory every scene in *The Secret Garden*. I know exactly where I was when I read that book. I remember not wanting anyone to interrupt me while I was reading, and I remember hoping that the book would never end. And, to this day, when I come upon a rusted garden gate, I believe that Mary, Dickon, and Colin are on the other side of that gate—secretly turning the garden into something beautiful.

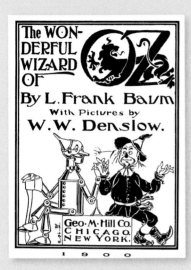

THE WONDERFUL WIZARD OF OZ

by L. Frank Baum,
illustrated by W. W. Denslow

In many cases, people who read a book and then see a movie always say, "The film wasn't as good as the book." But in some cases, such as *The Wizard of Oz*, people often love the movie as much as the book. Not only was the 1939 movie starring Judy Garland a critical and commercial success, it took the best qualities of the book and brought them to life. In the case of Baum's 1900 title, the author's greatest strengths lay in the plot and the imaginative world of Oz that he envisioned.

A tornado on the Kansas plains lifts Dorothy with her dog, Toto, and part of their house to the Land of Oz, where everything is lush and green. When the house lands, it kills the Wicked Witch of the East, and Dorothy takes the witch's silver slippers as her own. Then, with Toto, she sets off on the yellow brick road to see the wonderful Wizard, who may be able to get her back to Kansas. Along the way, she meets the Scarecrow who needs a brain, the Tin Man who desires a heart, and the Cowardly Lion who longs for courage. Before the Wizard grants their wishes, he sends them to kill the Wicked Witch of the West. Even before they accomplish this task, these characters exhibit brains, heart, and courage as they go along. Although a humbug, the Wizard actually provides the answers needed by everyone. In *The Wizard of Oz*, Baum wanted to create a modern American fairy tale. He succeeded brilliantly, and the book and its characters have entered into American culture and

(continued on page 15)

William C. DeVries

"For my part, I will bear all the unhappiness without a murmur, if you will give me a heart."

One of the first books my mother introduced me to was *The Wizard of Oz*. I read all of the books in the series and was very impressed by them. I particularly liked the Tin Woodman. In the book, the Wizard of Oz talks to the Tin Woodman about whether or not he really wants a heart. The Wizard believes that having a heart is not such a good thing: "It makes most people unhappy." But the Tin Woodman says, "For my part, I will bear all the unhappiness without a murmur, if you will give me a heart." In my work, I have thought about those lines many, many times.

"How about my heart?" asked the Tin Woodman.

"Why, as for that," answered Oz, "I think you are wrong to want a heart. It makes most people unhappy. If you only knew it, you are in luck not to have a heart."

"That must be a matter of opinion," said the Tin Woodman. "For my part, I will bear all the unhappiness without a murmur, if you will give me a heart."

"Very well," answered Oz meekly. "Come to me tomorrow and you shall have a heart. I have played Wizard for so many years that I may as well continue a little longer."

"And now," said Dorothy, "how am I to get back to Kansas?"

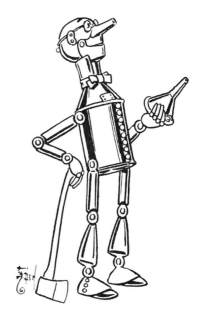

"We shall have to think about that," replied the little man. "Give me two or three days to consider the matter and I'll try to find a way to carry you over the desert. In the meantime you shall all be treated as my guests, and while you live in the Palace my people will wait upon you and obey your slightest wish. There is only one thing I ask in return for my help—such as it is. You must keep my secret and tell no one I am a humbug."

They agreed to say nothing of what they had learned, and went back to their rooms in high spirits. Even Dorothy had hope that "The Great and Terrible Humbug," as she called him, would find a way to send her back to Kansas, and if he did she was willing to forgive him everything.

THE WIZARD OF OZ by L. Frank Baum, illustrated by W.W. Denslow

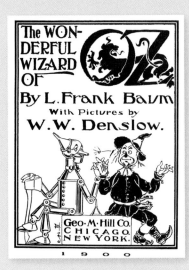

become part of our literary landscape. *Wicked*, Gregory Maguire's clever adaptation of the story, remains a long-running Broadway hit—and the movie a cherished film icon. But for Dr. William C. DeVries, the cardiothoracic surgeon who performed the first successful permanent artificial heart implantation, the book provided another kind of inspiration. Scholar Michael Patrick Hearn, author of *The Annotated Wizard of Oz*, has devoted a lifetime of study to Oz.

Michael Patrick Hearn

Brains, heart, and courage— the brains, heart, and courage within me

It was my sister's fault. She brought the Oz books home before I was old enough to check them out of the library myself. I was hooked from the start.

The Wizard of Oz was not the first or the last of the Oz books I read. But it was the best. The opening paragraphs about Dorothy's dull, gray life on the great, gray prairie did not prepare me for what immediately lay ahead. The violent upheaval of the Kansas cyclone introduced me to the unforgettable power of literature. The vivid image of Dorothy in danger at the very center of this natural disaster still haunts me. Then there was the welcome quiet after the storm when the cyclone landed her house very gently—for a cyclone—in that extraordinary land somewhere over the rainbow.

The writing of *The Wizard of* Oz was as clear-eyed and focused as the little heroine herself. Baum's quiet, reassuring voice was never intrusive. Like all masters of English prose, he knew exactly what to say. Baum was so convincing to me that he was not telling a story. He was relating history. He never distracted me with stylistic tricks or gratuitous commentary. He possessed a gift for providing the telling detail that brought a character, place, or incident vividly to life. He was sure to explain step by step exactly how Dorothy and her companions overcame one hardship after another. There was always something marvelous and unexpected around every curve of the yellow brick road. Something that seemed insignificant earlier in the story often turned up later to be of the utmost importance. Just as it appeared that Dorothy's journey might be winding down, Baum threw in some new twist in the plot that kept it moving swiftly along. I could not stop reading.

I never felt I was Dorothy, but I saw the new world of Oz through her bright, innocent eyes just as she was discovering it. I identified with the Scarecrow who thought he was stupid but was really quite smart. He turned out to be "the wisest man in all the Land of Oz." Whenever someone called me "stupid," I always reminded myself of the Scarecrow. I knew the truth about him and about myself. I longed for friends like the tenderhearted Tin Woodman and the not so Cowardly Lion. I knew we, too, could conquer all wicked witches and unmask the humbug wizards of the world.

Oz was not the real world, but it prepared me for the disasters and disappointments that lay ahead. I have always allowed myself to be guided by brains, heart, and courage—the brains, heart, and courage within me—just as the Scarecrow, the Tin Woodman, and the Cowardly Lion did. And I continue to battle the wicked witches and unmask the humbug wizards of this world.

The wind, with a wild cry, slipped under the umbrella, pressing it upwards as though trying to force it out of Mary Poppins's hand. But she held on tightly, and that, apparently, was what the wind wanted her to do, for presently it lifted the umbrella higher into the air and Mary Poppins from the ground. It carried her lightly so that her toes just grazed along the garden path. Then it lifted her over the front gate and swept her upwards towards the branches of the cherry-trees in the Lane.

"She's going, Jane, she's going!" cried Michael, weeping.

"Quick!" cried Jane. "Let us get the Twins. They must see the last of her." She had no doubt now, nor had Michael, that Mary Poppins had gone for good because the wind had changed.

They each seized a Twin and rushed back to the window.

Mary Poppins was in the upper air now, floating away over the cherry-trees and the roofs of the houses, holding tightly to the umbrella with one hand and to the carpet bag with the other.

The Twins began to cry quietly.

With their free hands Jane and Michael opened the window and made one last effort to stay Mary Poppins's flight.

"Mary Poppins!" They cried. "Mary Poppins, come back!"

But she either did not hear or deliberately took no notice. For she went sailing on and on, up into the cloudy, whistling air, till at last she was wafted away over the hill and the children could see nothing but the trees bending and moaning under the wild west wind. . . .

MARY POPPINS by P. L. Travers, illustrated by Mary Shepard

MARY POPPINS

by P. L. Travers,
illustrated by Mary Shepard

A serious journalist and writer, P. L. Travers grew up in Australia, came under the spell of George Russell (who wrote under the pen name Æ) in Ireland, traveled in the early 1930s to the Soviet Union, and spent her adult life in London. Along with the effects of this travel on her writing, the spiritual influences of the East also informed her most famous books, the series about the nanny Mary Poppins, because Travers became a follower of the mystic Gurdjieff.

In *Mary Poppins*, the nanny Mary Poppins arrives at Number Seventeen Cherry Tree Lane, blown in by a strong east wind, carrying a carpetbag. She takes charge of the four Banks children and creates a series of incredible outings. She levitates everyone so that they can have a tea party on the ceiling, glues stars to the sky, and dances under the full moon at the zoo. Like Dr. Doolittle, she can even talk to the animals. Mysterious, vain, salty, unsentimental, and acerbic, this nanny never admits to the children that anything unusual might have happened.

In fact, Mary Poppins in the book bears no resemblance to the same character created in the Hollywood movie, starring Dick van Dyke and Julie Andrews. Fortunately *New York Times* best-selling novelist Anita Diamant discovered the real Mary Poppins as a child.

Anita Diamant

Being a free spirit— the best magic of all

When I was a child, one of my favorite books was *Mary Poppins*. Hollywood turned her into a cream puff in the movie, and her name now conjures up the image of a perfect nanny—a woman who sweetly charms and pacifies her charges. But children who read the Pamela Travers series know that Mary Poppins is, in fact, opinionated, sharp of tongue, and not always nice. However, she is a good egg and, much more important, a witch with a magic satchel and knowledge of secret doorways into the many enchanted places hidden in plain sight throughout London.

Travers had a light touch for the supernatural: newborn babies who could converse with the wind, sunbeams, and birds; an ancient candy-store owner whose self-regenerating fingers are made of barley sugar. But Mary Poppins herself was the best magic of all: a free spirit who comes and goes as she sees fit; a well-traveled person with a fabulous past; an ordinary-looking woman who adores her own appearance and whose self-regard is as unassailable as the Himalayas. She was all that and more. I never wanted Mary Poppins to be my nanny. I wanted to be Mary Poppins when I grew up.

There stood an enormous bird. David had been to the zoo, and at home he had a book of birds with colored pictures. He knew the more common large birds of the world: the ostrich, the condor, the albatross, eagles, cranes, storks. But this bird—! Its shape was like that of an eagle, but stouter. Its neck had the length and elegant curve of a swan's neck. Its head was again like an eagle's, with a hooked bird-of-prey beak, but the expression in its brown eyes was mild. The long wings were blunt at the tips, the tail was short and broad. The legs, feathered halfway down, ended in taloned feet. An iridescent sheen sparkled on its plumage, reflecting sunlight from the scarlet crest, the golden neck and back, the breast of silver, the sapphire wings and tail. Its size alone would have been enough to take David's breath away. He could have stood beneath the arch of that neck with room to spare.

But the most astonishing thing was that the bird had an open book on the ground and was apparently trying to learn part of it by heart.

"Vivo, vives, vive," the bird read, very slowly and distinctly, staring hard at the book. "Vivimos, vivis, viven. That is simple enough, you blockhead! Now, then, without looking." It cleared its throat, looked away from the book, and repeated in a rapid mutter: "Vivo vives vi—ah—vivi—oh, dear, what is the matter with me?" Here the temptation to peek overcame it for an instant, and its head wavered.

But it said, "No, no!" in a firm tone, looked carefully the other way, and began once more.

"Vivo, vives, vive—quite correct so far. Ah—vi—ah—Oh, dear, these verbs! Where was I? Oh, yes. Vivo—"

David's head reeled as he watched this amazing performance. There was no need to pinch himself to see if he were dreaming: he was perfectly wide awake. Everything else around him was behaving in a normal way. The mountain was solid beneath him, the sunlight streamed down as before. Yet there was the bird, unmistakably before him, undeniably studying its book and speaking to itself. David's mind caught hold of a phrase and repeated it over and over again: "What on earth? What on earth?"

DAVID AND THE PHOENIX by Edward Ormondroyd, illustrated by Joan Raysor

DAVID AND THE PHOENIX

by Edward Ormondroyd,
illustrated by Joan Raysor

Published in 1957, *David and the Phoenix*
by Edward Ormondroyd presents a very
satisfying friendship between a young
boy and an almost 500-year-old mythical
bird. On vacation, young David climbs a
mountain, only to find a miraculous creature
on a remote outcropping. Reading to himself
in Spanish, a pompous but endearing
Phoenix begins a conversation with the lonely
boy. Although Phoenix had been planning
to leave for South America, he stays with
David to educate the boy about legendary
creatures—a gryffin, witch, banshee,
Leprechaun, faun, and sea monster. However,
since the Phoenix is being pursued by a
stubborn scientist intent on capturing the
exotic bird, their adventures take a serious
turn as they seek to outwit the scientist.

Out of print for many years, *David and
the Phoenix* became available again after
the success of Harry Potter, delighting old
fans and gaining many new ones. For a
slightly younger audience than the Potter
series, the book serves as an excellent
introduction to fantasy and mythological
creatures. When Professor Gerald Early of
Washington University discovered the book
as a young boy, he found added wisdom in
this lighthearted and humorous story.

Gerald Early

An understanding of the Christian story

The book that most deeply affected me as a child was Edward Ormondroyd's *David and the Phoenix*. I read the book when I was about ten, I think, which means sometime in the early 1960s. So, the book was still recent, although in my childish mind 1957 seemed some time ago. I remember distinctly that I read the book while I was home from school for a week with a bad case of the flu. Because I suffered from asthma, my mother was particularly concerned that the illness would set off an attack, so I was confined to bed, surrounded by most of the objects I liked: my toy guns and holster (modeled after those used by Paladin on a television show called *Have Gun—Will Travel*), my comic books, my toy soldiers, my marbles, my baseball cards, and a toy robot called Great Garloo, which I think was manufactured by Marx as the owner's "personal slave." It is striking that I had so many possessions because I grew up in such modest economic circumstances. My mother, a widow, worked part-time, so I was home by myself for a good portion of the day.

I don't remember how I came to *David and the Phoenix*. I just found it one day wandering around the house when my mother wasn't home. She had gotten a remainder copy from a secondhand shop in our neighborhood. It was priced on the inside cover at ten cents, but my mother rarely bought us books, so I suspect that the woman who owned the shop, named Laura, simply gave it to her as something for her children. "You have such good children," she would say. My sisters and I were very well liked in the neighborhood. We were thought to be very well-behaved and exceptional, bright Negro children. (I grew up in a largely Italian working-class neighborhood.)

I read the book slowly but persistently, savoring it. I loved it from the start. Of course, I identified with David, and every child wishes to have a secret friend like the Phoenix, a caring, older teacher who is a bit pompous but also more than a little funny. I did not understand many of the big words that the Phoenix used, but neither did David, so that intensified my identification with him

The death of the Phoenix at the end moved me more deeply than anything I had read or experienced to that point in my life. Its rebirth was a dramatic triumph that, unconsciously, made the Christian resurrection story far more real to me than anything in the Gospels themselves. "To lose your life and what you had and knew in order to be renewed": The Phoenix's death and rebirth made me cry. *David and the Phoenix* made me understand Christianity in a way that nothing else—certainly not the Bible—had. And the book was certainly not ostensibly a Christian but rather a pagan, mythological book.

After I finished reading it, I immediately reread it. For months afterward, I carried it around with me and reread selected parts. It has stayed with me a very long time, throughout my adult life.

So they rode till they came to a lake, which was a fair water and a broad, and in the middest of the lake King Arthur was ware of an arm clothed in white samite, that held a fair sword in the hand. "Lo," said Merlin, "yonder is that sword that I spake of." With that they saw a damsel going upon the lake.

"What damsel is that?" asked Arthur. "That is the Lady of the Lake," said Merlin; "and this damsel will come to you anon, and then speak ye fair to her that she will give you the sword." Anon withal came the damsel unto Arthur and saluted him, and he her again.

"Damsel," said Arthur, "what sword is that, that yonder the arm holdeth above the water? I would it were mine, for I have no sword."

"Sir king," said the damsel, "that sword is mine, and if ye will give me a gift when I ask it you, ye shall have it."

"By my faith," said Arthur, "I will give you what gift ye will ask."

"Well," said the damsel, "go ye into yonder barge and row yourself to the sword, and take it and the scabbard with you, and I will ask my gift when I see my time."

THE BOY'S KING ARTHUR edited by Sidney Lanier, illustrated by N. C. Wyeth

Fred Friedman

I wanted to grow up and become one of those knights who fought for the underdog against bullies.

THE BOY'S KING ARTHUR

edited by Sidney Lanier

It would be difficult for any modern reader to understand contemporary culture without knowledge of the Arthurian legends. References to the stories of King Arthur, his knights, his castle Camelot, and Queen Guinevere appear daily in newspapers, books, television, and movies. Fortunately, Sir Thomas Malory's *Le Morte d'Arthur*, Alfred, Lord Tennyson's *Idylls of the King*, and other books that helped evolve the legends have been frequently adapted for young readers.

Depending on the text, the Arthur stories usually include the legitimizing of his kingship when he pulls the sword Excalibur from a stone. As the wizard Merlin provides advice, Arthur establishes the Knights of the Round Table and its code of chivalry; he marries the beautiful Guinevere; the various knights (Launcelot of the Lake, Percival, Kay, Tristram, and Gawain) develop their own sagas. Then the knights engage in a quest for the Holy Grail. Two early-nineteenth-century publications—Howard Pyle's four-volume Arthurian saga and Sidney Lanier's *The Boy's King Arthur*—set the standard for later adaptations for children. Founder of the Brandywine School of Illustration, Pyle crafted books particularly noteworthy for their bold black-and-white portraits of the knights and scenes from the legends; Lanier's volume was brilliantly illustrated in 1945 by N. C. Wyeth.

After reading these books, Public Defender Fred Friedman, host of Minnesota Public Radio's *Fool Fred*, decided he wanted to become one of the Knights of the Round Table.

The stories that influenced me the most were those about King Arthur and of the Knights of the Round Table. While other books, and there were plenty of them, taught me lessons or stirred my imagination or provided knowledge or gave me the will and skills to follow current events, Arthurian legends gave me all of this and more.

The first two King Arthur books I read were by Howard Pyle, *The Story of King Arthur and His Knights*, and Sidney Lanier, *The Boy's King Arthur*. I still have them fifty-one years later. Actually I wore out a copy of the Pyle book in the Village Woods school library in Fort Wayne, Indiana. On a weekend trip to Chicago, I took the "L" from my Uncle Mitchell's to Kroch's and Brentano's downtown on Wabash Avenue, right under the train tracks, and purchased my own Lanier.

King Arthur's tales provided me with lessons on the value of mentoring (Arthur's relationship with Merlin). They taught me about loyalty through the various knights and their allegiance to Arthur. They taught me about the importance of friendship (Launcelot). They stirred my admiration for the code of defending the weak and powerless. They introduced me to early and medieval Christianity. Why would everyone leave home and health and safety and family to quest for some cup called the Holy Grail? It got pretty difficult for a not-yet teenager to figure out the conflicts between love of wife (Guinevere) and love of best friend (Launcelot). And why would Arthur's own son say terrible things that resulted in the destruction of Arthur and his reign?

Today I feel that the King Arthur books were unnecessarily unkind to women. Too many of the women in the stories were bad news, especially Morgan Le Fay, Arthur's sister. How could he be deceived into having relations with his sister? And Vivian who seduced Merlin into a cave. With that scene I realized why Arthur was in the fiction section: Merlin was way too smart a wizard to be tricked by any sorceress. No way, I thought, would a smart older guy fall for the charms of a younger woman.

Of course, when you are in fourth grade in a new school in a new town and have the sophistication of coming from the big city (Chicago) with museums and ball clubs in both leagues, you know pretty much all there is to know. Imagine how smart I sounded a few years later when the writers were referring to the Kennedy administration as "Camelot."

After reading the King Arthur stories, I knew that I wanted to grow up to become one of those 150 knights who fought for the underdog against bullies with too much power.

Everybody knows that Maniac Magee (then Jeffrey) started out in Hollidaysburg and wound up in Two Mills. The question is: What took him so long? And what did he do along the way?

Sure, two hundred miles is a long way, especially on foot, but the year that it took him to cover it was about fifty-one weeks more than he needed—figuring the way he could run, even then.

The legend doesn't have the answer. That's why this period is known as The Lost Year.

And another question: Why did he stay here? Why Two Mills?

Of course, there's the obvious answer that sitting right across the Schuylkill is Bridgeport, where he was born. Yet there are other theories. Some say he just got tired of running. Some say it was the butterscotch Krimpets. And some say he only intended to pause here but that he stayed because he was so happy to make a friend.

If you listen to everybody who claims to have seen Jeffrey-Maniac Magee that first day, there must have been ten thousand people and a parade of fire trucks waiting for him at the town limits. Don't believe it. A couple of people truly remember, and here's what they saw: a scraggly little kid jogging toward them, the soles of both sneakers hanging by their hinges and flopping open like dog tongues each time they came up from the pavement.

But it was something they heard that made him stick in their minds all these years. As he passed them, he said, "Hi." Just that—"Hi"— and he was gone. They stopped, they blinked, they turned, they stared after him, they wondered: *Do I know that kid?* Because people just didn't say that to strangers, out of the blue.

MANIAC MAGEE

by Jerry Spinelli

Jerry Spinelli's *Maniac Magee* pulls readers in immediately: "They say Maniac Magee was born in a dump. They say his stomach was a cereal box and his heart a sofa spring. They say he kept an eight-inch cockroach on a leash." Jeffrey Lionel Magee, an orphan, runs away from his guardians and refuses to live by anyone's rules. As he keeps doing one amazing thing after another, the legends about this idiosyncratic hero grow and evolve. He begins, however, to make a difference in the small town of Two Mills, Pennsylvania, where he longs to have an address that he can call home. Humor, heart, and wit underscore the narrative, as well as serious issues about the nature of family and the nature of prejudice. Winner of the Newbery Medal in 1991, *Maniac Magee* has attracted a wide audience of children.

Singer-songwriter and actor Tyler Hilton of the popular television show *One Tree Hill* tells how he was beguiled into reading by *Maniac Magee*.

Tyler Hilton
A new role model

Every now and then a book comes along that grips your attention and stays with you long after the book is put down. When I was ten or eleven, I read *Maniac Magee* by Jerry Spinelli and found it to be that kind of book. I had never thought I could be so excited about a book. After all, a book wasn't a toy or anything fun like that! But then I met Maniac Magee, a mysterious young wanderlust of a kid, and knew that I had a new role model. This was the first book, from what I can remember, that I actually talked about to other kids my age. It's just one of those that get you talking. The best kind.

They waited patiently for what seemed a very long time, stamping in the snow to keep their feet warm. At last they heard the sound of slow shuffling footsteps approaching the door from the inside. It seemed, as the Mole remarked to the Rat, like some one walking in carpet slippers that were too large for him and down-at-heel; which was intelligent of Mole, because that was exactly what it was.

There was the noise of a bolt shot back, and the door opened a few inches, enough to show a long snout and a pair of sleepy blinking eyes.

"Now, the very next time this happens," said a gruff and suspicious voice, "I shall be exceedingly angry. Who is it this time, disturbing people on such a night? Speak up!"

"O, Badger," cried the Rat, "let us in, please. It's me, Rat, and my friend Mole, and we've lost our way in the snow."

"What, Ratty, my dear man!" exclaimed the Badger, in quite a different voice. "Come along in, both of you, at once. Why, you must be perished. Well I never! Lost in the snow! And in the Wild Wood, too, and at this time of night! But come in with you."

The two animals tumbled over each other in their eagerness to get inside, and heard the door shut behind them with great joy and relief.

The Badger, who wore a long dressing-gown, and whose slippers were indeed very down-at-heel, carried a flat candlestick in his paw and had probably been on his way to bed when their summons sounded. He looked kindly down on them and patted both their heads. "This is not the sort of night for small animals to be out," he said paternally. "I'm afraid you've been up to some of your pranks again, Ratty. But come along; come into the kitchen. There's a first-rate fire there, and supper and everything."

He shuffled on in front of them, carrying the light, and they followed him, nudging each other in an anticipating sort of way, down a long, gloomy, and, to tell the truth, decidedly shabby passage, into a sort of a central hall,

out of which they could dimly see other long tunnel-like passages branching, passages mysterious and without apparent end. But there were doors in the hall as well—stout oaken comfortable-looking doors. One of these the Badger flung open, and at once they found themselves in all the glow and warmth of a large fire-lit kitchen.

THE WIND IN THE WILLOWS by Kenneth Grahame, illustrated by Ernest Shepard

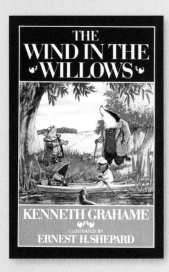

THE WIND IN THE WILLOWS

by Kenneth Grahame,
illustrated by Ernest Shepard

A distinguished banker by profession, Kenneth Grahame became a father at the age of forty-one, and he began telling his son bedtime stories. Even when away from home, Grahame sent updates by mail. Eventually his wife convinced him to turn this sprawling story into a book, *The Wind in the Willows*.

In an idealized English countryside, Mole, Rat, Badger, and Toad of Toad Hall engage in a series of adventures and antics. Toad's escapades capture the attention of young readers: He discovers the joy of riding around in cars, steals one, lands in prison, and escapes by dressing up as a woman. But the other characters explore more of the philosophical issues of the book—the love of hearth and home, the nature of friendship.

Published in 1908 in England, Theodore Roosevelt, president of the United States, discovered *The Wind in the Willows* and brought a copy back to his own publisher, Charles Scribner's Sons. A. A. Milne, author of *Winnie-the-Pooh*, became another early advocate of the title and adapted it for the London stage. Now, for over a century, children and adults have come to echo Grahame's own words about the book, spoken to illustrator Ernest Shepard: "I love these little people; be kind to them." Children's book creator Thacher Hurd first discovered the book as a child.

Thacher Hurd
If things are torn apart, we can make our world right again.

The Wind in the Willows was given to me at Christmas when I was seven by my grandfather, John H. Thacher. I loved the settings, the coherent little world in which everything happened in a soothing way. I was fascinated by what Mr. Toad (surely the id personified) was going to do next. What new way was he going to find to get into trouble? But the subtler story is the friendship between Rat and Mole, a wonderful relationship that really anchored the book for me. I could see all the ways in which they cared about each other. The Ernest Shepard illustrations were also an important part of the book; these illustrations expressed the emotions perfectly.

I had such a feeling for the place of the story, with a river going through the whole book, and those incredible houses. Mole and Rat are lost in the woods, slightly terrified, and all of a sudden there is Badger in his down-at-the-heel slippers, welcoming them to his cozy home. Grahame wrote with such calm serenity; Grahame's characters go out, have adventures, but they come back to these cozy little houses.

When I was in college, I lived in a communal household with six or seven people. One night we gathered in a tiny bedroom at the back of the house. We scrunched together on the bed and around the floor, and we read *The Wind in the Willows* aloud to each other. The book cast a spell over us—a soothing, peaceful aura to our gathering—as it always does when one gives oneself over to the world of Rat, Mole, Badger, and Toad. So I read this book as a child, in college, and as an adult. At all these ages, I have responded to the deep reassurance of its stories. It has made me feel as if all is well in the world—that everything will be fine. These characters are so sturdy; they are so resourceful; they care about what is going on in the world; they keep their houses shipshape. At one point Rat and Mole come into Mole's disheveled house, where he hasn't been for months, and Mole is all weepy. But Rat says they can fix it up and make it better. What I learned from *The Wind in the Willows* is that subtle message: We can fix it, solve it, make it better. If things are torn apart, we can make our world right again.

For a moment after Mr. and Mrs. Darling left the house the night-lights by the beds of the three children continued to burn clearly. They were awfully nice little night-lights, and one cannot help wishing that they could have kept awake to see Peter; but Wendy's light blinked and gave such a yawn that the other two yawned also, and before they could close their mouths all three went out.

There was another light in the room now, a thousand times brighter than the night-lights, and in the time we have taken to say this, it has been in all the drawers in the nursery, looking for Peter's shadow, rummaged the wardrobe and turned every pocket inside out. It was not really a light; it made this light by flashing about so quickly, but when it came to rest for a second you saw it was a fairy, no longer than your hand, but still growing. It was a girl called Tinker Bell exquisitely gowned in a skeleton leaf, cut low and square, through which her figure could be seen to the best advantage. She was slightly inclined to embonpoint.

A moment after the fairy's entrance the window was blown open by the breathing of the little stars, and Peter dropped in. He had carried Tinker Bell part of the way, and his hand was still messy with the fairy dust.

"Tinker Bell," he called softly, after making sure that the children were asleep. "Tink, where are you?" She was in a jug for the moment, and liking it extremely; she had never been in a jug before.

"Oh, do come out of that jug, and tell me, do you know where they put my shadow?" The loveliest tinkle as of golden bells answered him. It is the fairy language. You ordinary children can never hear it, but if you were to hear it you would know that you had heard it once before.

Tink said that the shadow was in the big box. She meant the chest of drawers, and Peter jumped at the drawers, scattering their contents to the floor with both hands, as kings toss ha'pence to the crowd. In a moment he had recovered his shadow, and in his delight he forgot that he had shut Tinker Bell up in the drawer.

PETER PAN by J. M. Barrie, illustrated by F. D. Bedford

PETER PAN

by J. M. Barrie

Although the character of Peter Pan first appeared in 1902 in James Barrie's book *The Little White Bird*, Barrie developed Peter's personality on the stage in 1904. In this play he created some of the great iconic characters of the twentieth century—the crocodile with a ticking clock, Captain Hook, the Lost Boys, and of course everyone's favorite fairy, Tinker Bell. One night Wendy, John, and Michael Darling leave home and soar into the sky with Peter Pan, the boy who never grows up. They land on an enchanted island, Neverland, filled with fairies, mermaids, and pirates. All narrowly escape having to walk the plank; together they defeat Peter's archenemy, the villainous Captain Hook.

In 1911 Barrie created a book, *Peter and Wendy*, which provided added background and events. In a generous bequeath, he left the funds from the play and book to the Great Ormond Street Hospital for Children. An act of Parliament extended those rights indefinitely, providing care for sick children as long as the hospital remains in operation.

New York Times best-selling writer Gail Carson Levine viewed life differently after she read the novel version of Peter's story.

Gail Carson Levine
How precious is our term on earth.

I was a good child, too good for my own good. *Peter Pan* showed me other possibilities. Peter is self-absorbed, conceited, thoughtless, brave, and completely lovable. Tinker Bell is passionate: She tries to kill Wendy and saves Peter's life. Wendy and her brothers abandon their parents without a note or a backward look. They aren't orphans. They *choose* to leave. Wow!

After reading *Peter Pan* again and again and again, I was still mostly an obedient kid, but sometimes not. Sometimes I joined the league of heartless, selfish children. It was beneficial for me, if not for my parents.

Of course, there is more to *Peter Pan* than mischief. The book is subtle and wry. I had to become subtle myself to get it. Here's Barrie describing the Lost Boys who are twins: "Peter never quite knew what twins were, and his band were not allowed to know anything he did not know, so these two were always vague about themselves."

I've left the best for last: the poignancy of Neverland, where no one grows old. Wendy leaves, but I wanted to stay; I discovered how precious youth is and how precious is our term on earth.

Cat counted the Dog's teeth (and they looked very pointed) and he said, "I will be kind to the Baby while I am in the Cave, as long as he does not pull my tail too hard, for always and always and always. But still I am the Cat that walks by himself, and all places are alike to me!"

"Not when I am near," said the Dog. "If you had not said that last I would have shut my mouth for always and always and always; but now I am going to hunt you up a tree whenever I meet you. And so shall all proper Dogs do after me."

Then the Man threw his two boots and his little stone axe (that makes three) at the Cat, and the Cat ran out of the Cave and the Dog chased him up a tree; and from that day to this, Best Beloved, three proper Men out of five will always throw things at a Cat whenever they meet him, and all proper Dogs will chase him up a tree. But the Cat keeps his side of the bargain too. He will kill mice, and he will be kind to Babies when he is in the house, just as long as they do not pull his tail too hard. But when he has done that, and between times,

and when the moon gets up and night comes, he is the Cat that walks by himself, and all places are alike to him. Then he goes out to the Wet Wild Woods or up the Wet Wild Trees or on the Wet Wild Roofs, waving his wild tail and walking by his wild lone.

THE JUNGLE BOOK

JUST SO STORIES

by Rudyard Kipling

Today Rudyard Kipling's legacy rests on four titles, dramatically different in feeling and scope. *The Jungle Book* and *The Second Jungle Book*, published in 1894 and 1895, consist of interlinking stories set in the Highlands of India. In these volumes, a human boy, Mowgli, is raised by wolves and instructed in the legends of the jungle. In *Just So Stories* Kipling provides humorous accounts of the development of certain animals. In *Kim*, a thrilling spy story, Kipling's most famous hero, Kimball O'Hara, an Irish orphan raised in India, joins a holy man from Tibet on a spiritual quest for "The River of the Arrow." As thirteen-year-old Kim grows up, he must reconcile his worldly life and his religious one.

Born in Bombay, India, in 1865, Rudyard Kipling was raised by an *ayah*; Hindustani served as his first language. Sent to England for his education, Kipling returned to India and worked as a journalist. But he wrote *The Jungle Book* and its sequel while living in Brattleboro, Vermont, where he moved because of his American wife. Eventually, Kipling returned to England; in 1907 he became the first English language writer to win the Nobel Prize for Literature.

Although his work has received harsh criticism for its British colonial attitudes, Kipling's stories for children have continued to delight young readers. Animals (such as the mongoose Rikki-tikki-tavi and the Bi-Coloured-Python-Rock-Snake), memorable places ("the great grey-green, greasy Limpopo River"), and completely satisfying

(continued on page 30)

Peter Matthiessen
The yearning for wild places and wild experiences

As a child, I found a strange and fascinating passage into another world in Rudyard Kipling's *Just So Stories* and *The Jungle Book*. His tales are filled with wild creatures—aloof, enigmatic, and even dangerous. In those days, my family lived in rural Connecticut, in a country of woodland and rocky hills, meadow and clear streams—a great variety of habitats for wild creatures, which seemed extraordinarily abundant. That was a time of boyhood expeditions in search of snakes and turtles and salamanders—small and harmless creatures, never scary like the wild animals of faraway jungles. But Kipling showed me a different world, in which the wildest of all the wild animals was the Cat. In Kipling's own black-and-white illustration, a black cat is walking away down a white snow track between bare black winter trees, and its wild tail is held high in the air; one can almost see that black tail twitch in exasperation. "I am the Cat who walks by himself, and all places are alike to me." That poetic and succinct statement of essential feline principles has drifted in my brain like a sliver of old song all these years.

In these books the young reader is gladly borne away to "the great grey-green, greasy Limpopo River, all set about with fever trees." The actual Limpopo River, now in Zimbabwe, is said to have many crocodiles, and is still, so far as I know, set about with fever trees (the beautiful yellow-barked acacia, found throughout much of subtropical Africa).

In *The Jungle Book* many of the stories have eerie qualities, beginning with the strange names of the book's denizens—Chuchundra the house rat, who never dares leave the wall for fear of the great cobras, Nag and Nagina; Rikki-tikki-tavi the mongoose, whose eyes turn red when he is angry and who "knew that all a grown mongoose's business in life was to fight and eat snakes."

Kipling was not simply a great storyteller but a gifted writer. I know the stories in these books instilled in me the yearning for wild places and wild experiences that was to become so important in my life. After Nag and Nagina, it seems to me no coincidence that my brother and I, as boys, became enthralled by snakes and caught any number of them. Today my brother is a marine biologist, while I am a writer who has observed and studied wildlife on every continent as well as undersea. Not surprising, one of my favorite places for research has been the jungle of *The Jungle Book* in India. Childhood reading can truly have a formative effect on later life.

Ursula K. Le Guin

Great writing—language that revels in its own gorgeous exaggeration, humor, nonsense, beauty, and perfect accuracy

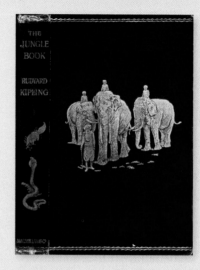

Rudyard Kipling's politics are out of fashion, but he was a marvelous writer for young people, a source of endless delight and example. The *Just So Stories* offer young kids something they get all too seldom: really great writing—language that revels in its own gorgeous exaggeration, humor, nonsense, beauty, and perfect accuracy. "I am the Cat who walks by himself, and all places are alike to me."

The two volumes of the Jungle Books are worlds in themselves—not only the beautiful, tragic Indian jungle where we live among the wolves with Mowgli, but other unforgettable stories like "Rikki-tikki-tavi" and "The White Seal," where Man is only one among the wonders of creation. And then there is *Kim*, a grand, fascinating adventure, that reaches out into real mysticism in a way no other book accessible to children does, and accompanies its reader, like a wise, fascinating companion, through the rest of life.

places ("the great grey-green, greasy Limpopo River"), and completely satisfying stories such as "The Elephant's Child" stand outside philosophy or politics.

Kipling's work provides for many children, as they did for naturalist and writer Peter Matthiessen, "a strange and fascinating passage into another world." His books also can be enjoyed again in the adult years; as Hugo and Nebula Award winner Ursula K. Le Guin says, *Kim* "accompanies its reader, like a wise, fascinating companion, through the rest of life."

Understanding

As he saw it, Chauntecleer did not ask much in return for his constant, abiding, and well-intentioned leadership. Good dinners. Loyalty. A little color in his life. Sleep: unbroken sleep, to be sure. And a morning sunbath, undisturbed. As matters would have it, that sunbath was, once in a while, disturbed.

One morning, several weeks after the appearance of a Dog who carried his baggage in front of his face, Chauntecleer the Rooster was strutting in front of his Coop, enjoying the bright sunlight and the day which went with it. Minor clucks in his throat announced his good pleasure. He had fluffed out his golden feathers so that the sun could shine down to the skin and warm it. His wings were ruffled and loose at his sides. And lazily he went scratching about in search of a proper dry sink of dust into which he would settle, nestle, and rest. This was the sweet progress of his sunbath; he had a dreamy smile on his face.

But suddenly someone in the Coop behind him began to gabble to a whole series of despairing clucks. All the other clucks went quiet while that one cry stuttered on with a true pain in it; and then it, too, fell silent, and the Coop was still. And that was wrong. An early morning Coop is almost never silent.

Chauntecleer was irritated. His pleasure had lost its rhythm, and he knew by the silence behind him that he was about to be involved. Yet, for a certain spite, he would not turn around and face the door of the Coop, but continued with the motions of his sunbath, though the spirit of the thing had gone out of it.

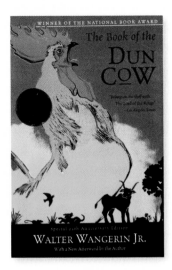

THE BOOK OF THE DUN COW

by Walter Wangerin Jr.

In 1978, a few years after Richard Adams' fantasy about rabbits, *Watership Down*, became a best-seller, Walter Wangerin Jr. turned a rooster, Chauntecleer, into the subject matter of an epic fantasy exploring the age-old struggle of good and evil. Inspired by Chaucer's "The Nun's Priest's Tale," this saga occurs in a nonhuman world where animals protect the earth from the ancient evil Wyrm, trapped in the earth's center. As Wyrm struggles to gain dominance, the evil Cockatrice is born, a creature part chicken and part snake. Around the same time, the Dun Cow, a Christlike figure, appears to give aid to Chauntecleer and his subjects. Ultimately, Chauntecleer, Mundo Cani, a depressed dog, and all the other farm and woodland animals must battle Cockatrice and his army of evil basilisks. In the end, only the sacrifice of Mundo Cani decides the outcome.

Winner of the National Book Award, *The Book of the Dun Cow* has either been loved or hated by adult critics over the years, but as a young boy Dave Eggers, who himself became a highly original writer, found inspiration in this inventive fantasy.

Dave Eggers
The startling power of a book

One of the first books I remember giving me a wholly immersive reading experience was Walter Wangerin's *The Book of the Dun Cow*. I had read a lot of books by then, but the majority were of the Encyclopedia Brown variety—totally enjoyable stories set in a familiar context like suburban America and not necessarily dealing with grand themes.

When we read *The Book of the Dun Cow* in sixth grade, I got caught up in it—despite its suffering from being assigned. After reading the epic battle scene between Chauntecleer and Cockatrice and then the resolution of the book, I distinctly remember walking around the school that day in a daze, as if I'd come back from the moon. Everything in my life seemed comparatively small and pedestrian.

That book was such a small thing—a lightweight paperback book—but the power contained within was really startling to me. I had dreams about the book, thought about it constantly. I kept it out of view for some time. Even seeing the cover threw me back into that world again, and the story was too strong to casually stumble upon. Only a book has that power.

The windows and shutters were fixed
and once again they painted her
a lovely shade of pink.
As the Little House settled down
on her new foundation,
she smiled happily.
Once again she could watch
the sun and moon and stars.
Once again she could watch
Spring and Summer
and Fall and Winter
come and go.

Once again
she was lived in
and taken care of.

Never again would she be curious about
    the city . . .
Never again would she want to live
    there . . .
The stars twinkled above her . . .
A new moon was coming up . . .
It was spring . . .
and all was quiet and peaceful in
    the country.

THE LITTLE HOUSE by Virginia Lee Burton

THE LITTLE HOUSE

by Virginia Lee Burton

Virginia Lee Burton lived most of her adult life in a house in Cape Ann, Massachusetts. To improve the property, Burton had moved the house back from the road, and placed it in the fields, streams, and woods to its advantage. This incident became the inspiration for her Caldecott Award–winning book that was dedicated to her husband "Dorgie," as his sons called him—George Demetrois, a world-renowned sculptor.

As a young woman, Burton had arrived at Demetrois's house to ask if she could study with him. According to family legend, he fainted when he saw this New England beauty. After they were married, they acquired property in Cape Ann and raised their two sons in "the little house," a place that saw constant dances, parties, and meals around a huge stone table. Burton on the cover page tells us that this is "Her Story," the story of a house. Little House first enjoys her perch on the hill. But as the landscape changes around her, Little House finds herself crowded out by city buildings, and her telltale eyes show all her misery. Finally movers transport Little House to the country, where she can again live in peace and tranquility.

Throughout the book, Little House remains in exactly the same spot in each artistic composition—it is only the landscape that changes around her. This complex exploration of change and time has resonated with millions of readers over the years. One of them, Pulitzer Prize winner Anne Tyler, found her own wisdom in the book.

Anne Tyler
Nothing could ever stay the same.

For my fourth birthday, I was given a copy of *The Little House* by Virginia Lee Burton. I have returned to that book over and over, sinking into its colorful, complicated pictures all through childhood and adolescence and adulthood. First my parents read it to me; then I read it to myself. When my children came along I read it to them, and now that they've outgrown it (as if you could ever really outgrow it!), I read it again to myself. I don't turn the pages anymore; I lift them up and sort through them. The binding fell apart long ago. The spine is a strip of naked cardboard, and the green cloth cover is bleached and ragged.

I believe the book spoke to me about something I hadn't yet consciously considered: the passage of time. And it introduced me to the feeling of nostalgia—the realization of the losses that the passage of time can bring. It's not that I hadn't yet experienced time, heaven knows. (Time passes so slowly for children; they experience it more than adults do.) But I'd experienced it unreflectively, and changes came as sudden jolts in my existence. So here was this story that spelled out for me all the successive stages. The sun rises and sets across one entire page, and a whole month of moons wheels across another. The seasons march in order, defined by the length of the days.

Like a child, the Little House has her periods of restlessness. And like a child, she finds even longed-for changes both exciting and saddening. Alone at night in the city that has always seemed to beckon, she missed "the field of daisies and the apple trees dancing in the moonlight."

When I see those words now (and when I hear them, murmuring across the decades in my mother's voice), I recall the feeling of elderly sorrow that came over me at age four. At age four, listening to *The Little House*, I had a sudden spell of . . . wisdom, I guess you could say. It seemed I'd been presented with a snapshot that showed me how the world worked: how the years flowed by and people altered and nothing could ever stay the same.

So Horton kept sitting there, day after day.
And soon it was Autumn. The leaves blew away.
And then came the Winter . . . the snow and the sleet!
And icicles hung
From his trunk and his feet.

But Horton kept sitting, and said with a sneeze,
"I'll stay on this egg and I won't let it freeze.
I meant what I said
And I said what I meant. . . .
An elephant's faithful
One hundred per cent!"

HORTON HATCHES THE EGG by Dr. Seuss

HORTON HATCHES THE EGG

by Dr. Seuss

America's best-selling children's book author, Theodore Geisel—Dr. Seuss—did not have an easy time getting his first book published. After *And to Think That I Saw It on Mulberry Street* had been rejected by more than two dozen publishers, he decided to go home and burn the manuscript. On his way, he ran into an old Dartmouth classmate on the street in New York. As he told this friend a tale of woe, Seuss found his fate suddenly reversed. His friend, it turned out, had just been appointed the children's book editor of a small press, Vanguard. He was hunting for books; Seuss had one. And the rest, as they say, is history. But Seuss always maintained that had he been walking down the other side of the street that day, he would have ended up in the dry-cleaning business.

In Seuss's fourth book, *Horton Hatches the Egg*, published in 1940, a good-for-nothing, lazy bird, Mayzie, convinces a gullible elephant Horton to sit on her egg while she flies away to enjoy the sun of Palm Beach. No matter what happens, Horton hangs on to the nest—even when hunters threaten his life and later consign him to a circus. But Horton holds on to his simple ethos: "I meant what I said! And I said what I meant. . . An elephant's faithful / One hundred per cent!" For his devotion he receives an amazing reward, an elephant bird that looks just like Horton. This seemingly straightforward story works on many levels. Some appreciate one of its implicit messages—even if your mother might not love you or want to stay with you, you can find someone who will. Someone important, like Horton. Newbery Award winner Karen Hesse found a role model in this book.

Karen Hesse
A grasp on morality

I met my first genuine humanitarian in the elephant Horton, and I embraced him and his way of being with every cell in my body, every curl on my head, every freckle across my cheeks.

Horton showed such sensitivity: He solved his problems with a sweet willingness that enchanted me, that endeared him to me. His determination to stick to his word, to his task, no matter how unpleasant, informed me, shaped me. He was ridiculed by his peers, and yet he still honored his commitment. To meet such a character when I was searching for a grasp on morality, for a handle on ethics and humanity—it was most fortuitous.

I wanted to be like Horton. I wanted the world to be populated by Hortons. I wanted all the children of the world to be treated with the same loving devotion with which Horton treated the egg.

If you look at my work, it all comes back to Horton.

"The first thing to do," said Freddy, "is to Visit the Scene of the Crime."

The smaller animals always helped Mrs. Bean with the housework, and were in and out of the house a good deal all day, so when Jinx and Freddy went in the kitchen door and up the back stairs, Mrs. Bean merely glanced up from the peas that two rabbits were helping her shell and said: "Be careful of those stairs, animals. They're pretty steep. I don't want you should hurt yourselves."

The children's room was the front bedroom over the porch, next to Mr. and Mrs. Bean's. Jinx started to walk across the floor, but Freddy stopped him. "Please don't disturb anything," he said, "until I have finished my investigation."

"Oh, I'm not disturbing anything. What's the matter with you?" demanded the cat.

"You're disturbing the clues," replied the pig testily. "All crimes have clues, and if you follow the clues, you find the criminal."

"If I knew what clues were, I'd know better what you were talking about," said Jinx.

But Freddy did not answer. He was being a detective for all he was worth. He went very carefully over the floor, and then he examined the bed and the window-sill, and finally he got a tape measure out of Ella's little sewing-basket and measured the height of the sill and the distance from the bed to the window and several other things. Jinx sat down by the door and watched, trying hard to look superior and sarcastic. But it's hard to look superior and sarcastic all by yourself when nobody's paying any attention to you, so after a while he gave it up and went to sleep.

A little later he woke up again. Freddy was standing looking out of the window, wrapped in thought. "Well," said Jinx, "found any of those—what do you call 'em?—clues you were looking for?"

"I have," said Freddy importantly. "What's more, I know who stole the train."

FREDDY THE DETECTIVE by Walter R. Brooks

FREDDY THE DETECTIVE

by Walter R. Brooks

"If L. Frank Baum has a successor, it is [Walter] Brooks," wrote critic Roger Sale. Certainly Walter Brooks's books about Freddy the Pig, who made his first appearance in 1927 in *To and Again*, epitomized American fantasy epics with their homespun humor and a large cast of animal characters. If Brooks has a successor, it would be E. B. White and *Charlotte's Web*.

Brooks brought a simple yet profound understanding to his books for children, "Children are people; they're just smaller and less experienced [than adults]. They are not taken in by the smug playfulness of those who write or talk down to them as if they were dull-witted and slightly deaf."

A book reviewer, columnist, and short story writer who contributed to *The New Yorker* and *Esquire*, Brooks created Ed the Talking Horse, the basis for a popular 1960s television show. But his animal fantasies have been his most lasting contribution to American letters. Initially in the series, Freddy travels with a group of his farm friends—Mrs. Wiggins, the cow; Hank, the horse; Charles, a bragging rooster—to experience a winter vacation in Florida. But then he takes over as the chief protagonist of the group and masters a variety of professions, including a detective business based on the solid principles established by Sherlock Holmes.

For a period of time, the Freddy books went out of print, although they were never out of favor with an active "Friends of Freddy" fan club. Fortunately, in the late 1990s Overlook Press began reprinting the volumes, making these gentle, funny books available once again for families and classrooms. Writer Adam Hochschild discovered the books as a child and found the philosophy behind them radically ahead of its time.

Adam Hochschild

The most subversive politics of all: a child's instinctive desire for fair play

The moral center of my childhood universe, the place where good and evil, friendship and treachery, honesty and humbug were defined most clearly, was not church, not school, and not the Boy Scouts. It was the Bean Farm.

The Bean Farm, as all right-thinking children of my generation knew, was the upstate New York home of Freddy the Pig and his fellow animals. Freddy's readers have called him a porcine prince, a pig of many parts, a paragon of porkers, a Renaissance pig. As the problems he faces require, he is by turns a cowboy, a balloonist, a magician, a campaign manager, a pilot, and a detective. But he is the most unheroic of heroes: he oversleeps, daydreams, eats too much, and, when not suffering from writer's block, writes flowery poetry for all occasions. His tail uncurls when he gets scared. Although lazy, he accomplishes a lot because "when a lazy person once really gets started doing things, it's easier to keep on than it is to stop."

Almost all the other villains foiled by Freddy are representatives of the Establishment. Poking fun at generals, realtors, bank presidents, and the like was unusual fare for children's books of the 1940s and 1950s. Other volumes make a few digs at the space program and at the FBI—Freddy's bumbling Animal Bureau of Investigation often misses the evidence right under his snout. In a subtle way the books even prefigured the spirit of the 1960s.

Small wonder, then, that some of the children who grew up on these books went on to found alternative newspapers, to march for civil rights, and to become ardent environmentalists. Still, you don't have to be in the 1960s generation to appreciate Freddy. As with all books that last, their attraction is broader and deeper. Essentially, they evoke the most subversive politics of all: a child's instinctive desire for fair play.

A man had three sons and he was fond of them all. He had no money, but the house in which he lived was a good one.

"To which of my three boys shall I leave my house?" thought the old man. "They have all been good sons to me and I want to be fair to them in every way."

Maybe you think the simplest thing would have been to sell the house and then divide the money among the three boys. It would have been simpler but nobody wanted to do this. The house had been in their family for many years—not only the three boys, but their father, their grandfather, and their great-grandfather had been born in it. It was their home; they knew and loved every room, every window, every nook and cranny of it, and they could not

bear to sell it to a stranger. So the old man had to think of a way out, and he did.

He called his three boys and said: "This is the way we'll do it. All of you must go out into the world. Each can choose a trade after his own heart and learn it well. In a year we will meet here together, and he who has learned his trade best shall have the house. Would you like to decide it that way?"

"Yes," said his sons, "that is fair enough."

And the oldest said, "I think I will become a blacksmith. That is the kind of work I like best."

"And I," said the second, "have always wanted to be a barber. That's what I'll set out to be."

"And I," said the third, "would like best of all to become a fencing master."

They agreed to return at the appointed time, and then they all went their separate ways. It happened, too, that they all found able masters who could teach them the higher branches of their trade.

TALES FROM GRIMM translated and illustrated by Wanda Gág

TALES FROM GRIMM

translated and illustrated by Wanda Gág

Wanda Gág was nurtured as a child on the fairy tales of Jacob and Wilhelm Grimm: "Often, usually at twilight, some grown-up would say, 'Sit down, Wanda-chen, and I'll read you a Marchen' . . . A tingling, anything-may-happen feeling flowed over me." In 1936 after she was well established as a children's book creator for picture books such as *Millions of Cats*, Gág returned to the legends of her youth and went back to the original German text to create new translations. She adapted the stories for a younger audience than they had been created for; even the title page states "freely translated and illustrated." But she stayed true to the spirit if not the letter of the original text. Aware of the goriness in these classic fairy tales, she refused to render them saccharine.

Tales from Grimm includes some of the best known of the stories: "The Musicians of Bremen," "Hansel and Gretel," "Rapunzel," "Cinderella," and "Snow White and Rose Red." But it also presented some less-frequently recounted favorites of Gág's, among them "The Three Brothers." When professor and radio host John Cech first encountered this particular story, he thought it had been written specifically for him. In this tale a child finds a wise solution, one not even apparent to adults.

John Cech

The adult world is not always in possession of the best solutions.

The first book that I remember reading—on my own and for myself— was Wanda Gág's *Tales from Grimm*. One story in particular said to me, "This is for you. I'm telling this story just for you." The tale was "The Three Brothers." In it three young men go out into the world to gain some extraordinary skill; that skill eventually helps them win the family home that their aging father is offering to the winner of this eternal, fraternal competition. The first young man becomes a master barber. He can style the chin whiskers of a passing hare in a manner fit for the king's court, without the rabbit ever breaking stride. The second brother becomes a superb blacksmith—so good that he can make minuscule golden horseshoes for the feet of a gnat and then shoe the creature as it passes by with tiny, tiny, tiny gold nails. The third brother takes up fencing and becomes so unbelievably quick with his sword that he can deflect the raindrops in a downpour with his blade, keeping himself perfectly dry under his flying foil. Although amazed by the virtuoso skills of all his sons, the father awards the house to the youngest, the fencer. But rather than claim the prize solely for himself, the young man invites his siblings to share the beloved family house with him and their father. And here the story leaves them, "liv[ing] happily together for the rest of their lives."

I can still remember the smell of the book and the feel of its soft, thick pages, and I know just the place where I read it in the public library. There was something about the writing—alive, funny, personal, as though it was whispering to you. Later I learned that both Gág and I came from Bohemian stock, where whispered stories are as essential as a roasted potato or a *kolacki* with a dab of apricot preserve in the middle of its flaky, powdered-sugar dough. Her stories were pure comfort food.

Yet why did this particular story speak to me? Like most kids, I was drawn to the fantasy of the everyday, heroic act of doing something so out-of-the-ballpark spectacular that it would take the collective breath away. And here, too, was the ancient yearning to be recognized by one's father as the outstanding one of all the siblings. Finally, in this tale, no one is excluded or exiled or evicted from the home. The story resolves itself in peace and harmony and in a solution that runs now, as it did when I first read it, against the winner-take-all mentality that tends to dominate our public life. And it is the youngest one in this family circle—the child, essentially—who sees this possibility and has the astonishing recognition that the adult world is not always in possession of the best solutions.

Beaver

Coming to it from the country,
proud that I finally had sidewalks to walk
and indoor plumbing.
Little strip of street called Beaver:
Hardware, laundromat, market,
post office, Kool-Kup, and Moon-Glo motel.
Beaver Creek holding it all together,
and me at the edge.
Like the water, muddy and rolling.
Growing in Beaver.

WAITING TO WALTZ: A CHILDHOOD by Cynthia Rylant, illustrated by Stephen Gammell

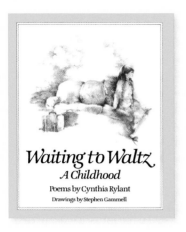

WAITING TO WALTZ: A CHILDHOOD

by Cynthia Rylant,
illustrated by Stephen Gammell

Because of divorced parents, Cynthia Rylant lived with her grandparents in Cool Ridge, West Virginia, and experienced poverty, pain, and loss. Growing up in her Appalachian community, she had never read children's books and had to find other ways to deal with her emotions. Finally in her twenties, while working in the children's section of the library, she read children's books, every night, all night, with passion and enthusiasm. She could not get enough of them, and realized that they were a perfect forum for her.

Her first picture books, *When I Was Young and in the Mountains* and *The Relatives Came*, capture the beauty and wealth of her Appalachian experience. *Waiting to Waltz: A Childhood*, a series of poems published in 1984 and illustrated by Stephen Gammell, evokes an incredible sense of place. The reader gets to know the people and sights of this small Appalachian town, viewing it from the eyes of a young girl who delights in it but also longs for other experiences.

In an amazing act of generosity, Cynthia Rylant decided to send to her editor, Dick Jackson, a manuscript that she had been given to read, because Rylant felt it was good enough to be put into print. Future McArthur Fellow Angela Johnson received a surprise letter accepting a book for publication that she had not even submitted. In her essay Johnson expresses what first drew her to Rylant's work, and why it still resonates so strongly two decades later.

Angela Johnson
Childhood is fraught with discovery, disappointment, and hope.

When the unnamed narrator in Cynthia Rylant's *Waiting to Waltz* talks about the town she calls home—with its laundromat, Moon-Glo motel, The Kool-Kup, and the other accoutrements that make up countless small towns—I began to understand my place in the world.

I was searching to own my small-town past and not leave it behind. The girl in the book understood where she was. To the unquestioning eye, that place was just an ordinary little town. But in her poem "The Brain Surgeon," she imagined that a homeless, handsome man by a creek had been a brain surgeon who'd lost his old life and wife on their honeymoon. I saw my own childhood more clearly. I reveled in others' need to make sense of the lives around them as I had tried.

The girl's early bouts with religion, unearthing bravery, tired mothers, love, loss, and a longing for a world elsewhere reminded me that childhood is always fraught with discovery, disappointment, and hope. I wanted to remember that. I feared being an adult who idealized childhood's precious pains. But I also wanted to remember the humor—trying to be older, boys who loved you and didn't seem to mind that you didn't love them back, friends you thought you'd have forever.

I wanted to remember that we were all waiting—if not to waltz, then just to dance.

Like most farm boys of the era, Robbie Trent was expected to help his father with both the morning and the evening chores, and on Saturday to accomplish two-thirds the work of a full-grown man. Both his father and his mother worked very hard. Robbie felt no

resentment about carrying his just share of the load. Meanwhile his mind was free to roam the woods and to imagine the joy of finding and capturing a wolfling.

Robbie did not tell his parents about his project. From long experience he knew exactly what they would say:

"A pet wolf on a farm where sheep are raised?"

"Are you crazy, lad?"

His mother would be a little more gentle, a trifle more consoling. But Robbie must plan very shrewdly if he wished a wolf whelp for a companion.

During the sixty-three days that Robbie marked on his calendar in the loft, the great globe curved one-sixth of its way around the distant sun. The boy knew from what he had been told by Professor Kumlien that the miracle of spring was due to the tilt of the earth, and the greater abundance of sunlight now lavished upon the Northern Hemisphere. This light and warmth first melted the snows of winter. It sent a stir of life into the seeds and roots of grass and flowers, pulled the sweet sap of the sugar maples to the very tips of the budding branches. It stimulated the water birds and songsters into their seasonal migration northward, and told the wolves and many other animals that it was time to mate and to bring forth their young.

THE WOLFLING by Sterling North, illustrated by John Schoenherr

THE WOLFLING

by Sterling North,
illustrated by John Schoenherr

Sterling North had a distinguished career as an essayist, critic, and publisher, but two works of fiction have been his most lasting contribution to children's books—the first based on his father's experience, *The Wolfling*, and the second on North's own childhood, *Rascal*.

"We have only one life to live," North begins *The Wolfling*, published in 1969. "Let us hope that we all live it meaningfully." Robbie Trent desires a wolf cub so much that he braves crawling into a wolf's den to seize one. Then Robbie, his own dog, and the neighborhood dogs raise Wolf, teaching him about what is and what is not allowed on the farm. Although the story basically recounts the love affair between a boy and his pet, it also incorporates a great deal of the history of America in the 1870s: the fate of Civil War soldiers, the Great Chicago Fire, the homesteading of Wisconsin, and the Panic of 1873.

Meticulously re-created from the letters of North's father, and with extensive footnotes that ground the novel in reality, *The Wolfling* provides a brilliant picture of a time and place, southern Wisconsin, as well as the age-old story of a boy's love for an unusual pet. For bookseller Becky Anderson, who grew up in the Midwest, this luminous story changed the kinds of books she read.

Becky Anderson

The power of being connected to the land, to nature, and other living creatures

From the time I was very young, everything I wanted to do was usually done by boys. Being the only girl sandwiched between two older brothers and one younger made me the odd girl out. So playing army, baseball, softball, and even tackle football, complete with helmet and shoulder pads, was my way of fitting in. My reading choices went along with my tomboy sports life, and I read every sports biography I could lay my hands on. Books on the Babe, Lou Gehrig, Babe Didrikson Zaharias, and Don Drysdale flew out of my elementary school library into my hands. I was in a reading rut until a boy and his wolf came to my rescue.

The author Sterling North had lived across the street from my great-grandparents in Downers Grove, Illinois, and my mother used to play with his children when she was a girl. It was years later when I was about nine that my grandmother gave me a new book called *The Wolfling*. The cover had a wonderful illustration of a boy and a wolf in the warm hues of autumn. Robbie Trent learns of a wolf den that has a litter of puppies. Wanting one for his own, Robbie proves to his parents that Wolf is as loyal and hardworking as any dog could ever be, despite the fact that all of their neighbors would rather kill a wolf than have one for a pet. The story takes place in 1870's Wisconsin and features as one of its main characters the great Swedish-American naturalist Thure Kumlien. Thure teaches Robbie all about the birds, trees, and fauna of the woods and fields.

Oh, to be Robbie and to have a wolf pup as a friend. To wander the woods and learn everything of the world where we would play. A whole new world of reading was opened up to me. I went on to read all I could; *Ring of Bright Water* by Gavin Maxwell, all of Marguerite Henry, all of Walter Farley, and *That Quail, Robert* by Margaret Stanger—a story about a family and their pet quail. Soon after my reading life changed, my family took off on a camping trip from Illinois to California. The six of us and our gear were stuffed into the station wagon. Stopping somewhere in Nebraska to get gas, we got out of the car; my dad pointed out to us that there was a dead bird on the front grill of the car. "Doesn't it look like a quail?" he said. That was all it took for the floodgates to open, and I cried all the way to California.

The *Wolfling* showed me the power of being connected to the land, to nature, and to other living creatures. It showed me that animals share with us the universal language—the language of love. To this day I still occasionally dream about running through the woods with a wolf by my side.

Currumpaw is a vast cattle range in northern New Mexico. It is a land of rich pastures and teeming flocks and herds, a land of rolling mesas and precious running waters that at length unite in the Currumpaw River, from which the whole region is named. And the king whose despotic power was felt over its entire extent was an old gray wolf.

Old Lobo, or the king, as the Mexicans called him, was the gigantic leader of a remarkable pack of gray wolves, that had ravaged the Currumpaw Valley for a number of years. All the shepherds and ranchmen knew him well, and, wherever he appeared with his trusty band, terror reigned supreme among the cattle, and wrath and despair among their owners. Old Lobo was a giant among wolves, and was cunning and strong in proportion to his size. His voice at night was well-known and easily distinguished from that of any of his fellows. An ordinary wolf might howl half the night about the herdsman's bivouac without attracting more than a passing notice, but when the deep roar of the old king came booming down the canyon, the watcher bestirred himself and prepared to learn in the morning that fresh and serious inroads had been made among the herds.

Old Lobo's band was but a small one. This I never quite understood, for usually, when a wolf rises to the position and power that he had, he attracts a numerous following. It may be that he had as many as he desired, or perhaps his ferocious temper prevented the increase of his pack. Certain is it that Lobo had only five followers during the latter part of his reign. Each of these, however, was a wolf of renown, most of them were above the ordinary size, one in particular, the second in command, was a veritable giant, but even he was far below the leader in size and prowess. Several of the band, besides the two leaders, were especially noted. One of those was a beautiful white wolf, that the Mexicans called Blanca; this was supposed to be a female, possibly Lobo's mate. Another was a yellow wolf of remarkable swiftness, which, according to current stories had, on several occasions, captured an antelope for the pack.

WILD ANIMALS I HAVE KNOWN by Ernest Thompson Seton

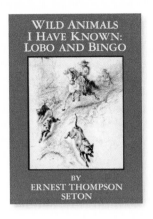

WILD ANIMALS I HAVE KNOWN

ROLF IN THE WOODS

by Ernest Thompson Seton

As a young boy, Ernest Thompson retreated to the woods to draw and study animals as a way to avoid his abusive father. Ultimately, he changed his name, adding Seton as a way to distance himself from his parent. The study of nature became his lifelong passion. Seton's personal story parallels that of his protagonist Rolf in *Rolf in the Woods*, published in 1911. This book, dedicated to the Boy Scouts of America, was based, in part, on Seton's long-held belief that indigenous people provided the best role models for America's youth.

Seton is usually remembered today for his collection of eight true stories about various animals: *Wild Animals I Have Known*, a book that has remained in print for 110 years. These stories focus on the relationship between humans and animals and contain some great individual creatures—Lobo the wolf, Silverspot the crow, Raggylug the cottontail rabbit. In Seton's world, nature is raw in tooth and claw; "The life of a wild animal always has a tragic end," he stated. In this book these tragic heroes have been given amazing dignity. In the most famous story, "Lobo, the King of the Currumpaw," Seton hunts down and kills a wolf; later he

(continued on page 49)

Jack Prelutsky
You never know where things are going to lead.

Growing up in the Bronx, a gritty borough of the city of New York, I thought that wild animals meant pigeons, sparrows, rats, mice, and squirrels. As a little boy I didn't know anything about the truly wild creatures that share this world with us. I had an older cousin who was a bird-watcher, and he invited me to go birding with him. I didn't want to because I'd already seen all of the birds that I thought existed—sparrows, pigeons, canaries, parakeets, chickens, and turkeys. Of course, I'd also heard about eagles.

When I was thirteen and in the seventh grade, I found *Wild Animals I Have Known* in the school library at the beginning of the year. It was exactly the right book for me at the time, and may have been the only book that I read in the seventh grade outside of my class work. I hid it in the shelves behind other books so I'd always find it whenever I was in the library. All year long I went to the library and read and reread it. Seton really knew something about nature—Silverspot the crow, Lobo the wolf. I started wondering about the creatures in the book, and about other wildlife beyond its pages.

My own first book was a book of animal poems. Susan Hirschman, then editor-in-chief of Macmillan Children's Books, had seen a manuscript of mine about imaginary animals and suggested that I might try writing about real ones. That brought to mind my junior high school reading of *Wild Animals I Have Known*. Largely because of Seton's book, I felt confident that I could meet her challenge—and I did. That was how my first book of original poems, *A Gopher in the Garden*, came to be published.

You never know where things are going to lead. In the past few years, I've become an avid bird photographer. So far I haven't photographed any rare or exotic beauties that hide in jungles or nest in the arctic tundra, just ordinary ones that I encounter every day, like robins, crows, gulls, and jays. In my photos, I relate the birds to other objects, both natural and manmade, as I try to find the "birdness" of the bird. At the same time, I've been working on an extremely silly book about birds. I've been teaching myself computer graphics, and hope to illustrate this manuscript myself. None of this would be happening if I hadn't read *Wild Animals I Have Known* more than fifty years ago.

A tin-lined copper pot hanging over the fire was partly filled with water; then, when it was boiling, some samp or powdered corn and some clams were stirred in. While these were cooking, he took his smooth-bore flint-lock, crawled gently over the ridge that screened his wigwam from the northwest wind, and peered with hawk-like eyes across the broad sheet of water that, held by a high beaver-dam, filled the little valley of Asamuk Brook.

The winter ice was still on the pond, but in all the warming shallows there was open water, on which were likely to be ducks. None were to be seen, but by the edge of the ice was a round object which, although so far away, he knew at a glance for a muskrat.

By crawling around the pond, the Indian could easily have come within shot, but he returned at once to his wigwam, where he exchanged his gun for the weapons of his fathers, a bow and arrows, and a long fish-line. A short, quick stalk, and the muskrat, still eating a flagroot, was within thirty feet. The fish-line was coiled on the ground and then attached to an arrow, the bow bent—zip—the arrow picked up the line, coil after coil, and transfixed the muskrat. Splash! And the animal was gone under the ice.

But the cord was in the hands of the hunter; a little gentle pull and the rat came to view, to

be dispatched with a stick and secured. Had he shot it with a gun, it had surely been lost.

He returned to his camp, ate his frugal breakfast, and fed his small, wolfish-looking yellow dog that was tied in the lodge. He skinned the muskrat carefully, first cutting a slit across the rear and then turning the skin back like a glove, till it was off to the snout; a bent stick thrust into this held it stretched, till in a day, it was dry and ready for market. The body, carefully cleaned, he hung in the shade to furnish another meal.

ROLF IN THE WOODS by Ernest Thompson Seton

put down his gun, picked up a camera and pencil, and adopted a different relationship with animals in the wild.

Although now dated and somewhat difficult to read, Seton's work has had lasting effect on many children throughout the years. America's first children's poet laureate, Jack Prelutsky, developed a love of birds when he encountered Silverspot the crow. Legendary folksinger Pete Seeger appreciated the basic philosophy underlying Seton's work and drew on it for his own music.

Pete Seeger

A close relationship with nature may save the human race.

When I was seven, I lived in Nyack, New York, and the local librarian, who knew I enjoyed hiking in the woods, introduced me to the novels of Ernest Thompson Seton. These books changed my life. Seton became my guru. I saw an ad that asked, "Could you survive in the woods with nothing but a pocket knife and an axe? Seton can." I read every one of a set of nine books. From ages seven to thirteen I devoured Seton's writings.

The first book I read was *Rolf in the Woods*. Rolf, fifteen years old in 1810, is being beaten by his uncle. His mother dies. He runs away and finds a wigwam with a middle-aged Indian, Quonab, living in it, trapping animals and exchanging their skins at the hardware store for tools. The boy asks if he can stay; Quonab agrees; and Rolf falls asleep for the first time in a teepee. Eventually Rolf and Quonab flee north for the wilderness. Although Rolf understands books, the Indian can teach the boy from the book of nature.

I saved my nickels and bought myself enough unbleached muslin to build a teepee, 12 by 24 feet in size. I pegged it out, hemmed it up, and laced up the front. I set this out in my grandparents' cow pasture and had to install a fence around it so the cows didn't break it down. Slept in it overnight, using spruce branches for a bed. Learned to cook my food in it on a tiny fire. Later I took my teepee to school and put it in another pasture, introducing others to the idea of outdoor life. Living outdoors provided a better education for me than any school or university. I am still convinced that a close relationship with nature may save the human race.

Seton believed that if young people wanted role models they did not need to go to Europe. In America we had native people who showed us the way. If there was food, everybody shared; if there was no food, everybody, including the chief and his family, went hungry. And I thought: "That's the way to live—no rich, no poor."

Mona went on reading. Rush went on playing. Oliver went on drawing his fourteenth battleship.

"I think I have a good idea," repeated Randy patiently, and they looked at her.

"Well?" said Mona, her finger in her book.

"Let's start a club!" suggested Randy.

"Oh, look at all the clubs we've had already," said Rush. "The Mystery-Solving Club. The Tropical Fish Collectors Club. The Helping-Cut-Down-the-Electric-Light-Bill Club. What ever happened to any of them? They were all the same. Mona was always president and we never had more than two meetings."

"But this one will be different," persisted Randy. "Listen, Rush. Each of us (except Oliver, of course) gets fifty cents allowance every Saturday. Now. You want to go to Carnegie Hall and hear some music. Mona wants to go to a play. I want to see those French pictures Father was talking about. Every single one of those things costs more than fifty cents. Now what I was thinking was this. We're all old enough to be allowed to go out by ourselves—except Oliver—if we promise to be careful and not get run over or talk to people or anything. So why don't we put all our allowances together once a week and let one of us spend them? I mean, for instance, Mona would get a dollar and a half next Saturday and she could go to a play. Then the next week you'd get it, and the week after that it would be my turn. See? Only one rule would be that we couldn't save it, or just spend it on things like candy or a movie. We'd have to do something really good with it; something we'd always wanted to do."

"Say, that's not a bad idea at all." Rush looked excited. "We could pool our resources—that's what it's called, pooling your resources. Gee whiz, that would mean a dollar and a half for each of us if we pooled our resources!"

"We'd have to ask Father," said Mona.

"Oh, he'd say yes. He believes in children being independent."

"We'd have to ask Cuffy."

"Well, if we asked Father first and he said yes Cuffy would say yes too. You know she would."

"And what about shoelaces and pads and the dimes we owe?" Mona meant to find every flaw in the plan before she was won over. "There are always things like that."

"We'll just have to be careful," replied Rush.

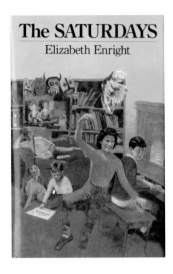

THE SATURDAYS

by Elizabeth Enright

The niece of architect Frank Lloyd Wright, Elizabeth Enright came to writing by a circuitous route. After studying dance with Martha Graham and illustration at the Art Students League of New York and Parsons, this multitalented young woman found that she liked writing books more than she enjoyed illustrating them. In 1939, at the age of thirty, she won the Newbery Medal for *Thimble Summer*, becoming one of the youngest writers to be given that award. Today, however, she is best known as the author of the Melendy Quartet, a series of books that began with *The Saturdays*, published in 1941.

Four Melendy children—two boys and two girls—live with their widowed father and housekeeper Cuffy in a New York City brownstone. A well-educated, intelligent, and lively group, they decide to pool their allowance money so that one Saturday a month each of them can do something really important. *The Saturdays* contrasts the need for economy on the part of the children with the opulence of the city they explore. One of the outings eventually leads to their being invited by a wealthy matron to spend a summer at the lighthouse she owns. As Enright said, the Melendys were concocted out of "wishes and memory and fancy." This blend of reality and fantasy held tremendous appeal for two midwestern children, film critic Roger Ebert and Newbery Award winner Linda Sue Park.

Linda Sue Park
The city seemed an exotic, adventurous place.

When I was ten years old, I discovered *The Saturdays* by Elizabeth Enright. Enright was the author of *Thimble Summer*, which I had read and liked, so I went looking in the library for other books by the same author—as I always did, and still do today! The characters in *The Saturdays* were especially appealing. The four children included Mona, the eldest and most glamorous; Rush, on whom I had a terrible crush; Randy (Miranda), a girl I wished to have as a best friend; and Oliver, who was both serious and funny. The stories in the book are made up of episodic chapters—one Saturday per chapter—detailing the children's outings in New York City. I can still remember every one of those outings: the first Saturday making the Grand Plan; Randy at the art museum; Rush at the opera; Oliver at the circus; Mona at the hairdresser's; the boating escapade in Central Park; —all delightful and memorable.

As a writer, I remain in awe of Enright's perfect touch with detail. She uses exactly what is needed to make the story come alive without bogging it down. For example, Randy has tea at a hotel and eats petits fours—little French cakes—for the first time. The petits fours are described as having "frilled paper collars . . . with silver peppermint buttons on top" and, just like Randy, I wanted to eat one immediately!

The portrayal of New York City, where the family lived, was also masterful. To me, a child of the Midwest suburbs, the city seemed an exotic, wonderful, adventurous place. The book was one of several that made me want to live in New York—and when I grew up, I did.

Roger Ebert
Stories could be wonderful.

Miss Fiske was the librarian at the Urbana Free Library, my own library when I was growing up. She ran the book club, the Saturday morning puppet shows, book fairs, and she read stories. She never had to talk to me about her love of books; she simply exuded it and instilled that passion in me.

I still search used bookstores for the adventures of the Melendy family by Elizabeth Enright—*The Saturdays*, *The Four-Story Mistake*, *Then There Were Five*, and *Spiderweb for Two*. Those books were the first real ones I ever read. They taught me that stories could be wonderful—that Miss Fiske was absolutely right to love books.

Even in ancient times people were wonderful builders. Seven of the things they built were so remarkable that they are called the Seven Wonders of the World. Some of the Seven Wonders were tombs or temples, and some were giant statues. The walls of a city were one of the wonders, and a lighthouse was another.

These ancient wonders were remarkable because in those days builders did not have giant machines to help them. They did not have steel and many of the other materials we have now to work with.

With our machines and materials we have built many wonders. The pictures on this page show a few. Among the many others are the artificial satellites we have made for exploring space.

THE GOLDEN BOOK OF SCIENCE FOR BOYS AND GIRLS by Bertha Morris Parker, illustrated by Henry McNaught

THE GOLDEN BOOK OF SCIENCE FOR BOYS AND GIRLS

by Bertha Morris Parker,
illustrated by Henry McNaught

As Golden Books developed in the 1950s, the publisher began to tackle increasingly complex projects, ones that might make others balk at both the expense and the expansiveness. Not all of these could be produced by the staff, so subject area experts were added to the stable of writers. Bertha Morris Parker, an innovator in elementary school science instruction, taught at the University of Chicago Lab School and created a series of science unit booklets from the 1930s through the 1960s. The author of more than seventy children's books and a president of the National Council of Elementary Science, Parker developed an entire encyclopedia for Golden Books; published in 1959, ten years in the making, the volumes cover 1,400 subject entries. Although less ambitious, some of her earlier titles, like *The Golden Book of Science for Boys and Girls*, were encyclopedic in their approach. Addressing such topics as animals with hair, animals with fur, magnets, clouds, weather, and toys that work, the book, illustrated in 1956 by Henry McNaught, was chock full of the kind of information that young children seek.

Although we usually view Golden Books as a particularly American phenomenon, many of these titles were translated into other languages and gained popularity particularly in the Netherlands and Japan. Hence, as a child in England, *New York Times* best-selling author and Macarthur Award winner David Macaulay found one of the Golden Books that he has kept by his side ever since. The jacket on this page comes from his personal hard-earned copy of *The Encyclopaedia of Science for Boys and Girls*, *The Golden Book of Science for Boys and Girls* in America.

David Macaulay

Everything is interesting if you stop and look at it.

As a child living in Bolton, England, I collected money for the Methodist Missionary Society. Every Saturday morning, I'd have a set number of subscribers that I visited and gathered money from, maybe only one or two pennies a week. By the end of the year, I had collected six pounds, sixteen shillings, and seven pence to help support various programs in Africa. As a reward, I was allowed to go to the local bookstore and choose any book I wanted; my parents paid half of it and the church the rest.

I located a new, big science book, called in England *The Encyclopaedia of Science for Boys and Girls*. The book was large, 12 inches by 15 inches, and impressive. On the cover it featured inventions like headphones and included many subject areas (air, seas, inventions, plants, and animals). My instant response was that it must include everything I would ever need to know.

I had to wait to receive the book at a ceremony. But I really wanted to get my hands on it and was very happy when I finally did. This book was an organized version of my childhood life, much of which was spent in the nearby woods exploring and gathering. Between what I saw and what I imagined, it all seemed to be contained, organized, and catalogued in this book.

But the double-page spread that most intrigued me was called "Wonders of Today and Tomorrow." The Empire State Building filled most of the left-hand page. It seemed enormous. Below it an ocean liner, much like the S.S. *United States*, was shown steaming into New York City. For me this picture was America, and when my family finally came here in 1957 on the S.S. *United States*, I expected the Empire State Building to be so large I would be able to see it as we passed Ireland. Later when I looked at the book as an adult, understanding illustration, I realized that clever Mr. McNaught had left a misty line between the building and the skyline, making the size of the building ambiguous and letting him off the hook for misleading this impressionable child.

Not only did I bring the book to another country as a child, I have kept it all these years. From it I learned that everything is interesting if you stop and look at it; I was introduced to a whole range of topics, many of which I would one day explore and discover for myself. The book's connection to my own titles, such as *The Way Things Work*, seems quite obvious to me many years later. I was so positively affected by this book that I wanted to make others like it; it's the kind of book I found fascinating as a child and still do as an adult. *The Encyclopaedia of Science for Boys and Girls* gave me ownership of my world by making a world of information accessible, fun, and exciting.

The March Hare took the watch and looked at it gloomily: then he dipped it into his cup of tea, and looked at it again: but he could think of nothing better to say than his first remark, "It was the best butter, you know."

Alice had been looking over his shoulder with some curiosity. "What a funny watch!" she remarked. "It tells the day of the month, and doesn't tell what o'clock it is!"

"Why should it?" muttered the Hatter. "Does your watch tell you what year it is?"

"Of course not," Alice replied very readily: "but that's because it stays the same year for such a long time together."

"Which is just the case with mine," said the Hatter.

Alice felt dreadfully puzzled. The Hatter's remark seemed to her to have no

sort of meaning in it, and yet it was certainly English. "I don't quite understand you," she said, as politely as she could.

"The Dormouse is asleep again," said the Hatter, and he poured a little hot tea upon its nose.

The Dormouse shook its head impatiently, and said, without opening its eyes, "Of course, of course: just what I was going to remark myself."

"Have you guessed the riddle yet?" the Hatter said, turning to Alice again.

"No, I give it up," Alice replied. "What's the answer?"

"I haven't the slightest idea," said the Hatter.

"Nor I," said the March Hare.

Alice sighed wearily. "I think you might do something better with the time," she said, "than wasting it in asking riddles that have no answers."

ALICE'S ADVENTURES IN WONDERLAND by Lewis Carroll, illustrated by Sir John Tenniel

ALICE'S ADVENTURES IN WONDERLAND

THROUGH THE LOOKING-GLASS

by Lewis Carroll,
illustrated by Sir John Tenniel

First published in 1865, *Alice's Adventures in Wonderland* began its journey with a modest printing of 2,000 copies but immediately established itself as a cultural icon and has always been in print. The book originated as a tale invented by Oxford don Charles Dodgson for the three Liddell children on a boat trip. Since Alice Liddell begged him to write down the saga, he did so and chose Lewis Carroll as his pen name. In this highly unusual and humorous story, Alice falls down a rabbit hole into a surreal world where all logic seems reversed. In the 1871 sequel *Through the Looking-Glass, and What Alice Found There,* Alice discovers that she is a pawn in a bizarre chess game, dominated by the Red Queen. Sir John Tenniel's illustrations for the two books now seem inseparable from these texts—although Tenniel squabbled incessantly with Carroll as the books were being created.

These idiosyncratic books, translated into more than 125 languages, contain many lines and characters that have entered into cultural consciousness: "Curiouser and curiouser . . . Off with their heads," the March Hare, Cheshire Cat, White Rabbit, Tweedledee, Tweedledum, and the Jabberwock. A diverse group of individuals, from Queen Victoria to the rock group Jefferson Airplane, have fallen under Alice's spell—one that continues to be cast on children, college students, writers, and scientists. A specialist in the field of children's learning, Professor Alison Gopnik of the University of California at Berkeley, believes that the Alice books have charted the course of her life.

Alison Gopnik
Science and fiction have a shared foundation.

Alice's Adventures in Wonderland and *Through the Looking-Glass* were among the first books I read as a child. I was Alice: I shared her name, long hair, dreamy absentmindedness, and preference for logic and imagination over common sense. I, too, was bewildered by the blindness of grown-ups, especially their failure to recognize that children were smarter than they were. I still am.

At twenty Alice changed my life. I went to the University of Oxford instead of Massachusetts Institute of Technology, and I became an empiricist psychologist instead of a Chomskyan philosopher—all because of a sun-dappled row down the Thames and a glimpse of gardens through a gate.

At fifty Alice is with me again in my work on theories, imagination, and consciousness. The books exemplify the link between logic and imagination, and between logic and imagination and the wide-ranging consciousness of childhood. Our unique ability to understand our world by creating theories is the same ability that lets us imagine possible worlds. Science and fiction have a shared foundation.

For children, theorizing and imagining are intense activities; they spend every minute learning and pretending. Charles Dodgson, shy Oxford don and mathematical logician, and Lewis Carroll, wild, uninhibited master of nonsense and imagination, were united in the little girl in the garden.

I think every scientist and every child is the grave, wide-eyed little girl who fearlessly follows evidence and logic wherever it leads—even through the looking-glass and down the rabbit hole.

Buck's first day on the Dyea beach was like a nightmare. Every hour was filled with shock and surprise. He had been suddenly jerked from the heart of civilization and flung into the heart of things primordial. No lazy, sun-kissed life was this, with nothing to do but loaf and be bored. Here was neither peace, nor rest, nor a moment's safety. All was confusion and action, and every moment life and limb were in peril. There was imperative need to be constantly alert; for these dogs and men were not town dogs and men. They were savages, all of them, who knew no law but the law of club and fang.

He had never seen dogs fight as these wolfish creatures fought, and his first experience taught him an unforgettable lesson. It is true, it was a vicarious experience, else he would not have lived to profit by it. Curly was the victim. They were camped near the log store, where she, in her friendly way, made advances to a husky dog the size of a full-grown wolf, though not half so large as she. There was no warning, only a leap in like a flash, a metallic clip of teeth, a leap out equally swift, and Curly's face was ripped open from eye to jaw.

It was the wolf manner of fighting, to strike and leap away; but there was more to it than this. Thirty or forty huskies ran to the spot and surrounded the combatants in an intent and silent circle. Buck did not comprehend that silent intentness, nor the eager way with which they were licking their chops. Curly rushed her antagonist, who struck again and leaped aside. He met her next rush with his chest, in a peculiar fashion that tumbled her off her feet. She never regained them. This was what the onlooking huskies had waited for. They closed in upon her, snarling and yelping, and she was buried, screaming with agony, beneath the bristling mass of bodies.

THE CALL OF THE WILD by Jack London, illustrated by Wendell Minor

THE CALL OF THE WILD

by Jack London

When the Klondike gold rush began in Alaska, tens of thousands came over the Chilkoot Pass, swept up in mass hysteria. Because sled dogs provided the only reliable transportation in this formidable climate, canines were stolen from the lower forty-eight states and worked to death by those hunting for their fortunes. During the gold rush young Jack London worked himself as a beast of burden, carrying bags and packages. But he took what he observed firsthand and turned it into *The Call of the Wild*. Rather than telling the events from the point of view of the men who experienced the gold rush, London chose to focus on the events from the point of view of a dog, Buck.

Weighing 140 pounds, Buck begins his life as a pampered pet. Then kidnapped and beaten, he struggles to survive in a savage environment, realizing he must adapt to intolerable circumstances or die. Starved, whipped, mistreated by humans, Buck at one point is saved by a man and becomes devoted to him. But the man's death frees Buck to follow his own path, becoming part of a wolf pack that survives on its own terms. London captures the veniality of humans and the magnificence and grandeur of dogs. First published as an adult book in 1903, the novella quickly became a staple of childhood. It has been published in many editions, one of the most exquisite with illustrations by Wendell Minor. Literary crusader Jim Trelease, author of *The Read Aloud Handbook*, fell in love with this book as a child.

Jim Trelease

A dose of "virtual reality" decades before the phrase was coined

When I was eleven years old, a book came into my life that transported me from the world of childhood reading into the much wider one I enjoy to this day: I read Jack London's classic *The Call of the Wild*. Nothing before or since has equaled its impact.

I have no idea why I chose to read it. My brothers and I were living with our parents in a tiny two-bedroom apartment in New Jersey—no house, no car, and no pets. So why did I respond to a book about a half–St. Bernard/half-sheepdog kidnapped (or was it dognapped?) from California and dragged to the numbing Canadian Klondike for the gold rush? How does a young altar boy identify with a wilderness adventure overflowing with violence, starvation, brutality, betrayal, death, and the love of a dog?

Until I met that book, everything I'd read was, in a word, childish. The books were unthreatening and kept me sheltered. And then along comes this novel that smacks me awake, that grabs my insides with one hand and my soul with the other hand, that demands that I pay attention, a book that snarls, "So you want to see the secret stuff the world is made of? Okay, kid, here it is." The Klondike was a long way from formulaic backyard Hardy Boys adventures, and I couldn't get enough of it.

Until *The Call of the Wild*, I'd always been aware I was reading a book; that is, I'd yet to be "lost" in one. Jack London gave me my first dose of "virtual reality" decades before the phrase was coined. I went immediately to his *White Fang* and then Jack O'Brien's Silver Chief series.

For years afterward I believed the whole experience was peculiar to me. It wasn't until I was in my fifties and read an old essay by Clifton Fadiman that I discovered the experience wasn't peculiar at all, that nearly all lifetime readers experience it with a singular book at some point. Fadiman explained that such a book is like one's first big kiss or first home run—they're unforgettable, and we spend the rest of our lives trying to duplicate or surpass them.

In recent years, when my friend Stephen Krashen, the reading researcher, explored Fadiman's theory, he found it to be firmly grounded: teenagers who were avid readers could almost always name their "home run" book while unenthusiastic or reluctant readers could not. In a nutshell, Jack London's *The Call of the Wild* had been my home run book.

Today when I hold an unread book in my hands and ponder whether it will be worth reading, left unsaid, but nonetheless there, is always the hope or question of whether it could be as good as *The Call of the Wild*.

How to Make Fire Without Matches

The following article on "Fire by Friction" is not a requirement but every Scout will want to master this method which is widely used to start Council Fires.

EDITORIAL NOTE—For years the experts of the Smithsonian Institution in Washington, D. C. have given technical advice to the Boy Scouts in fire-by-friction research. Dr. Walter Hough and others have given valuable information on the fire making tools of primitive man and the continuous quest for the best wood and material. This article by Mr. W. N. Watson, author of "Early Fire Making Methods and Devices," is in step with the Smithsonian findings.

Modern man makes more fires in a single day than the Stone Age man made in a lifetime. The daily consumption of matches in the United States exceeds half a billion. An automobile at a speed of 70 miles per hour makes over a million fires or explosions per hour. For early man, the making of a fire was a task that required persistence and skill and once made, fire was a thing to be carefully tended and kept.

The methods of fire making used before the invention of the friction match are becoming lost arts in many parts of the world. The Scouts who can make fire by the methods used by the early Indians has the right to be proud of his achievement. Friction fire making is an art and requires much practice. A working knowledge of these methods commands great respect for the fire craft of primitive man who was able to make his fires without matches under all conditions of life in the wilderness.

The methods of fire making by wood friction are divided into three classes: (1) Drilling, (2) Sawing, and (3) Planing. The bow drill is by far the most satisfactory method for the Scout.

BOY SCOUT HANDBOOK

Although Ernest Thompson Seton was adored by generations of readers for his novels and nature stories, his most important contribution to American culture came in 1910 when he pulled together the first edition of what became the *Boy Scout Handbook*. Created as a guide for the Boy Scout organization, for which Seton served as Chief Scout from 1910 to 1915, *The Official Handbook for Boys* relied for much of its content on Lord Baden-Powell's *Scouting for Boys* and Seton's *The Birch Bark Roll of the Woodcraft Indians*.

Revised many times, and with many other writers contributing, *Handbook for Boys* already had millions of copies in print by the 1940s, when Professor Peter Neumeyer discovered it; by that point this 680-page book contained enough activities to keep any boy in America occupied for years.

Peter Neumeyer
Everything a ten-year-old boy wanted to know

I still own and look at, from time to time, one of my favorite books from childhood, a classic of sorts: the *Boy Scout Handbook* or *Handbook for Boys* (1940). With ads for "troop flags," "patrol flags," "white L-Kraft knife," "folding candle lantern," "official pack basket, Mohawk Indian style," "Official 'signaler' [Morse code machine]," "official chow kit, with flashlight," and "Fingerprint Set," this book is an expanded version of the first edition of 1911, which had undergone consultation with 4,600 names, said to comprise "everybody . . . in America who was related to boys' work." It begins with chapters defining scouthood—a chapter titled "The Good Turn and Knighthood"—amplified by examples of those good turns, such as "let a dog out of a trap," "watered chickens at store," or "found and restored lady's pocketbook." It also covers cooking (fowl, game, green sweet corn, Seneca Indian dinner, "twist" baked on a stick), first aid, Indian sign language, tree and bird identification, stars and constellations, weather, insects, snakes, electricity, salesmanship, scholarship—in short, everything that a ten-year-old wanted to bury his nose in.

Small wonder that in 2007 the *New York Times* best-seller list includes *The Dangerous Book for Boys*, "skipping stones, tying knots and other essential activities," more or less the *Boy Scout Handbook*, redux. That idealistic and practical 1940 book spoke to me most directly when I was eleven. It addressed what every boy wanted to know. Decades later, boys are still intrigued by the very same things.

Peter led the private detective to the Tigers' clubhouse, an unused tool shed behind Mr. Sweeny's Auto Body Shop. The Tigers were busy racing garter snakes.

Bugs made a face when he saw Encyclopedia.

"So Mr. Brains is now a Civil War know-it-all," said the Tigers' leader. "Well, well! Maybe you can tell me what Stonewall Jackson did at the Battle of Bull Run."

"Which battle at Bull Run?" asked Encyclopedia. "There were two—one in 1861, the other in 1862."

"Good for you," said Bugs, grinning. "Now don't say this sword isn't the real thing."

Encyclopedia walked to the table on which the sword lay.

Bugs said, "This sword was given to Stonewall Jackson a month after the First Battle of Bull Run."

"If that's true," Peter whispered to Encyclopedia, "the sword is worth ten bikes like mine."

"Twenty," corrected Encyclopedia.

"Read what is says on the blade," said Bugs. Encyclopedia read:

To Thomas J. Jackson, for standing like a stone wall at the First Battle of Bull Run on July 21, 1861. This sword is presented to him by his men on August 21, 1861.

"The sword certainly has seen a lot of use," said Encyclopedia.

"Did you expect it to look new and shiny?" sneered Bugs. "It's more than a hundred years old."

"It doesn't look like it ever was worth five dollars," Encyclopedia said.

"Never mind how it looks," said Peter. "Do you think it belonged to General Jackson?"

Before Encyclopedia could answer, Bugs spoke up. "I sure hate to part with the sword," he said. "But Peter wants it so much I just had to say I'd trade it for his bike."

"Trade? You won't trade with Peter," said Encyclopedia. "This sword never belonged to General Stonewall Jackson!"

HOW DID ENCYCLOPEDIA KNOW THAT?

ENCYCLOPEDIA BROWN, BOY DETECTIVE by Donald J. Sobol, illustrated by Leonard Shortall

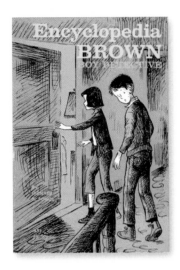

**ENCYCLOPEDIA BROWN,
BOY DETECTIVE**

by Donald J. Sobol,
illustrated by Leonard Shortall

Published in 1963, the first of Donald
J. Sobol's Encyclopedia Brown series,
Encyclopedia Brown, Boy Detective introduces
a character who has intrigued young sleuths
ever since. The son of the local police chief,
Leroy Brown—called Encyclopedia because
of his vast knowledge—lives in Idaville,
Florida. His father is considered a genius by
the town, but Encyclopedia bears a great
deal of responsibility for that reputation.
Secretly, he helps his father solve crimes;
local residents also pay Encyclopedia, "no
case too small," for his services.

A young Sherlock Holmes, he uses
observation, deduction, and logic to solve
mysteries. So he quickly determines that a
Civil War sword could not have belonged to
Stonewall Jackson or that a thief has been
lying to his father. Encyclopedia sometimes
receives aid as a bodyguard from Sally
Kimball, his Watson; he often finds himself
pitted against the town bully, Bugs Meany.
Each book contains ten cases; every chapter
includes logical or factual inconsistencies;
all the solutions have been printed in the
back of the book. Many reluctant readers
find themselves totally engaged by Sobol's
pithy writing and challenging puzzles. ESPN
commentator Rick Reilly was won over as a
young boy.

Rick Reilly

I never got any of the answers right at first, but I started to learn.

When I was seven or eight, I first read Donald J. Sobol's *Encyclopedia Brown,
Boy Detective*. I loved the fact that all the clues for the mystery were right
there in the story, and the answer was waiting in the back. How cool was that?
Of course, I never got any of the answers right at first, but I started to learn.
When in doubt, I realized that Bugs Meany, the neighborhood bully, was up to
no good.

Imagine my broken heart when I got to the end of the book. And
imagine my joy when I discovered it was a series! I'd love to shake Donald
Sobol's hand someday. He made reading interesting and fun for me.

He sold the bag of wool.
He sold the shawl his wife made.
He sold five pairs of mittens.
He sold candles and shingles.
He sold birch brooms.
He sold potatoes.
He sold apples.
He sold honey and honeycombs,
turnips and cabbages.
He sold maple sugar.

He sold a bag of goose feathers.
Then he sold the wooden box he
carried the maple sugar in.
Then he sold the barrel he carried the
apples in.
Then he sold the bag he carried the
potatoes in.
Then he sold his ox cart.
Then he sold his ox, and kissed him
good-bye on his nose.

OX-CART MAN by Donald Hall, illustrated by Barbara Cooney

OX-CART MAN

by Donald Hall,
illustrated by Barbara Cooney

Donald Hall had served as poetry editor of the *Paris Review* and taught at the University of Michigan before he moved to his family's farm in New Hampshire to write full-time in 1975. While writing adult poetry, he also turned his hand to a picture-book text for children, *Ox-Cart Man*, based on a family story. "I heard the story from my cousin, who had heard it when he was a boy from an old man, who told him that he had heard it when he was a boy, from an old man."

Describing a New Hampshire farming family's life, in a cyclical fashion, the book begins in October as an unnamed farmer, referred to only as "he" in the text, fills up a wagon, attaches it to an ox, and takes the family produce to Portsmouth Market. There he sells all that they have, purchases a few items for the family, and walks the ten miles back to his home. Then the family begins to create again the items they will sell next fall. The spare, poetic text was illustrated by another New England artist, Maine's Barbara Cooney; she rendered the illustrations for the nineteenth-century story in a style similar to the primitive New England painters of the era. Together the combined talents of author and illustrator re-create a sense of time and place. In an age when children often fail to understand how any of their food gets produced, the book describes in detail a self-sustaining, frugal society, where people consume what they produce.

WGBH producer Carol Greenwald discovered *Ox-Cart Man* as an adult and realized that it gave her a way to look at her own work.

Carol Greenwald
Aesthetics are crucial.

When I first read *Ox-Cart Man* to my children many years ago, we all loved the story of the cycle of the seasons on a New England farm in colonial times. But the book became a favorite not because of its subject matter but because of the way the language and the illustrations combine into an elegant and evocative whole. Donald Hall communicates so much in very concise words and phrases—we could all easily imagine the hard work the family did to make the shingles, the maple syrup, and the flax that the farmer sells at Portsmouth Market. We felt the pang of sadness as he says good-bye to his good ox and "kisses him on the nose." And we could practically feel those "soft as clouds" goose feathers dropping into the barnyard on the lovely spring day. His words were made palpable and enhanced by the detail and personality that shine through Barbara Cooney's simple yet graceful illustrations. We could almost feel the chill in the air in the image of the farmer making his long way home from Portsmouth through the starkness of the trees and the dark hills.

While all of us learned some pretty useful information about that cycle of the seasons on a New England farm, there was perhaps an even more important message about aesthetics that was implicit in the story. In my business, children's television, there's a real temptation to give aesthetics short shrift. Some people think that the language has to be dumbed down and that little effort needs to be put into what things look like. As long as the colors are bright and there's lots of action, children will watch it. To some extent that's true; children are not the most discriminating audience. But I think aesthetics are crucial because, like it or not, kids are developing a world view from their television shows. We need to be thoughtful about exposing them to language that's carefully constructed and visuals that are designed with thought about the artistry and style. That way, they can learn how to appreciate and understand the beauty of language and art and, perhaps, even see a model of how to create it themselves. Donald Hall and Barbara Cooney set the bar for me, as I have worked with other authors to create television programs for children that don't just entertain them but also enrich their ears and eyes.

"This is the land of Narnia," said the Faun, "where we are now; all that lies between the lamp-post and the great castle of Cair Paravel on the eastern sea. And you—you have come from the wild woods of the west?"

"I—I got in through the wardrobe in the spare room," said Lucy.

"Ah!" said Mr. Tumnus in a rather melancholy voice, "if only I had worked harder at geography when I was a little Faun, I should no doubt know all about those strange countries. It is too late now."

"But they aren't countries at all," said Lucy, almost laughing. "It's only just back there—at least—I'm not sure. It is summer there."

"Meanwhile," said Mr. Tumnus, "it is winter in Narnia, and has been for ever so long, and we shall both catch cold if we stand here talking in the snow. Daughter of Eve from the far land of Spare Oom where eternal summer reigns around the bright city of War Drobe, how would it be if you came and had tea with me?"

"Thank you very much, Mr. Tumnus," said Lucy. "But I was wondering whether I ought to be getting back."

"It's only just round the corner," said the Faun, "and there'll be a roaring fire—and toast—and sardines—and cake."

"Well, it's very kind of you," said Lucy. "But I shan't be able to stay long."

"If you will take my arm, Daughter of Eve," said Mr. Tumnus, "I shall be able to hold the umbrella over both of us. That's the way. Now—off we go."

And so Lucy found herself walking through the wood arm in arm with this strange creature as if they had known one another all their lives.

THE LION, THE WITCH AND THE WARDROBE by C. S. Lewis, illustrated by Pauline Baynes

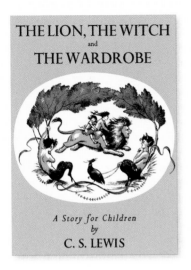

**THE LION, THE WITCH
AND THE WARDROBE**

by C. S. Lewis,
illustrated by Pauline Baynes

Clive Staples Lewis, a medievalist and Oxford don, met with colleagues in Oxford as part of the informal literary group the Inklings. Another of the members, J. R. R. Tolkien, admired Lewis's work in general but hated his children's books about Narnia. Although they didn't quite measure up to Tolkien's standards, the series, beginning with *The Lion, the Witch and the Wardrobe*, began enchanting children in the 1950s when they were first published and have grown in popularity in the twenty-first century, aided by popular movie adaptations.

Lewis penned many other books, including *The Screwtape Letters*, a science-fiction trilogy, and essays on Christian faith. But of all his creations, Narnia has captivated the largest number of readers, having sold more than 100 million copies in forty-one languages. These seven books chronicle the adventures of four children who have been evacuated from London during World War II to stay with an elderly professor. In one of the rooms they discover a wardrobe that leads to Narnia, a kingdom of talking animals, an evil witch, gnomes, and mythical creatures. The ruler of Narnia—Aslan, a magnificent lion—has arrived to free the land from the spell of the White Witch.

Often when adults are asked what they remember from the books, they immediately respond "Turkish delight," a candy used to entice the children. But *Salon* cofounder Laura Miller became so intrigued by the series that she wrote *The Magician's Book* to explore Narnia's impact throughout her life.

Laura Miller
There were other people who had the kind of imagination that I had.

In one of the most vivid memories from my childhood, nothing happens. On a clear, sunny day, I'm standing near a curb in the quiet suburban California neighborhood where my family lives, and I'm wishing, with every bit of myself, for two things. First, I want a place I've read about in a book to really exist, and, second, I want to be able to go there. I want this so badly I'm pretty sure the misery of not getting it will kill me. For the rest of my life, I will never want anything quite so badly again.

The place I longed to visit was Narnia, the setting for a series of novels by C. S. Lewis. There are things about these books that I, at age nine, did not yet understand and did not even realize were there to be understood. My relationship to Narnia would turn out to be as rocky as any love affair: a story of enchantment, betrayal, estrangement, and reunion.

This momentous passage in my reading life came when I was in second grade. Wilanne Beldon, a teacher I idolized, handed me a slim hardcover bound in gray fabric with the image of a little stag stamped on the front and said, "I think you'll like this one." It was her copy of *The Lion, the Witch and the Wardrobe*. When I returned it to her, I told her that I didn't know there were other people who had the kind of imagination that I had. It was this book that made a reader out of me. It showed me how I could tumble through a hole in a world I knew and into another, better one, a world fresher, more brightly colored, more exhilarating, more fully felt than my own.

The novelist Graham Greene, who marveled at the now-alien world of his boyhood reading, once wrote, "Perhaps it is only in childhood that books have any deep influence on our lives. . . . In childhood, all books are books of divination, telling us the future." The books we happen to latch on to as children help to furnish our imagination and, to a certain degree, our identity.

One day Stanley got a letter from his friend Thomas Anthony Jeffrey, whose family had moved recently to California. A school vacation was about to begin, and Stanley was invited to spend it with the Jeffreys.

"Oh, boy!" Stanley said. "I would love to go!"

Mr. Lambchop sighed. "A round-trip train or airplane ticket to California is very expensive," he said. "I will have to think of some cheaper way."

When Mr. Lambchop came home from the office that evening, he brought with him an enormous brown-paper envelope.

"Now then, Stanley," he said. "Try this for size."

The envelope fit Stanley very well. There was even room left over, Mrs. Lambchop discovered, for an egg-salad sandwich made with thin bread, and a toothbrush case filled with milk.

They had to put a great many stamps on the envelope to pay for both airmail and insurance, but it was still much less expensive than a train or airplane ticket to California.

FLAT STANLEY by Jeff Brown, illustrated by Tomi Ungerer

FLAT STANLEY

by Jeff Brown,
illustrated by Tomi Ungerer

Like so many children's books, *Flat Stanley* began its journey as a bedtime story. One evening Jeff Brown discovered that one of his sons feared that the big bulletin board in his bedroom might fall on him while he was sleeping. So Jeff made up stories for his boys about what would happen if the bulletin board fell and one of them ended up flat. Both thought this idea wildly funny, and he continued to tell them stories about Stanley Lampchop, as he was named by his son J. C. As the story evolves in the book, flatness proves to be a great advantage for the boy—he can slip into places that real children can't, actually becomes a kite, and can be mailed in envelopes for his vacations.

Although not all reviewers warmed to this decidedly offbeat tale when it was published in 1964, *Flat Stanley* stayed in print for many years, largely because children loved his quirky story. Then in 1995 a third-grade teacher in Canada used the book to help students make connections with others around the world, so they mailed friends, families, and pen pals a drawing of *Flat Stanley* in an envelope and kept a journal of all the places Stanley had visited. The project became an international sensation, and in the ensuing years *Flat Stanley* has traveled the globe. After receiving top security clearance, he visited the White House; he traveled in the *Discovery* space shuttle; he made many appearances at the 2006 Olympic Games; and Clint Eastwood took him to the Academy Awards. *Flat Stanley* may now be used to help children improve writing and communication skills, but the book caused Kansas State University Professor Philip Nel, an authority on children's literature, to think about the appropriate use of imagination.

Philip Nel

The power of imagination— and that there are more and less socially acceptable ways of imagining

In first grade, *Flat Stanley* was my favorite book. Flattened by his bulletin board, Stanley becomes two-dimensional, able to slide under doors and to be mailed to his friend. What a great idea! Bolstering my six-year-old's willingness to believe in stories, illustrator Tomi Ungerer rendered Stanley *nearly* two-dimensional—"half an inch thick," just as Brown says. This slight concession to a third dimension made Stanley's flatness seem not just plausible, but possible. Maybe I could become like Flat Stanley.

So, one day, I was walking across my elementary school lunchroom, pretending to be two-dimensional. I alternated pushing my stomach outward (while bending my back backward) and then sucking it backward (while arching my back forward). I was convinced that my body looked just like a vertically held piece of paper, its center arcing to and fro, convex to concave, over and over again. Yes, I was just like Flat Stanley . . . until I walked past classmate Stephanie Reed. She paused and looked me in the eye with an expression that said, "Phil Nel, you are a freak." Defiant, I continued my freakish undulations for a few more paces, but then began walking normally, suddenly conscious of the gap between the ideas inside my head and how odd I must look to other people.

The experience made me aware of the power of the imagination. It didn't make me less imaginative, but it did help me learn that there are more and less socially acceptable ways of imagining. So, I wrote stories. I drew pictures. I even impersonated my favorite characters, but not in the lunchroom.

The Bethel Church sat atop a long, low-rise, not much to the eye—but it told on a light mare pulling against a heavy stallion, and it was here Black Prince began to close in; before the rise was half covered, the stallion's nose was pressing toward the buggy's back near wheel.

Jess had given up encouraging. He was urging now. Eliza lifted the hat off his head. Come what might, there wasn't going to be any more hat-whacking if she could help it—but Jess was beyond knowing whether his head was bare or covered. He was pulling with his mare now, sweating with her, sucking the air into scalding lungs with her. Lady had slowed on the rise—she'd have been dead if she hadn't—but she was still a-going, still trying hard. Only the Quaker blood in Jess' veins kept him from shouting with pride at his mare's performance.

The Reverend Godley didn't have Quaker blood in his veins. What he had was Kentucky horse-racing blood, and when Black Prince got his nose opposite Lady's rump Godley's racing blood got the best of him. He began to talk to his cob in a voice that got its volume from camp-meeting practice—and its vocabulary, too, as a matter of fact—but he was using it in a fashion his camp-meeting congregations had never heard.

They were almost opposite the Bethel Church now; Black Prince had nosed up an inch or two more on Lady and the Reverend Godley was still strongly exhorting—getting mighty personal, for a man of his convictions.

But Lady was a stayer and so was Jess. And Eliza, too, for that matter. Jess spared her a glance out of the corner of his eye to see how she was faring. She was faring mighty well—sitting bolt upright, her Bible tightly clasped, and clucking to the mare. Jess couldn't credit what he heard. But there was no doubt about it—Eliza was counseling Lady. "Thee keep a-going Lady," she called. Eliza hadn't camp-meeting experience, but she had a good clear pulpit voice and Lady heard her.

She kept a-going. She did better. She unloosed a spurt of speed Jess hadn't known was in her. Lady was used to being held back, not yelled at in a brush. Yelling got her dander up. She stretched out her long neck, lengthened her powerful stride, and pulled away from Black Prince just as they reached the Bethel Church grounds.

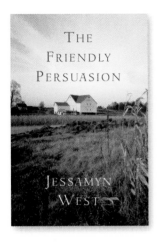

THE FRIENDLY PERSUASION

by Jessamyn West

Many of the essays in this book attest to what children's book professionals always seek: the right book, for the right child, at the right time. Since the range of books that can work is extraordinary, those serving children have to be flexible and creative in their selections.

Louis Clark, president of the Government Accountability Project, was once a struggling third-grade reader. Because of his problems, he might well have been presented with dumbed-down texts for reluctant readers, as so many young people are. But his teacher did something different—she gave him a much more sophisticated book, one originally written for adults that reflected some of the issues of his own life, Jessamyn West's *The Friendly Persuasion*.

After two years in a terminal ward of a tuberculosis sanitorium, Jessamyn West was released so that she could "die among her loved ones." But her mother refused to accept this prognosis, slowly nurturing her daughter back to health and entertaining her with family stories about their Indiana Quaker forebears. As West slowly recovered, she took her mother's reminiscences and begin to craft a series of stories about an Indiana Quaker farm couple. By the time she had regained her health, she had published several pieces about them in *The Atlantic Monthly, Harper's Bazaar,* and *The Ladies Home Journal.* Then she collected these pieces and shaped a book about Jess and Eliza Birdwell, *The Friendly Persuasion*, which spans a period from before the Civil War to the turn of the century. Family love, human foibles, and warmth and humor permeate the book. Adapted for a popular movie starring Gary Cooper, and often a selection for a "one town reads" book, *The Friendly Persuasion* had a profound effect on a third-grade boy—the right book at the right time.

Louis Clark

The personal power that flowed whenever I released myself from one world to inhabit another

As the freshly arrived preacher's son, I entered my third-grade classroom sick with worry. Having somehow been spawned into a family on which every limb of the family tree was sprinkled with either well-educated ministers or teachers, I devolved early into a chronic underachiever.

My previous lackluster academic performance was but icing on my petrified little soul, however. I was far more focused on avoiding any situations in which I would have to actually say something and, thereby, reveal my speech impediment, endure the inevitable snickering, and soon experience the nightmarish taunting at recess. I could not pronounce most words, including my first name, although I could nail my middle name, Alan, and my last name, Clark.

Now, as I sat waiting for my first humiliation, I cursed fate that my sister was no doubt already adjusting to her new fourth-grade class. Then the idea struck. No one knew me. When my new teacher asked my name, I became Alan Clark, although I knew I was only buying time. Mrs. Rayle, one of Dad's new parishioners, paused, looked up, seemed puzzled, and then simply said, "Well, Alan, welcome."

She won my heart that day. As the year progressed, she also won my soul. One day she took me aside, as no other teacher had ever done, and pressed the book *The Friendly Persuasion* into my eager hands. She said these stories by Jessamyn West were about a small Indiana rural community like our own, but long ago. I read the book from cover to cover that first time to please my mentor as I navigated the unfamiliar thickets of Quaker dialect and bursts of unfamiliar poetic prose.

The second reading landed me on the shore of a new world. Like my real world, this one was largely populated with Quakers and Methodists, dripping with piety but also harboring intense personal ideals and social consciences. Through learning of their humorous and sometimes poignant struggles, I also experienced for the first time the personal power that flowed whenever I released myself from one world to inhabit another. For a time that first serious book served as my life raft from a sea of alienation that threatened my young being. Soon reading, and the academic achievement that flowed from its fruits, became a longer-lasting salvation.

Two years later, one morning I excitedly returned from speech therapy. My fifth-grade teacher suggested I knock on the door of my mom's sixth-grade class. When she opened the door, I said but one word, delivering it in perfect English: "Louis."

The smoke cleared away and Miss Moody was staring at the biggest, ugliest creature she had ever seen.

"Thank you, madam," it said. "Too bad you didn't make a wish. You could have had anything you wanted—gold, jewels, a palace. I could have made you a queen or a president. Now I must get to work."

"Work?" said the astonished Miss Moody.

"Lots of work. When anyone wants to steal or cheat or lie or hurt someone else or start a nice little war, I help them do it." The creature laughed. "Just for fun, I get into people's dreams. Children wake up screaming."

"That's just what you are," said Miss Moody. "A bad, bad dream."

"Why aren't you afraid of me?"

"Because I'm not afraid of anything I don't believe in. And I don't believe in you for a minute."

The creature grew bigger and uglier. "Now are you afraid of me?" it said.

"No," said Miss Moody.

DO NOT OPEN by Brinton Turkle

DO NOT OPEN

by Brinton Turkle

Brinton Turkle studied theater in college and in later years worked with marionettes and local stage productions. Hence he brought a strong sense of drama and storytelling tension to his work when he began writing and illustrating picture books. In *Do Not Open*, published in 1981, Turkle drew upon a folklore concept—the genie or power in a bottle—to relate a highly original story. Miss Moody and her cat, Captain Kidd, live by the sea where she salvages objects for her cozy cottage. Then late one September afternoon, a huge storm descends on her domain. In the morning she begins a treasure hunt on the beach. Finding a deep purple bottle that says, "Do Not Open," Miss Moody hears a child crying inside, pulls out the stopper, and unleashes a terrible creature. "When anyone wants to steal or cheat or lie or hunt someone else or start a nice little war, I help them do it," the huge dark shape tells her. But Miss Moody proves the equal, in terms of ingenuity, to any monster.

Children's literature specialist Maria Salvadore had always loved this book and had shared it with her son when he was small. But after the events of September 11, 2001, she grew to appreciate the power of a single book in a totally different way.

Maria Salvadore

Even though the world will spin in its own, unfathomable direction, readers—for a time—control at least a part of their universe.

As a child, my reading was eclectic. I read what my older sister read—often thinking her taste in books was way off base—or what my mother recommended, what I could put my hands on at the library, or books that I was given as gifts. It made me read widely, with not one but lots of book titles coming to mind, each with its own peculiar impact.

It wasn't until my son came along that I realized the influence of a single book on an individual. The power of a seemingly simple picture book became clear to me on September 11, 2001.

My son was well beyond the picture book age when the entire world changed that day. But he would not stop searching every shelf in the house (and there are lots of them) until he found Brinton Turkle's *Do Not Open*. I think he found comfort in the familiarity of the story we'd read dozens and dozens of times; each time safe, together, and relaxed. But more, in rereading this book, he found himself again with a solitary old woman who is able to contain the evil found in a bottle.

From *Do Not Open* and my son's response, I learned that readers are able to control a part of their world for as long as it takes to read (or reread) a book. Even though the world will spin in its own, unfathomable direction, readers—for a time—control at least a part of their universe.

With my stepping ashore I began the most unhappy part of my adventures. It was half-past twelve in the morning, and though the wind was broken by the land, it was a cold night. I dared not sit down (for I thought I should have frozen), but took off my shoes and walked to and fro upon the sand, bare-foot, and beating my breast with infinite weariness. There was no sound of man or cattle; not a cock crew, though it was about the hour of their first waking; only the surf broke outside in the distance, which put me in mind of my perils and those of my friend. To walk by the sea at that hour of the morning, and in a place so desert-like and lonesome, struck me with a kind of fear.

As soon as the day began to break I put on my shoes and climbed a hill—the ruggedest scramble I ever undertook—falling, the whole way, between big blocks of granite, or leaping from one to another. When I got to the top the dawn was come. There was no sign of the brig, which must have lifted from the reef and sunk. The boat, too, was nowhere to be seen. There was never a sail upon the ocean; and in what I could see of the land was neither house nor man.

I was afraid to think what had befallen my shipmates, and afraid to look longer at so empty a scene. What with my wet clothes and weariness, and my belly that now began to ache with hunger, I had enough to trouble me without that. So I set off eastward along the south coast, hoping to find a house where I might warm myself, and perhaps get news of those I had lost. And at the worst, I considered the sun would soon rise and dry my clothes.

KIDNAPPED by Robert Lewis Stevenson, illustrated by N. C. Wyeth

KIDNAPPED

by Robert Lewis Stevenson

First published in *Young Folks* in 1886, *Kidnapped* combined real characters such as Alan Breck (Stewart) with those imagined in a rich historical novel set in eighteenth-century Scotland. In the beginning young David Balfour, an orphan, is given a letter to deliver to the House of Shaw. There he meets his deranged uncle Ebenezer, who at first tries to kill him and then schemes to have David kidnapped and placed on the *Covenant*, a ship bound for America. On the vessel David develops an allegiance to Alan Breck (Stewart), a brave Jacobite who wants to return a Scottish king to the throne. After the *Covenant* sinks off the coast of the Isle of Mull in the Scottish Highlands, the two witness the murder of Colin Roy Campbell, a real event in history. Then they must flee from the British dragoons through the heather, mountains, and moors of the highlands.

Plot driven from the first chapter until the end, the story has been written with a thick Scottish dialect that takes some patience for the reader. Stevenson always claimed, however, that he downplayed the brogue, so that non-Scottish readers could enjoy the book. The novel works simply as a sea and land adventure story, but it also contains a great deal of historical information. Readers see a sympathetic portrayal of the plight of the Highland Scots who at this period of time could not wear their clan tartans; and one poignant scene shows a boat leaving for America and families being torn apart. The book has been re-created in many different forms, from movies to the graphic novel.

From a French-Canadian background, Ned Berube, who has spent his career explaining computers and computer technology, developed an appreciation of Scottish culture and history from the book.

Ned Berube

A keen appreciation and understanding of a people, culture, and country

I come from a blue-collar family that was not very book oriented, so my parents and siblings were quite surprised at my early bookishness. My dad was a general contractor, who had apprenticed to a Swedish cabinetmaker when he first came to the U.S. from Quebec, Canada when he was seventeen years old. My mother was a traditional housewife with six kids, but I suspect she read a great deal, only because of the unusual, somewhat literary names she gave to us—Maurice, Olivette, Vietta, Norbert, Edgar, and Jeannine.

I didn't speak or read English until I was about six years old, as we lived in one of the French-Canadian enclaves in Fall River, MA. What sparked my interest in books was a series of Classic Comic books that belonged to my cousins. I read those illustrated classics from cover to cover, just devouring those tales about exotic places and characters in stories like *The Song of Hiawatha*, *Robinson Crusoe*, and *Kidnapped*.

Soon I was old enough to get a library card of my own and to take the bus to the Fall River Public Library downtown. What a treasure trove in those stacks! Delighted, I rediscovered Robert Louis Stevenson's *Kidnapped* in book form, and I was transported once again to Scottish highlands and lochs.

Kidnapped had a particular resonance for me—the story of a boy, David Balfour, undergoing perilous adventures both at sea and in the wilds of Scotland. David and his Scots protector, Alan Breck, became my heroes despite the strange Scottishisms of the text. I could see myself in the hold of the ship being tossed about on the waves of the Little Minch off of the gray misty coasts of the Isle of Skye, and scurrying with Alan and David through the heather and mountains of Appin, avoiding the red-coated dragoons, while making their way back toward Queensferry. At the time I had no idea of the politics of the era, nor what a Whig or much less what a Jacobite was, but David's steadfastness under duress and Alan's Scottish humor and masterful swordplay captured my heart and imagination.

Stevenson's tale transported me to a country that I would eventually visit several times as an adult, and fall in love with again and again. From my experience with *Kidnapped*, I realize that this single book, read in childhood, fostered a keen appreciation and understanding of a people, culture, and country even before I got to see and meet them firsthand. Stevenson's masterful description of the skirling of bagpipes, the snickersnee of flashing blades, and breathless dashes through the Scottish glens imprinted an affinity within me for a stalwart people who contributed so much in the forming and settling of America.

Just as Grandma set her cake out to cool, she heard the jingle of the ice cream cart. She hurried out.

"I'm sorry, Grandma," said Peter 'Possom, the ice cream man. "I could not bring your pink ice cream. The ice cream factory didn't make any pink ice cream today."

"But I must have pink ice cream," wailed Grandma. "You don't come tomorrow. What can I do?"

"Dunno," said Peter. "I go to Alkali Flats tomorrow. Wish I could help." He waved and pedaled away.

Grandma though and thought. Then she had an idea. She grabbed her next-to-best bonnet and rushed off toward Hackberry lodge to find Rufus Raven. Soon she heard his ructious laughter. When she called to him, he came right down.

"Hello, Grandma. What can I do for you?"

"Could you fly to Alkali Flats tomorrow and bring back some pink ice cream for Yomi and Tomi's birthday party?"

"Be glad to, Grandma," said Rufus with a big smile.

PINK ICE CREAM by Launa Latham

Pink Ice Cream

Written and Illustrated by
Launa Latham

PINK ICE CREAM

by Launa Latham

Usually when people discuss their favorite book, they pick a title that has been widely read, often a classic book that has also affected thousands if not millions of others. But not all books must be universally approved or applauded to bring meaning; books are, ultimately, the most personal of media. They can be important to only one person or to only a few people, and yet because of that they still have tremendous influence.

Pink Ice Cream by Launa Latham was privately published in a paperback edition in 1991. Latham grew up on a farm near Spur, Texas, and she delighted in watching the over a hundred inhabitants of the prairie dog town on her family farm. Other animals lived in these holes as well—cottontail rabbits, turtles, burrowing owls, and snakes. Once a teacher in a one-room schoolhouse, Latham used her childhood memories and her experience with children to write and illustrate stories about Grandma Prairie Dog and her boarding house in West Texas.

Lesley Stahl, longtime anchor of CBS's *60 Minutes*, found one of the rare copies of the book and was attracted to its insights about the power of imagination.

Lesley Stahl
You can remake your world by using your imagination.

When I was a little girl, my best friend stopped talking to me. It was a rejection so hurtful that I still shiver whenever I think about it. Her name was Ellen Whiteford, and we became friends again when her mother brought us together over scoops of vanilla and chocolate ice cream. Asked which flavor we liked, we said both. Then Mrs. Whiteford explained that people are similar to ice cream. They can look different on the outside, but that has nothing to do with our liking them for what's on the inside. It was Tolerance 101 for children.

It's no wonder that my favorite children's book is *Pink Ice Cream* by Launa Latham. When Grandma Prairie Dog asks the rabbit twins Yomi and Tomi what they want at the birthday party, they shout, "Pink ice cream!" Poor Grandma. There is no pink ice cream anywhere to be found on the plains of West Texas where she runs a boarding house. On the day of the party, the guests are distracted by contests. Just when Grandma is about to serve dessert, the idea comes to her. She quickly paints a light bulb with red fingernail polish. And voila! The vanilla ice cream turns pink.

Turning on a light can transform things. Put another way—you can remake your world by using your imagination to see it differently. A psychologist acquaintance who works with abused children uses this book in her practice. One of her small patients told her, "I wish there was a pink light in my whole life."

At the City Bath Houses, Ella, Henny, and Sarah undressed in one locker, while Mama shared another with Charlotte and Gertie. They got into their bathing suits quickly, took the sweaters, the lunch, and their bathhouse keys and went at once to the hot, sandy beach. It wasn't so easy to find a place in which to settle themselves and their belongings. The beaches were crowded with other mamas who had sought relief for their children. But finally, when they had walked a few beach blocks away from the bathhouse, a suitable spot was found. The children dropped their bundles and raced madly down to the water's edge.

"Ooh, it's cold," said Sarah as the water lapped at her toes.

"Aw, come on! Let's get wet all over quickly," suggested Henny. "Then we won't mind it so much."

The children agreed that this was the best plan. They stepped back to where the waves did not reach, then joining hands, they ran without stopping into the ocean until the water came up to Gertie's chest. "Ready, set, go!" Ella counted. Down they splashed, straight into the heart of a wave. Wet all over, they stood up spluttering.

"It's hard to believe now that it's terribly hot in the city," Ella said.

"Uh-huh," Charlotte agreed. "I'm glad Mama brought us here."

They splashed about happily. They formed a circle and played Ring-Around-The-Rosy. Mama had remembered to bring a ball, and they tossed it back and forth to one another. They ducked through some waves and rode on the backs of others. They had a glorious time.

Mama could hardly get them out. They stayed in the water till their lips got blue and their bodies shivered with the thorough chilling. That was when the sweaters came in handy. Mama spread the lunch and to the famished children, the simple food tasted wonderful. There were bread-and-butter sandwiches, Mama's kind, a slice of sour rye bread placed against a slice of pumpernickel. With these, they ate hard-boiled eggs and whole tomatoes sprinkled liberally with salt. For herself Mama had brought limburger sandwiches. The children found it hard to believe that they tasted better than they smelled.

"Ocean bathing certainly gives you children an appetite," Mama remarked as she watched the shoeboxes becoming empty one by one.

At the end, Mama had a wonderful surprise—store-bought cakes! Not just plain cakes like the ones Mama baked at home for the Sabbath, but fancy ones with icing—chocolate and vanilla!

ALL-OF-A-KIND FAMILY by Sydney Taylor, illustrated by Helen John

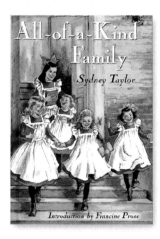

ALL-OF-A-KIND FAMILY

by Sydney Taylor,
illustrated by Helen John

In a New York Lower East Side tenement at
the turn of the twentieth century, a family
of two loving parents and five little girls
experience all the joys of life, even though
they are quite poor. Their adventures in *All-
of-a-Kind Family*, published in 1951, include
the simple pleasures of finding buttons while
dusting, buying penny candy, and visiting
the family's junk shop. But their greatest
enjoyment comes from celebrating all the
Jewish holidays, lovingly described as a child
would experience them. At the end of the first
book, a baby boy arrives, and the family's
saga continues in several other volumes.
During the latter part of the twentieth century,
these stories became the best-known books to
present the Jewish faith to children.

For this realistic chronicle, Sydney Taylor
drew upon her own personal experience.
Taylor also pursued a career as an actress
and professional dancer for the Martha
Graham Company, but today she is
remembered for her re-creation of the
vibrant and cohesive community that she
brought to life. Much like Betty Smith's *A Tree
Grows in Brooklyn*, the All-of-a-Kind Family
books demonstrate that a rich, exciting life
can be found in places where people own
few possessions. Novelist Meg Wolitzer
discovered these books as a girl, and still
remembers vividly the details of the story.

Meg Wolitzer
There is no single world— but many of them.

All-of-a-Kind Family was one of the most evocative books I read as a child,
and as a result I still think about it frequently, even now. It was the first in
a series about a family on New York's Lower East Side in the early 1900s,
and what I loved about it, in part, was that all the siblings were girls. Sydney
Taylor created a kind of island of femaleness in an urban setting. What went
on among the sisters reminded me of what went on between me and my
own sister in our modern suburban life: all the disagreements, love, and the
intensity of imaginative play. In one scene, two of the sisters lay in bed at
night eating the precious crackers and candy they had bought during the day.
Because the family had very little money, they needed to make them last,
and so one of the sisters instructed the other about which particular one they
were allowed to eat, and how many nibbles from the edge they were allowed
to take, etc.

The writer had such a deep sense of the complex lives of children—the
things that take place when parents aren't looking. The warmth of family life
was conveyed beautifully, too. What this novel has, most of all, is atmosphere,
and this has influenced me deeply as a writer ever since. (*Atmosphere!*
I sometimes remind myself when I'm working. *Fill up the thing with
atmosphere!*) Good children's books give you an early sense of the multiple
textures of the world. They remind you that there is, in fact, no single world—
but many of them.

Peter Wood

Testimony to something right in our world

Kate is outdoors on a blanket, bundled against the autumn chill in the photograph her parents sent for Christmas. It is midmorning daylight and about as far away from the great green room as a two-year-old may get, but still Kate is clutching her favorite book, *Goodnight Moon*.

When Margaret Wise Brown woke up one morning in 1945 with this story in her head, she mistakenly titled it *Goodnight Room*. But the title *Goodnight Room* would have impoverished the book by insisting too much on the interior. The great green room, capacious as it is, is not the World. Outside, glimpsed through the windows in Clement Hurd's pictures, are the moon and the stars. And the little story ends with a fading away from the local and the particular: "Goodnight stars / Goodnight air / Goodnight noises everywhere."

The chill of the outside universe is written and drawn into the story in other ways, too: the fire blazing in the fireplace, the blankets on the bed, the pair of mittens pinned to the drying stand, and the quiet old lady's winter knitting. The implied world beyond the walls is cold and snowy, but not hostile or dangerous.

In fact, the great green room has a hint of the Peaceable Kingdom. The two long-haired kittens gambol on the braided rug and play with the old lady's yarn, but ignore the mouse that scurries from rug to mitten stand, and from mush bowl to windowsill. The mouse provides one of several lines of near narrative that Hurd conjured with his illustrations out of Brown's minimal text. Hunting for the mouse from frame to frame is one of the child reader's pleasures.

The great green room doesn't win the hearts of small children because it is filled with the ordinary. It captures the child because it transforms the ordinary into something richer and more complete. Clement Hurd's pictures of the "great green room" and Margaret Wise Brown's ineffably quiet rhyme on the edge of sleep cast a spell that lasts long into the night.

Kate's delight in *Goodnight Moon* is a small testimony to something right in our world. Ultimately, children respond deeply to these images of peace and security because they feel them to be real. Beyond our wars, real and cultural, we provide that assurance. "Goodnight noises everywhere."

Principles & Precepts

There was indeed a house up ahead of us, on the right-hand side of the road. We could see it in the moonlight. But as we hurried toward it, in livelier spirits, I couldn't make myself believe that it was a farmhouse. Certainly, it was no ordinary farmhouse. For it was much too showy. I could count three stories and an attic. It was a stone house, too. And even if it had been built years and years ago, when labor and plaster were peddled around at bargain rates, I could not doubt that it had cost a fortune.

Who had been crazy enough, I wondered, curious over the unusual place, to build a house like this at the very end of the world? It didn't fit into the waste landscape at all.

Still, was my contented thought, the better the house the better the meal. It ought to work out that way. So we really were in luck to strike a place like this instead of a shack, which would have better matched the country.

Not only was the house itself built of stone, but it was inclosed by a stone wall at least three feet high. Where the private road turned in, smoothly graveled, the wall was lifted into a huge arched gateway. Looking in, I thought curious-like of the magic palace that the genii had built for Aladdin.

"Is it real?" I asked Poppy's opinion, wondering if it would be safe for us to go in. "Or is it a mirage, as you read about in stories of people crossing the desert?"

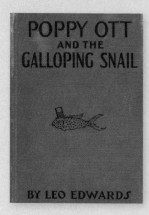

POPPY OTT

by Leo Edwards

Leo Edwards began his writing career penning serialized stories in *American Boy*; he would eventually create several popular series during the 1920s and 1930s–Andy Blake, Jerry Todd, Tuffy Bean, Poppy Ott, and Trigger Berg.

A master at intriguing titles and page-turning plots, Edwards brought lots of quirky and delicious elements into his books. *Poppy Ott and the Galloping Snail*, for example, contains a mysterious death, omnipresent ghost, missing heiress, creepy mansion, villainous lawyer, rattletrap car (the galloping snail), eccentric characters, and an unusual pet (a spotted gander).

Edwards also knew a great deal about communicating with his readers and building a devoted base of fans. Comic-book master Stan Lee, who has developed many classic characters—Spider Man and the Incredible Hulk—was particularly attracted to the work of Leo Edwards. Newbery Award Winner Betsy Byars became a member of the Secret and Mysterious Order of the Freckled Goldfish.

Betsy Byars
Cultivate friendships, and value them.

In 1935, at age seven, I sent off two two-cent stamps to Leo Edwards in order to become a member of the Secret and Mysterious Order of the Freckled Goldfish. The club took its name from Edwards's book *Poppy Ott and the Freckled Goldfish*. For my two stamps I was to receive a membership card adorned with a comical picture of the freckled goldfish, containing the club's rules along with Leo Edwards's autograph and a coveted club button.

I was living in a cotton mill community in rural North Carolina at the time. Pleasure reading was considered a sort of frivolity there, and there was no hope of my organizing a local chapter of the club as other readers were doing. The local chapter activities were reported in a special section called "Our Chatter-Box." Chapters sent word of their libraries and their fund-raisers, and one group even had their own robes with the freckled goldfish on the front and back. I would have given a lot to have had one of those robes.

Leo Edwards was my favorite author then. The stories and apparently the man himself teemed with energy and enthusiasm. And in the Our Chatter-Box section he did something unique among children's authors—he begged his readers to write him. Among other things, Leo Edwards taught me that it might be quite exciting to write books for children and to have fans who wanted to write to you. Leo Edwards was more than an author to me. He was a real person who taught me to cultivate friendships and to value them.

Stan Lee
Communicate with fans.

When I was young, I read everything I could lay my hands on. My mother used to say that if I didn't have a book to read while I was eating, I'd read the label on the ketchup bottle. But I particularly liked the books by Leo Edwards, the Poppy Ott series. There was a tremendous amount of humor and adventure in these books. They bore titles that were ridiculously imaginative–*Poppy Ott and the Stuttering Parrot, Poppy Ott and the Galloping Snail, Poppy Ott and the Freckled Goldfish*, and *Poppy Ott Hits the Trail*.

In each book were pages of letters, "Our Chatter Box"; Leo Edwards would write a message to the readers and print some of their letters with his own answers. He had a very informal style, and I loved the fact that books had letters and commentary by the author. For years I remembered the warm, friendly feeling of those letters pages. I learned about communicating with fans from Leo Edwards. He gave me the idea to create the "Bullpen Bulletins" pages in my own comics years later.

Everything had to be kept very secret, so when they found or bought anything to take on the trip they hid it behind a rock in the park. The night before my father sailed he borrowed his father's knapsack and he and the cat packed everything very carefully. He took chewing gum, two dozen pink lollipops, a package of rubber bands, black rubber boots, a compass, a toothbrush and a tube of tooth paste, six magnifying glasses, a very sharp jackknife, a comb and a hairbrush, seven hair ribbons of different colors, an empty grain bag with a label saying "Cranberry," some clean clothes, and enough food to last my father while he was on the ship. He couldn't live on mice, so he took twenty-five peanut butter and jelly sandwiches and six apples, because that's all the apples he could find in the pantry.

When everything was packed my father and the cat went down to the docks to the ship. A night watchman was on duty, so while the cat made loud queer noises to distract his attention, my father ran over the gangplank onto the ship. He went down into the hold and hid among some bags of wheat. The ship sailed early the next morning.

MY FATHER'S DRAGON by Ruth Stiles Gannett, illustrated by Ruth Chrisman Gannett

MY FATHER'S DRAGON

by Ruth Stiles Gannett,
illustrated by Ruth Chrisman Gannett

When a young boy with the euphonious name of Elmer Elevator rescues a stray cat, his life takes an unexpected turn. The cat, an escapee of Tangerina and Wild Island, persuades Elmer to travel to the jungles there and rescue a baby dragon in captivity. Even more important, the cat instructs Elmer on what to bring in his backpack—including two dozen pink lollipops and six magnifying glasses. Young readers for over fifty years have delighted in watching Elmer put everything he brings to good use while he outwits tigers, boars, a lion, and crocodiles before releasing the dragon.

Ruth Stiles Gannett wrote *My Father's Dragon*, with its wonderful balance between action and fantasy, on a two-week vacation between jobs. Before the project was completed, she enlisted her stepmother to illustrate the book and her fiancé to choose the type and draw the maps. The resulting book immediately became a childhood and classroom favorite, the perfect book to read aloud at the end of first grade or independently in third or fourth grade. In the case of Nick Clark, director of the Eric Carle Museum of Picture Book Art, he came under the book's spell after he found it in the school library.

Nick Clark
Use your noodle.

I always enjoyed reading under the covers with the flashlight when the lights were supposed to be out. When I was eight or nine, I went to a small private school in New York City with a very comfortable library, with lots and lots of books. There I stumbled upon Ruth Stiles Gannett's *My Father's Dragon*. I was delighted by the ingenuity of the protagonist Elmer Elevator. Having been given guidance by the cat about which items to take to the Island of Tangerina (chewing gum, rubber bands, a toothbrush, a jackknife, seven hair ribbons), he had to use these strategically as he worked his way through various challenges. I was also mesmerized by the art: There are wonderful images of the rhinoceros brushing its tusk, the lion with his marvelous mane braided with bows, and Elmer walking along a bridge of crocodiles. The illustrations are absolutely delicious and really take the text into another dimension, graphically extending it.

Books are so important in conveying messages to children. We may not fully appreciate the impact of a book until we are older, but there are things that we learn from our reading. From *My Father's Dragon* I learned that you have to use your noodle—and that the underdog can triumph in the end.

B abar, the young king of the elephants, and his wife, Queen Celeste, have just left for their wedding trip in a balloon.

"Good-by! See you soon!" cry the elephants as they watch the balloon rise and drift away.

Arthur, Babar's little cousin, still waves his beret. Old Cornelius, who is chief over all the elephants when the King is away, anxiously sighs: "I do hope they won't have any accidents!"

The country of the elephants is now far away. The balloon glides noiselessly in the sky. Babar and Celeste admire the landscape below.

What a beautiful journey! The air is balmy, the wind is gentle. There is the ocean, the big blue ocean.

Blown out over the sea by the wind, the balloon is suddenly caught by a violent storm. Babar and Celeste tremble with fear and cling with all their might to the basket of the balloon.

By extraordinary good fortune, just as the balloon is about to fall into the sea, a final puff of wind blows it on an island where it flattens out and collapses.

"You aren't hurt, Celeste, are you?" Babar inquires anxiously. "No! Well then look, we are saved!"

THE TRAVELS OF BABAR by Jean de Brunhoff

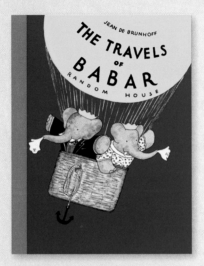

BABAR BOOKS

by Jean de Brunhoff

Babar the elephant first began in the mind of a mother, Cecile de Brunhoff, who told bedtime stories to her sons ages five and six. Then when their father Jean de Brunhoff heard the stories from his boys, he expanded them, illustrated the text, and published *The Story of Babar* in 1933. Possibly because de Brunhoff created his series of seven books about Babar while struggling with tuberculosis, the stories have a serious undertone. Babar sees his mother killed by hunters and flees. When he arrives in Paris, he is befriended by a rich old lady, becomes a Parisian dandy, and later returns to become King of the Elephants. De Brunhoff died in 1937; in the late 1940s one of the two sons, Laurent, an abstract painter, continued the saga, bringing Babar into modern life, sending him to the moon, and demonstrating his practice of yoga.

The Babar books, according to Maurice Sendak, "have a freedom and a charm, a freshness of vision that captivates and takes the breath away." First published in large, oversized volumes, perfect for the elephant protagonist, with a text printed in script, the books were frequently altered and shrunk over the years to save money. But the oversized volumes always worked the best for the books, providing the necessary space for de Brunhoff's delicate watercolors of his enormous hero. Fortunately in this century, they have been reissued in their original format.

Leslie Moonves, CEO of CBS, read the original Babar books as a child.

Leslie Moonves
The virtue of curiosity

I have fond memories of my childhood and the books that I encountered then. I was read to when I was very young. Then I went through a phase from about six until nine when I read sports books and sports biographies. But as a young child, around four, the Babar books by Jean de Brunhoff were my absolute favorites. My mother, an avid reader until this day, found them for me. To show how naïve I was, I didn't realize until many years later that they were French in origin.

For me these books provided noticeable life lessons. Babar the elephant is quite sensitive and quite exploratory. He is very interested in everything in the world. Babar goes to new places—Paris, the seashore, mountains—and travels in a balloon and on an ocean liner. I related to him because I wanted to be an adventurer; I was very curious. To this day I remain curious; it helps me every day that I am in my job and that I am on earth.

Because I am dealing with a world that is so rapidly changing in the media environment, it is important to value curiosity. I just spent a day up in Silicon Valley, meeting with people who are twenty-two years old and forming new companies. It is really fascinating and exciting to see what they are doing. Curiosity is required every day in my work, more now that ever before. I first learned to value that virtue as a child in the books about Babar.

Stephanie Loer
To care deeply about animals

ROBERT LAWSON

My father came home from the bookstore with a twinkle in his eye and a new book in his hand. "It's about rabbits," he announced. That evening he began reading *Rabbit Hill* to my brother and me. We spent many winter evenings listening to the haps and mishaps of the animals that lived on the Hill. The anticipated arrival of "New Folks" coming to live in the old house on the Hill built suspense with each chapter. Would the Folks be kind to the animals that called the Hill home? Robert Lawson's ability to create animal characters with human virtues and foibles made me care about them deeply.

As a child I lived on a large midwestern farm; animals, both domestic and wild, were a part of my life. So the creatures on Rabbit Hill were very real to me. I was quite sure animals did talk to one another. Today, I am fortunate to still live in rural surroundings. And when I chatter away to our horses, sheep, and chickens, I still listen—thoroughly convinced they will stop neighing, baaing, and clucking and actually begin speaking.

BABAR BOOKS

by Jean de Brunhoff

Babar the elephant first began in the mind of a mother, Cecile de Brunhoff, who told bedtime stories to her sons ages five and six. Then when their father Jean de Brunhoff heard the stories from his boys, he expanded them, illustrated the text, and published *The Story of Babar* in 1933. Possibly because de Brunhoff created his series of seven books about Babar while struggling with tuberculosis, the stories have a serious undertone. Babar sees his mother killed by hunters and flees. When he arrives in Paris, he is befriended by a rich old lady, becomes a Parisian dandy, and later returns to become King of the Elephants. De Brunhoff died in 1937; in the late 1940s one of the two sons, Laurent, an abstract painter, continued the saga, bringing Babar into modern life, sending him to the moon, and demonstrating his practice of yoga.

The Babar books, according to Maurice Sendak, "have a freedom and a charm, a freshness of vision that captivates and takes the breath away." First published in large, oversized volumes, perfect for the elephant protagonist, with a text printed in script, the books were frequently altered and shrunk over the years to save money. But the oversized volumes always worked the best for the books, providing the necessary space for de Brunhoff's delicate watercolors of his enormous hero. Fortunately in this century, they have been reissued in their original format.

Leslie Moonves, CEO of CBS, read the original Babar books as a child.

Leslie Moonves
The virtue of curiosity

I have fond memories of my childhood and the books that I encountered then. I was read to when I was very young. Then I went through a phase from about six until nine when I read sports books and sports biographies. But as a young child, around four, the Babar books by Jean de Brunhoff were my absolute favorites. My mother, an avid reader until this day, found them for me. To show how naïve I was, I didn't realize until many years later that they were French in origin.

For me these books provided noticeable life lessons. Babar the elephant is quite sensitive and quite exploratory. He is very interested in everything in the world. Babar goes to new places—Paris, the seashore, mountains—and travels in a balloon and on an ocean liner. I related to him because I wanted to be an adventurer; I was very curious. To this day I remain curious; it helps me every day that I am in my job and that I am on earth.

Because I am dealing with a world that is so rapidly changing in the media environment, it is important to value curiosity. I just spent a day up in Silicon Valley, meeting with people who are twenty-two years old and forming new companies. It is really fascinating and exciting to see what they are doing. Curiosity is required every day in my work, more now that ever before. I first learned to value that virtue as a child in the books about Babar.

When Meg woke to the jangling of her alarm clock the wind was still blowing but the sun was shining; the worst of the storm was over. She sat up in bed, shaking her head to clear it.

It must have been a dream. She'd been frightened by the storm and worried about the tramp so she'd just dreamed about going down to the kitchen and seeing Mrs. Whatsit and having her mother get all frightened and upset by that word—what was it? Tess—tess something.

She dressed hurriedly, picked up the kitten still curled up on the bed, and dumped it unceremoniously on the floor. The kitten yawned, stretched, gave a piteous miaow, trotted out of the attic and down the stairs. Meg made her bed and hurried after it. In the kitchen her mother was making French toast and the twins were already at the table. The kitten was lapping milk out of a saucer.

"Where's Charles?" Meg asked.

"Still asleep. We had rather an interrupted night, if you remember."

"I hoped it was a dream," Meg said.

Her mother carefully turned over four slices of French toast, then said in a steady voice, "No, Meg. Don't hope it was a dream. I don't understand it any more than you do, but one thing I've learned is that you don't have to understand things for them to *be*. I'm sorry I showed you I was upset. Your father and I used to have a joke about tesseract."

"What is a tesseract?" Meg asked.

"It's a concept." Mrs. Murry handed the twins the syrup. "I'll try to explain it to you later. There isn't time before school."

"I don't see why you didn't wake us up," Dennys said. "It's a gyp we missed out on all the fun."

"You'll be a lot more awake in school today than I will." Meg took her French toast to the table.

"Who cares," Sandy said. "If you're going to let old tramps come into the house in the middle of the night, Mother, you ought to have Den and me around to protect you."

"After all, Father would expect us to," Dennys added.

"We know you have a great mind and all, Mother," Sandy said, "but you don't have much *sense*. And certainly Meg and Charles don't."

"I know. We're morons." Meg was bitter.

"I wish you wouldn't be such a *dope*, Meg. Syrup, please." Sandy reached across the table. "You don't have to take everything so *per*sonally. Use a happy *medium*, for heaven's sake. You just goof around in school and look out the window and don't pay any attention."

"You just make things harder for yourself," Dennys said. "And Charles Wallace is going to have an awful time next year when he starts school. *We* know he's bright, but he's so funny when he's around other people, and they're so used to thinking he's dumb, I don't know what's going to happen to him. Sandy and I'll sock anybody who picks on him, but that's about all we can do."

"Let's not worry about next year till we get through this one," Mrs. Murry said. "More French toast, boys?"

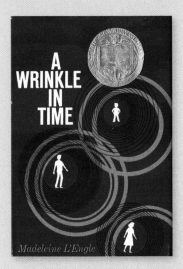

A WRINKLE IN TIME

by Madeleine L'Engle

Rejected by twenty-six publishers, *A Wrinkle in Time* came very close to never being published. Madeleine L'Engle herself had stopped sending the manuscript around. But then the book's guardian angel stepped in. L'Engle gave a party for her visiting mother and some of her friends; one of them knew John Farrar of Farrar, Straus and Giroux and convinced him to take a look. Farrar did, his children's editor did, and they decided that they couldn't resist this unusual mixture of fantasy and science fiction.

L'Engle's incredibly messy manuscript—she made major changes before it was published—remained inconsistent from a literary point of view. It begins with the most clichéd sentence in the English language, "It was a dark and stormy night." But the characters and the story line were quite unusual in 1962 and began to attract young readers immediately.

In the book Meg Murry and her precocious brother Charles Wallace join forces with three beings, Mrs. Whatsit, Mrs. Who, and Mrs. Which, to save Meg's father from the ultimate evil, a giant pulsing brain. Winning the Newbery Award and legions of devoted fans, *A Wrinkle in Time* remains one of the most cherished American classics. Facing its share of censorship over the years—whether for being too Christian in its orientation or for promoting witchcraft—the book rarely fails to work its magic with children. Photo detective Maureen Taylor, like many young readers, found a role model in Meg.

Maureen Taylor
Question everything.

Even before I learned how to read, books were an important part of my life. I had a small collection that I looked at every day. In kindergarten I quickly picked up reading, and as a child I read voraciously, with a stack of books beside me, often reading several at once. Every week I'd ask my mother, "When are we going to the library?" One summer I read so much that my father was convinced that something was wrong. He thought my mother should take me to the doctor, "just in case."

At the end of fifth grade my favorite childhood book was Madeleine L'Engle's *A Wrinkle in Time*. I read it through several times in one summer. I still own a copy. Meg was my hero. I immediately identified with her—we had poor handwriting, were clumsy, and wore glasses. I felt I understood her angst because we were both at an awkward age. I found it refreshing that a female protagonist could be intelligent and engage in scientific inquiry. It was a very powerful book for me.

That same summer I read the adult title C. W. Ceram's *God, Graves, and Scholars: The Story of Archaeology*. While Meg had her adventures in outer space, the archaeologists in Ceram's book traveled to exotic places locating lost history. Both books appealed to my fascination with scientific investigation and discovery, reading and learning, and problem solving.

As a child, I wanted to be an archaeologist more than anything in the world; I thought it must be so exciting to live like the men in Ceram's book. In college I decided that history had more allure. I couldn't space travel like Meg or dig up old artifacts, but I could make discoveries by researching historical details. Now as a photo detective, looking at photographs brings a new discovery every day I look at family photographs with a fresh eye. I try to see what the owners have forgotten about their ancestor's lives and use the photographic evidence to reveal their hidden past. The roots of this passion are in those books I read as a child.

From *A Wrinkle in Time* I learned to believe in myself and—from Meg I learned that it was important to question everything.

Miss Pickerell let out her breath and continued to climb.

Just as she thought she could go no farther, her fingers grasped a sort of sill. Miss Pickerell realized that she had reached the space ship.

She dragged herself up to the opening and lay there a moment, half in and half out, with her stomach pressed against the sill. She took one look backward at her cow, and as she did so, she saw something else, but she was too agitated from her climb to pay it much attention. What she saw was the blue-suited figure of Mr. Haggerty hurrying down the lane to the pasture gate, his large briefcase swinging in his hand.

Miss Pickerell pulled herself through the opening, and through a second doorway just behind it, and then, too weak to stand, she rested for a moment on her hands and knees.

She opened her eyes and looked up. She found herself inside a large, partly circular room. At the far side of this room, stood two men, looking up at a large panel with a mass of complicated-looking instrument dials. Nearby, at one side of her, Miss Pickerell saw several curved couches or bunks, with deep springs and cushions.

One of the men at the other side of the room turned his head partly around, as if he might have heard Miss Pickerell come in. She got to her feet, and as she did so, her dizziness overcame her and she collapsed into one of the bunks.

She heard someone say, "Well, there he is at last!"

Someone else called out, "Haggerty! Where in the world have you been all this time?"

Miss Pickerell opened her mouth to say that she wasn't Mr. Haggerty, but before she could speak, someone shouted, "Let 'er go!"

There was a heavy clanking sound as the two doors behind her closed. Then there came an ear-splitting hissing and a thunderous rumbling. The bunk beneath Miss Pickerell rose like an explosion. A tremendous force pushed her deep into the springs and cushions of the bunk. She felt as though she would be pushed right through. The force tore away her strength, her breath, everything.

She lost consciousness.

MISS PICKERELL GOES TO MARS by Ellen MacGregor, illustrated by Paul Galdone

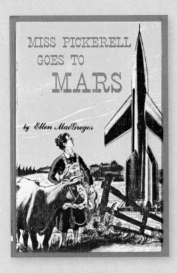

MISS PICKERELL GOES TO MARS

by Ellen MacGregor,
illustrated by Paul Galdone

During the late 1940s and early 1950s
Eleanor Cameron developed her Mushroom
Planet series and Louis Slobodkin wrote *The
Space Ship Under the Apple Tree;* hence
a few years before Americans actually
landed on the moon, American children
could absorb the idea of space travel from
their own books. The first of seventeen
volumes featuring Miss Pickerell, an eccentric
old woman who resembles Miss Marple,
appeared in 1951 in *Miss Pickerell Goes to
Mars.* This series, written initially by Ellen
MacGregor and continued after her death by
Dora Pantell, used the chapter book format
to explore issues of science and included
titles such as *Miss Pickerell Tackles the
Energy Crisis.* In all the books Miss Pickerell's
misadventures convey science lessons as well
as a large dollop of humor.

In *Miss Pickerell Goes to Mars,* the
protagonist's pasture had been selected as
a launch pad by some scientists intent on
reaching the red planet. After she encounters
one of them, she heads into the spaceship to
expel the others from her property because
they are annoying her cow. But things don't
turn out quite the way she expects, and she
finds herself headed to Mars, the first woman
to travel on a space mission.

Although now unfortunately out of print,
Miss Pickerell Goes to Mars, with its lively
illustrations by Paul Galdone, became a
favorite book of many children. Cancer
researcher Bert Vogelstein found personal
affirmation in this slim volume.

Bert Vogelstein
To keep my brain free for the important stuff

In Ellen MacGregor's *Miss Pickerell Goes to Mars* the protagonist, Miss
Pickerell, accidentally manages to board a spaceship that is going to Mars. She
travels there because of an absentminded scientist: He's so preoccupied that
he and his colleagues take a woman on the spaceship without knowing that
they are doing so. Miss Pickerell is flabbergasted that he is so scatterbrained,
but he says: "I save wear and tear on my brain. . . . I don't clutter it up with
little unimportant things. Anything . . . [else] I just write down. And then I
forget it." That idea stuck with me.

For better or worse, people often think I'm absentminded. If they get in a
car with me, I'm as likely to go somewhere completely different as I am to go
to the right place. But that is because I try to keep my brain free for important
stuff, rather than for trivial details. When I read *Miss Pickerell Goes to Mars*, it
made me aware that a scientist might think exactly the way I do.

"... Stolen at Dune Beach. Car is Swiftline cream sedan, believed heading south on Shore Road. Alert all cars! Repeat ..."

The bulletin had just come over the police band on Frank Hardy's motorcycle radio. He and his brother Joe, side by side on their dark-gray machines, were roaring northward along Shore Road to join school friends for a swim.

"Dune Beach!" Frank shouted, and the boys skidded to a halt on a sand shoulder. The car thief might pass them at any moment!

"Let's stop him!" Joe proposed.

The boys waited, scanning a deserted fishing pier on their right. Frank was eighteen, tall and dark-haired. Joe, a year younger, was blond. Both were excellent amateur detectives.

"Joe, do you realize this makes five car thefts in one week along Shore Road?"

The Hardys steered their motorcycles to the land side of Shore Road and faced them south, ready to move out quickly.

Several cars whizzed by, heading north. Then two police cars screamed past in the other direction.

After five more minutes had gone by, Frank frowned. "It looks as if we're not going to nab any thieves today."

Joe said, "Let's hope the police are on the right track!"

THE HARDY BOYS: THE SHORE ROAD MYSTERY by Franklin W. Dixon

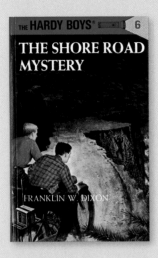

THE HARDY BOYS

by Franklin W. Dixon

In 1927 Edward Stratemeyer launched one of the most successful series of children's books of all times, the Hardy Boys, with three volumes: *The Tower Treasure*, *The House on the Cliff*, and *The Secret of the Old Mill*. During the 1920s, Stratemeyer had noted the popularity of adult detective fiction and thought children might be equally intrigued by the genre. He developed the outlines for these books featuring Frank and Joe Hardy, amateur detectives attempting to follow in their father's footsteps. They spend their days solving crimes rather than worrying about school. They also own a motorboat and motorcycles; in fact, they appeal in every way to the fantasy life of young boys.

Leslie McFarlane, under the pseudonym of Franklin W. Dixon, wrote the first volumes in the series; other ghostwriters continued this popular saga. Beginning in 1959 the Stratemeyer Syndicate started revising all the books to update them, although the revisions were so inferior to the originals that fans still consider the process "an act of literary vandalism." The original series, through the 1950s, dominated children's book sales. Numbered in sequence, costing around a dollar, the books could be purchased in all types of stores, in all kinds of locations. Even in communities where no bookstores existed, children used their hard-earned allowances to purchase Hardy Boys books.

Peter Lynch, who has demystified the process of investing for individuals in books like *One Up on Wall Street*, found in the Hardy Boys sagas some early role models.

Peter Lynch
Method and intellect, teamwork, and discussion

My childhood took place in the pretelevision era; when one of our neighbors got a television set, I actually went over and stood outside of their house just to watch it through a window. But we were a reading family, surrounded by books, and my mother was a great reader.

My mother also volunteered in the public elementary school in Newton, Massachusetts, that I attended, and they ran a thrift shop; people would bring in used clothing and books. I bought Hardy Boys mystery books there—*The Shore Road Mystery*, *The Secret of the Lost Tunnel*—for ten cents. That was a good buy even in the early fifties.

I remember the Hardy Boys series vividly, how much I enjoyed them. But even more than pleasure, I remember the excitement of reading them. What appealed to me were the situations; Joe and Frank Hardy had to think and react. The books didn't have complex plots, but the boys had to analyze a situation and take action. I was fascinated by the fact that they owned a motorcycle; I've never driven a motorcycle in my life, but a kid who owned a motorcycle was cool.

I really liked the fact that they worked with their father. My father took sick when I was seven and died when I was ten. Because my father died when I was so young, the Hardy Boys' partnership with their father had a lot of meaning and resonance for me.

During my career in the financial industry, I've spent my time researching companies. I spend a lot of time just looking at how solid a company is or if it could be fixed or improved. Because I have no prejudices or biases, I look at all kinds of companies, domestic and foreign, union and nonunion, in fast- or slow-growing industries. If you pick the best companies, you win at investment. But of course so much depends on how much research you do. Someone can invest on a whim; someone might spend two hours looking at a company and think that it looks fine. But I look at a wide variety of companies from a lot of different angles. Reading has allowed me to take that approach—to be flexible and cast a wide net.

In the Hardy Boys, I saw role models of boys who took action, were thoughtful, planned things out, and used their brains. There was no magical thinking in these books—no brawn, no super powers. There was method and intellect, teamwork, and discussion. These are all great values to take into the business world.

The Good Samaritan

A certain lawyer stood up, and, to try Jesus out, said, "Master, what shall I do to inherit eternal life?"

Jesus said to him, "What is written in the law? How do you read it?"

And he, answering, said, "You shall love the Lord your God with all your heart, and with all your soul, and with all your strength, and with all your mind, and your neighbor as yourself."

And Jesus said to him, "You have answered correctly; do this, and you shall live forever."

But he, wishing to justify his question, said to Jesus, "And who is my neighbor?"

Jesus, answering, said: "A certain man went down from Jerusalem to Jericho, and fell among thieves, who stripped him of his clothing, and beat him, and went off, leaving him half dead.

"By chance a certain priest came down that way, and when he saw him, he passed by on the other side.

"A Levite also, when he reached the spot, came and looked at him, and passed by on the other side.

"But a certain Samaritan, as he journeyed, came where he was. And when he saw him, he took pity on him, and went to him, and bound up his wounds, pouring in oil and wine. And he set him on his own beast, and brought him to an inn, and took care of him.

"The next day, when he departed, he took out some coins, and gave them to the innkeeper, and said to him, 'Take care of him, and whatever you spend beyond this, when I come again I shall repay you.'

"Now which of these three, do you think, was neighbor to him who fell among the thieves?"

And he said, "He who took pity on him."

Then Jesus said to him, "Go, and do the same yourself."

THE GOLDEN BIBLE FOR CHILDREN: THE NEW TESTAMENT edited and arranged by Elsa Jane Werner, illustrated by Alice and Martin Provensen

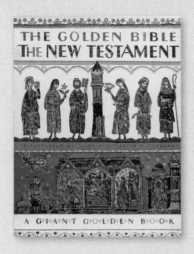

THE GOLDEN BIBLE FOR CHILDREN: THE NEW TESTAMENT

edited and arranged by Elsa Jane Werner, illustrated by Alice and Martin Provensen

Hundreds of the Golden Books were written by staff members to provide material for the talented illustrators who had been attracted to the imprint. In the 1940s editor Jane Werner, writing as Elsa Jane Werner, took on what she felt to be the most intellectually challenging and gratifying projects of her career, the adaptation of both the Old and New Testaments of the Bible. *The Golden Bible Stories from the Old Testament*, illustrated by Feodor Rojankovsky, was published in 1946 and was followed by *The Golden Bible for Children: The New Testament*, illustrated by Alice and Martin Provensen, in 1953. Both seemed obvious candidates for a new Golden Books format—Giant Golden Books—designed to stand apart from competitors' volumes on the shelf. Although priced slightly higher than the small Golden Books, these album-sized titles still boasted cover prices well below the average in the market.

Throughout their illustrating career, the Provensens worked seamlessly as a team. Alice and Martin, employed by rival California animation studios—Lantz (who created Woody Woodpecker) and Disney—met during World War II when they were developing U.S. Navy training films. Moving to New York at the end of the war, they brought to their work an understanding of animation as well as graphic art. Positioned between representative and modern abstract artists, these two not only conducted a great deal of research for each illustration, but they also understood how to keep young readers turning the pages. Since by the 1950s Golden Books completely dominated the home market for baby boomers, millions of children discovered the power of the Bible stories in these books, including the CEO of Forbes, Inc., Steve Forbes.

Steve Forbes
We should help others—even when there is no apparent advantage in doing so.

When I was a child, I didn't always enjoy reading, but I loved being read to. Around the age of five or six, my favorite book was one of the giant Golden Books, Elsa Jane Werner's *The Golden Bible for Children: The New Testament*, illustrated by Alice and Martin Provensen. I particularly loved "The Good Samaritan" and found its lesson fascinating, one we often forget as adults in the hurly-burly of life. That story about the Good Samaritan taught me then that we should help others—even when there is no apparent advantage in doing so. As a first-class example of practical compassion in action, it stresses the importance of charity.

So many stories stay with us, long after we encounter them as children; that book and story have had a lifelong effect on me.

In a town in Calabria, a long time ago, there lived an old lady everyone called Strega Nona, which meant "Grandma Witch."

Although all the people in town talked about her in whispers, they all went to see her if they had troubles. Even the priest and the sisters of the convent went, because Strega Nona did have a magic touch.

She could cure a headache, with oil and water and a hairpin.

She made special potions for the girls who wanted husbands.

And she was very good at getting rid of warts.

But Strega Nona was getting old, and she needed someone to help her keep her little house and garden, so she put up a sign in the town square.

And Big Anthony, who didn't pay attention, went to see her.

"Anthony," said Strega Nona, "you must sweep the house and wash the dishes. You must weed the garden and pick the vegetables. You must feed the goat and milk her. And you must fetch the water. For this, I will give you three coins and a place to sleep and food to eat."

"Oh, grazie," said Big Anthony.

"The one thing you must never do," said Strega Nona, "is touch the pasta pot. It is very valuable and I don't let anyone touch it!"

"Oh, si, yes," said Big Anthony.

STREGA NONA by Tomie dePaola

STREGA NONA

by Tomie dePaola

One of America's most popular illustrators, Tomie dePaola has created more than 200 books for children, filling them with stylized art full of energy and empathy. Since his first books, published in 1965, he has turned his hand to Mother Goose stories, nursery tales, folklore, Bible stories, autobiographical stories, and Christmas carols. His illustrations with dark brown outlines have been built with layer upon layer of acrylic paints, with an occasional touch of colored pencils. In all of his books, both the story and the art receive equal attention.

For *Strega Nona*, one of his best-known works published in 1975, dePaola drew inspiration from a staple of folklore—the magic cooking pot. According to children's book critic Barbara Elleman, dePaola served up the perfect ingredients for a humorous picture book that also provides a more serious message.

Barbara Elleman
Magic deserves a little caution.

The joy of life that slices through the books of Tomie dePaola is a spirit I greatly admire. His stories sometimes bubble up with laughter, sometimes simmer with sly wit, and sometimes burst with outright silliness. Cleverly, he matches image to mood. The pages, punctuated often with his signature hearts and white birds, are warmed with lively lines and vibrant colors, giving an upbeat feeling that pleases. Tomie, it seems, sees the world through a smile, and I, in turn, respond.

One of my favorites is *Strega Nona*, a tale that warms my heart a bit more at each reading. In telling his story, Tomie provides likeable, believable characters and sets them in situations ripe for humor. Strega Nona, or grandmother witch, has the magic touch; she makes potions for young husband-hunting girls and cures headaches with "oil and water and a hairpin." When her ever-inept helper Big Anthony attempts to duplicate Strega Nona's magical pasta-making spell—to help fill his ever-empty stomach—he nearly overwhelms the town with a flood of spaghetti. Through facial and body expressions, Tomie deftly pictures the hilarious results of Big Anthony's meddling. And, as the pasta pot refuses to quit delivering (he doesn't know he must blow three kisses), we find Big Anthony fumbling through a series of funny gyrations that only Tomie could bring off.

I chuckle through this merry chain of events, yet relish in Strega Nona's timely return, bringing order out of chaos. The best, however, is the conclusion: When the villagers suggest "stringing him up," Strega Nona decries "the punishment must fit the crime" and hands Big Anthony a fork. And eat he does! A final scene finds Big Anthony's bulging stomach and haggard face giving credence to his eating nightmare. Her reprisal against her bumbling assistant is so deserving—and so priceless.

Humor, Tomie seems to be saying, is a part of life, but magic deserves a little caution. It is a message I find worth noting; when temptations appear on my own horizon, I think of Strega Nona and Big Anthony and smile.

They stood at the bottom of an elm tree. It was perfectly enormous. It was easy to see why it looked so big. They were very small. It was delightful to be small! "Come on," said Edward, "let's climb."

Ned and Nora were looking for the treasure, too. They were already high up in the branches, far overhead. Eleanor and Edward could hear them laughing and calling to one another. Edward put his foot on a knotted root, sought for handholds in the ridged bark, and started to climb. Eleanor followed him close behind.

The going was easy. The trunk of the tree was knobbed and channeled in grooves, and there were networks of ribs between the grooves. They climbed lightly and quickly, and before long they were high above the ground.

The voices of Ned and Nora beckoned them on, and now and then, through hollow openings between branches, they caught glimpses of a red head, or a scrap of white dress, or a dangling leg. Up and up they climbed, tirelessly. At last they found themselves at a place where the huge trunk separated, and a tremendous limb split off, like a thumb projecting from a hand. They rested in the hollow for a while, and then climbed on. The main stem rose higher and then split into long fingering branches. Which way had the lost children gone? Their voices seemed to come from different places, now on this side, now on that.

Eleanor didn't care very much whether they found them or not, she was enjoying the climbing itself so much. It was as easy as going upstairs. The shaggy bark offered steps and leaning-places and outthrust chairs to sit on. She planned to climb to the topmost branch and blow around with the wind. Then, swaying back and forth, she would just let go and fly away! Just fly away, and soar and float all the way down to the ground!

THE DIAMOND IN THE WINDOW by Jane Langton, illustrated by Erik Blegvad

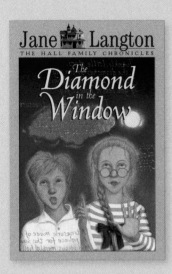

THE DIAMOND IN THE WINDOW

by Jane Langton,
illustrated by Erik Blegvad

In 1962 Jane Langton published the first of her eight books about Edward and Eleanor Hall, two orphans who live with their Aunt Lily in a remarkable Victorian home in Concord, Massachusetts. In the first story, *The Diamond in the Window*, property taxes on the residence remain unpaid, and the Halls face the demolition of this Victorian monstrosity, with its picturesque stained-glass window, towers, and turrets. Then Edward and Eleanor discover a secret attic room, a cryptic poem, and antique toys that send them on a mysterious quest. The history of Emerson, Thoreau, Alcott, and the town itself has been interwoven into their daytime life and their dreams, which draw them further into adventures. Langton excels in three-dimensional characters and a plot-driven story with a totally satisfying conclusion. Most children simply read the book for its intriguing events—a page turner that might be described as Mary Poppins meets the Transcendentalists. But the book works on a much deeper intellectual level as well. The new Gothic Revival Victorian that served as the inspiration for the book still stands at 148 Walden Street in Concord, about a mile away from the home of *New York Times* best-selling author Gregory Maguire.

Gregory Maguire

Consciousness, responsibility, honor, and even truth— Truth, with a capital *T*

I was ten. Ten, and hemmed round, as children can be, by restrictions. Hedged in by my six siblings (three older, three younger), by a certain financial restraint my parents needed to exercise, by their anxieties about health and safety, which curbed our play. (No crossing the street. At the age of ten!) Hedged in, also, by the monoculture of the Irish Catholic school and church we attended. For escape, for liberty of a sort, I burrowed into the public library, one of the few acceptable destinations in my narrow world.

Of the wealth I found there, what stands out is Jane Langton's *The Diamond in the Window*, a novel for grade-school readers. The two kids in the book are also penned in by circumstance: hard times in Concord, Massachusetts; financial need; dead parents; mysteriously missing relatives; and a guardian uncle who has gone vague in the head. Their life is broken open by the discovery—in their own home—of a secret room high under the roof beam, a room with little beds just their size, and a glass diamond fitted into a keyhole window.

By the light of the moon and stars streaming through the glass, the children fall asleep and dream themselves into a series of adventures that grow more beautiful and dangerous month by month. The mechanics of the plot—finding the treasure, rescuing the relatives—gripped my imagination. But the dreams themselves, achingly simple metaphors about consciousness, responsibility, honor, and even truth—Truth, a concept in itself, with a capital *T*—are what make the book unforgettable. Simple as parables, as easy to digest as nursery rhymes, the nine dreams constitute the education of the subconscious. I couldn't have said so at the time, of course: I merely lapped up the book as a thirsty schoolchild greets a water fountain.

All these years later, I live in Concord, hardly a mile from the house memorialized by the book. I dream a different series of dreams. Dreaming and examining what might be of value within the subconscious images is the start of my writing life every day. Thinking—about concepts with capital letters, like Truth, like Wickedness—powers my work till bedtime. In gratitude, I keep *The Diamond in the Window* and its sequels close to hand. My world, lit by diamonds, seems enormous these days.

She rummaged in her handbag and produced a letter and her reading-glasses. "This is her letter to me. I'm going to read you a passage from it." She slowly put on her glasses and began to read: "Jeschke is really a very decent, steady, good-hearted man. I don't know anyone else whom I would rather marry if I marry at all. My dear mother, I can confide in you that I would much rather remain alone with Emil. Of course he has no idea of this and I shall never let him know. But what else can I do? Something might happen to me, and what would become of Emil then? Or I might not earn so much, indeed I'm already earning less than I was. A hairdresser has opened a new shop near the market, and the tradesmen's wives have to go to him or his wife wouldn't trade with them. I must think of my boy's future. I shall be a good wife to Jeschke. I've made up my mind to that. He deserves it. But the only person I really love is my darling boy, my Emil."

The old lady put down the letter.

Emil had slung his arms round his knees. He looked pale. He gritted his teeth, but suddenly he dropped his head on his knees and began to cry.

"All right, my boy!" said his grandmother. "All right, my boy!" Then she sat there in silence, giving him time to weep. "She's the only one you love," she said after a while, "and you're the only one she loves. Each of you has deceived the other out of love, and in spite of your love you have each misjudged the other. It happens like that sometimes."

A jay flew screaming above the tree-tops.

Emil dried his eyes and looked at the old woman. "What am I to do, Granny?"

"One of two things, Emil. When you get home you can ask her not to marry. Then you'll kiss and the thing will be settled."

"Or?"

"Or you can keep silence, but the silence must last till the end of your days, and you must be cheerful in your silence and not go round with a face like a mourner at a funeral. You alone can decide which course to pursue. I can only tell you this: You're getting older and your mother is getting older. That sounds simpler than it really is. Will you be able in a few years' time to earn enough for both of you? And if so, where will you earn it? In Neustadt? No, my boy. One day you'll have to leave home, and even if you don't have to, you ought to leave home. Then she will stay behind, all alone . . . What will happen if in ten or twelve years you get married? A mother and a young wife don't belong under the same roof. I know. I've tried . . . once as the wife and once as the mother." The old lady's eyes seemed to be looking back far into the past. "If she marries she will be making a sacrifice for you. But one day that sacrifice will bring her happiness."

She got up, "Choose which you like . . . the one or the other. But think it over carefully. I am going to leave you alone now."

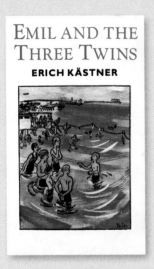

EMIL AND THE THREE TWINS

by Erich Kästner

First published in 1929 in Germany, Erich Kästner's book *Emil and the Detectives* re-creates details of Kästner's own German childhood in Dresden at the turn of the twentieth century. Emil's mother works extremely hard to set aside some money so that her beloved son can visit his grandmother in Berlin. Hence when the money is stolen, Emil must find it and follows a mysterious stranger in a bowler hat, setting off a madcap set of events. The same pacing continues in the sequel, *Emil and the Three Twins*.

Not only a writer for children, Kästner created novels, poetry, and plays that came under attack during Hitler's regime and were banned and burned. Later, in 1949, one of his children's books, *Lisa and Lottie* (renamed *The Parent Trap* in the Disney film), was also highly controversial; it was one of the first children's books to deal openly with the subject of divorce. But no matter what happened to him or his books, Kästner retained great faith in children and remained true to his own experience as a child. As he once wrote, "Truly to hold childhood in the memory means to know again . . . what is genuine and what false, what is good and what bad."

Author Philip Pullman, who knows as much about weaving a spellbinding tale for children as any writer today, responded to the emotional truth he found in the Emil books.

Philip Pullman

The value of self-control and reticence rather than me-first emotionalism

As *Emil and the Three Twins* opens, Emil is living with his widowed mother in the little town of Neustadt, where his mother earns a meager living as a hairdresser. He and his mother love each other very much; Emil is a good boy, conscientious, helpful, honest, though in some miraculous way neither boring nor priggish. He's mischievous, though; a couple of years before, he and some friends decorated the statue of the Grand Duke Charles by chalking a red nose on it, which has led Emil to be slightly wary of the local policeman, a formidable man called Sergeant Jeschke. However, as this book begins, Emil has a very large surprise: Sergeant Jeschke announces, with some awkwardness, that he would like to marry Emil's mother, if Emil does not mind.

Well, Emil does mind very much. He wants things to continue as they always have, and for him and his mother to live together and look after each other as they always have done. But he thinks that if his mother wants it, he ought not to stand in her way; so he agrees.

Then comes an invitation to stay with one of his friends from the *Detectives* book at his newly inherited house by the Baltic Sea, and the main plot gets under way: a story that involves a team of acrobats consisting of a man and his two sons, the Byrons. It turns out that they're not related at all, and that one of the "twins" is growing faster than the other and making their gymnastic routines more difficult; and the adult Byron is intending to abandon him and make off with the smaller one. Emil and his friends, indignant at this injustice, succeed in making everything all right.

But that's not what I most value in this book. Near the end, Emil has a conversation with his grandmother, a wise and sharp-tongued old woman who has sensed that Emil is not happy, and who has learned—by means of a letter from Emil's mother—the reason why. The wonderful thing about this conversation is that the grandmother never ceases to be her sharp, sardonic self, even while dispensing comfort.

I love this passage because it is full of wisdom, and because it celebrates the value of self-control and reticence rather than the me-first emotionalism that we see everywhere these days; and I hope I learned from it. The reason it resonated so strongly for me was that I was in a similar situation to Emil, though I had a brother and Emil didn't, and the man who became our stepfather didn't consult us beforehand as Sergeant Jeschke did. But I hope I was as good as Emil; I still believe everything that his grandmother says.

would think of him in each of the moments that revealed him to me. I would think of him most vividly in that single flashing instant when he whirled to shoot Fletcher on the balcony at Grafton's saloon. I would see again the power and grace of a coordinate force beautiful beyond comprehension. I would see the man and the weapon wedded in the one indivisible deadliness. I would see the man and the tool, a good man and a good tool, doing what had to be done.

And always my mind would go back at the last to the moment when I saw him from the bushes by the roadside just on the edge of town. I would see him there in the road, tall and terrible in the moonlight, going down to kill or be killed, and stopping to help a stumbling boy and to look out over the land, the lovely land, where the boy had a chance to live out his boyhood and grow straight inside as a man should.

And when I would hear the men in town talking among themselves and trying to pin him down to a definite past, I would smile quietly to myself. For a time they inclined to the notion, spurred by the talk of a passing stranger, that he was a certain Shannon who was famous as a gunman and gambler way down in Arkansas and Texas and dropped from sight without anyone knowing why or where. When that notion dwindled, others followed, pieced together in turn from scraps of information gleaned from stray travelers. But when they talked like that, I simply smiled because I knew he could have been none of these.

He was the man who rode into our little valley out of the heart of the great glowing West and when his work was done rode back whence he had come and he was Shane.

SHANE by Jack Schaefer, illustrated by John McCormack

SHANE

by Jack Schaefer,
illustrated by John McCormack

TRUE GRIT

by Charles Portis

Although very few classic Westerns have ever been written for young readers, the ones that exist have made lasting impressions. Originally published for adults in 1949, *Shane* was adapted by Jack Schaefer in 1954 for a book suitable for readers ages 12 to 14. In a Wyoming valley in 1889, a mysterious stranger, Shane, rides into town and helps the struggling Starrett family on their farm. The personification of the romantic West, antisocial and alienated, Shane fights the cattle baron who wants to take over the Starretts' land. "He was the man who rode into our little valley out of the heart of the great glowing West and when his work was done rode back whence he had come and he was Shane."

In 1968 Charles Portis published a highly unusual Western, *True Grit*, with a fourteen-year-old, pistol-packing, fast-talking heroine, Mattie Ross, intent on avenging her father's death. In a book that combines adventure with a sense of place—Indian Territory in the 1870s—the nonstop action and snappy dialogue keep readers engaged until the final pages. Both books made a tremendous impact on Nashville Hall of Fame songwriter Billy Edd Wheeler.

Billy Edd Wheeler
Qualities I admire: being soft-spoken, forthright, and honest

Two Western classics have influenced my life deeply, each in its own different way. Jack Schaefer's *Shane*, told through the eyes of young Bob Starrett, is best known as a classic movie starring Alan Ladd, Jean Arthur, and Van Heflin. But the book is even better. It features the heroic character, Shane, a reluctant gunfighter; he has qualities I admire and often dream of having myself. He is soft-spoken, forthright, and honest; he turns his back on money to do the right thing. *Shane* tells the age-old story of the duel between good and evil in a time when law and order was lacking; a man or woman, boy or girl, had to rely on personal courage and determination to survive.

Charles Portis's *True Grit* features as its heroine fourteen-year-old Mattie Ross, headstrong and as unforgettable a character as any you will ever meet in literature. After her father is killed, she hires the irascible and often-drunken U.S. Marshal "Rooster" J. Cogburn to track down the killer, Tom Chaney. They are joined by a young Texas Ranger, LaBoeuf, who also hopes to capture Chaney and collect reward money, and head into Indian Territory. But young Mattie can hold her own with both men, as she does in this conversation with Cogburn:

"Now make up your mind. I don't care anything for all this talk. You told me what your price for the job was and I have come up with it. Here is the money. I aim to get Tom Chaney and if you are not game I will find somebody who is game. All I have heard out of you so far is talk. I know you can drink whiskey and I have seen you kill a gray rat. All the rest has been talk. They told me you had grit and that is why I came to you. I am not paying for talk. I can get all the talk I need and more at the Monarch boardinghouse."

"I ought to slap your face."

"How do you propose to do it from that hog wallow you are sunk in?" With that dialogue, it is no wonder that this book was made into one of the great movie classics, starring John Wayne, Kim Darby, and Glen Campbell.

Shane and *True Grit* made an impression on me that has lasted a lifetime.

One evening, after thinking it over for some time, Harold decided to go for a walk in the moonlight.

There wasn't any moon, and Harold needed a moon for a walk in the moonlight.

And he needed something to walk on.

He made a long straight path so he wouldn't get lost.

And he set off on his walk, taking his big purple crayon with him.

But he didn't seem to be getting anywhere on the long straight path.

So he left the path for a short cut across a field. And the moon went with him.

The short cut led right to where Harold thought a forest ought to be.

He didn't want to get lost in the woods. So he made a very small forest, with just one tree in it.

It turned out to be an apple tree.

The apples would be very tasty, Harold thought, when they got red.

So he put a frightening dragon under the tree to guard the apples.

It was a terribly frightening dragon.

It even frightened Harold. He backed away.

HAROLD AND THE PURPLE CRAYON by Crockett Johnson

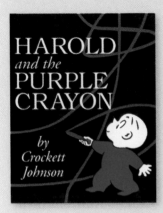

HAROLD AND THE PURPLE CRAYON

by Crockett Johnson

A book of amazing longevity, with two million sold and never out of print, *Harold and the Purple Crayon* at first failed to impress Crockett Johnson's editor Ursula Nordstrom. "It doesn't seem like a good children's book to me," she wrote, although admitting that she might turn down Tom Sawyer the way she felt that day. She later apologized to her talented artist for her "lukewarm and unenthusiastic" reading and went ahead to publish the book. Johnson, the *nom de plume* of David Johnson Leisk, had worked with Nordstrom on other books, such as *The Carrot Seed*, written by his wife Ruth Krauss.

A cartoon artist and creator of the popular 1940s newspaper Barnaby comic strip, Johnson on occasion turned his hand to inventing children's books. He had a genius for distilling figures and landscape to the bare minimum to tell a story, although he once confessed that he drew people without hair because it was easier. In his most popular children's book, Harold sets out for a walk one evening and with a well-worn, stubby purple crayon draws an entire adventure for himself—a dragon, sailboat ride, a picnic with the nine types of pie he loves best, a balloon trip, and his return home. The book celebrates the power of the imagination and the creative spirit of children.

Not surprising, the book has spoken to legions of artists because Harold can create an entire universe with his beloved crayon. Maurice Sendak, creator of *Where the Wild Things Are*, personally learned book making and illustration from Krauss and Johnson and admires *Harold and the Purple Crayon* for its lightness of touch. Chris Van Allsburg, creator of *The Polar Express*, loves the idea behind the book.

Maurice Sendak
Just let the kid do his own thing.

Crockett Johnson's *Harold and the Purple Crayon* is just immense fun. Harold does exactly as he pleases. There are no adults to demonstrate or remonstrate. The book comes out of a particular theory of children's books: Just let the kid do his own thing; let him have fun. Books shouldn't teach. They shouldn't give lessons. Kids should feel that they can do what they want to do and no one will punish them. They can just be kids and enjoy reading and looking at a book.

Chris Van Allsburg
I could create my own world.

When I was child, I didn't draw much. My principal activity was building models—cars, boats, electric trains, planes, everything. I was very good at it. While I was building them, they worked on my imagination. If I built the HMS *Victory*, I imagined myself fighting side by side with Lord Horatio Nelson, commander of the British fleet. Or I'd sail with Charles Darwin to the Galapagos Islands on the HMS *Beagle*.

As a child my favorite book was *Harold and the Purple Crayon* by Crockett Johnson. The book is based on a perfect visual concept: A little boy builds a world out of purple lines, and then that world becomes real. If he wants to take a ride in a sailboat, he draws it. I believe that the empowerment of Harold appealed to me as a reader—I loved the idea that I could be in control and create my own world.

I have remembered the book since childhood for two reasons. First, for the theme: The book explores the power of imagination, the ability to create with imagination. Second, the book contains a fairly elusive, mysterious idea but presents it so succinctly through these simple drawings that this idea registers clearly.

When I first started making picture books, I thought about the books of Crockett Johnson. These books contained stories that kids would remember all their lives; they were the kind of books I wanted to make.

With slow and stately tread the Red Buck began a circuit of the garden. The Doe and their Fawn walked behind him. Obediently all the other Animals fell into line. There came Phewie and the Gray Fox, side by side, waddling Porkey and Uncle Analdas, Mother and Father with Little Georgie between them, his arms around their necks, the Pheasant and his wife, with their mincing, rocking-chair walk, feathers glimmering bronze-gold in the moonlight. There came all the Fieldmouse tribe, the Raccoon and the Opossum, the Chipmunks and the Squirrels, gray and red. And alongside them, on the very edge of the garden, the quivering and humping of the earth showed the progress of the Mole and his three stout brothers.

Slowly, solemnly the procession circled the garden until they had all returned to the little lawn where the Good Saint stood. The Red Buck snorted again, and all gave attention as he spoke.

"We have eaten their food." His voice rang out impressively. "We have tasted their salt, we have drunk their water, and all are good." He tossed his proud head in the direction of the garden. "From now on this is forbidden ground."

RABBIT HILL by Robert Lawson

RABBIT HILL

by Robert Lawson

In the 1940s Robert Lawson turned to writing *Rabbit Hill* after some prodding from his editor May Massee, who had always wanted a rabbit story from Rabbit Hill, Lawson's home near Westport, Connecticut. In this saga, a new family moves into the house on the property, and all the animals are both excited about their arrival and worried about the consequences. Other owners have not taken care of the land, and there is a need for a good steward in the home. By the end, they discover that "there is enough for all"; these creatures great and small find a way to coexist in this small ecosystem.

From the beginning, the book received praise from critics, the Newbery Award, and the devotion of children. With its strong ecological message, its vision of humans living in harmony with the land, the novel seems timelier today than when first published. Former Director of Reading at Ball State University, J. David Cooper took the book into inner-city classrooms and was amazed with the results. Journalist Stephanie Loer first heard the book as a child.

J. David Cooper

We all need to share, get along with others, and cooperate.

I first read Robert Lawson's *Rabbit Hill* when I was a boy; I remember it being given to me as a present around Easter. We didn't have many books in the house, so owning a copy was special.

I was the first person in my family to attend college. After graduating, I taught in inner-city Louisville, Kentucky. My first school was very close to the stockyards. I had some children who still lived in houses with dirt floors. Some came and went several times during the year because they worked on farms. Some of my students had parents in the Kentucky School for the Blind and the Kentucky School for the Deaf. This was a great teaching experience for me, which I have drawn on for many years. I knew that any book I could get to work in this particular environment had to have special qualities.

My students were motivated, but they just didn't have access to books. It was important that I made that possible for them. We got library cards for all the children and took field trips to the public library not far away. We would have a story time in the library; we went four or five times a year and connected those trips to our thematic projects.

I always read *Rabbit Hill* out loud in class. The final chapter is entitled "There Is Enough for All." My mother was always a proponent of getting along with other people; she didn't like controversy, and she didn't believe it was necessary. My students were in a neighborhood where they desperately needed this lesson. Lawson brilliantly shows, in this chapter, that we all need to share, get along with others, and cooperate.

As a child I read *Rabbit Hill*; when I took children's literature, I wrote about it. Then I experienced the reactions of students as I taught it. The book has sustained me throughout my life—that is what the great books do.

Stephanie Loer
To care deeply about animals

My father came home from the bookstore with a twinkle in his eye and a new book in his hand. "It's about rabbits," he announced. That evening he began reading *Rabbit Hill* to my brother and me. We spent many winter evenings listening to the haps and mishaps of the animals that lived on the Hill. The anticipated arrival of "New Folks" coming to live in the old house on the Hill built suspense with each chapter. Would the Folks be kind to the animals that called the Hill home? Robert Lawson's ability to create animal characters with human virtues and foibles made me care about them deeply.

As a child I lived on a large midwestern farm; animals, both domestic and wild, were a part of my life. So the creatures on Rabbit Hill were very real to me. I was quite sure animals did talk to one another. Today, I am fortunate to still live in rural surroundings. And when I chatter away to our horses, sheep, and chickens, I still listen—thoroughly convinced they will stop neighing, baaing, and clucking and actually begin speaking.

MY FATHER'S DRAGON

by Ruth Stiles Gannett,
illustrated by Ruth Chrisman Gannett

When a young boy with the euphonious name of Elmer Elevator rescues a stray cat, his life takes an unexpected turn. The cat, an escapee of Tangerina and Wild Island, persuades Elmer to travel to the jungles there and rescue a baby dragon in captivity. Even more important, the cat instructs Elmer on what to bring in his backpack—including two dozen pink lollipops and six magnifying glasses. Young readers for over fifty years have delighted in watching Elmer put everything he brings to good use while he outwits tigers, boars, a lion, and crocodiles before releasing the dragon.

Ruth Stiles Gannett wrote *My Father's Dragon*, with its wonderful balance between action and fantasy, on a two-week vacation between jobs. Before the project was completed, she enlisted her stepmother to illustrate the book and her fiancé to choose the type and draw the maps. The resulting book immediately became a childhood and classroom favorite, the perfect book to read aloud at the end of first grade or independently in third or fourth grade. In the case of Nick Clark, director of the Eric Carle Museum of Picture Book Art, he came under the book's spell after he found it in the school library.

Nick Clark
Use your noodle.

I always enjoyed reading under the covers with the flashlight when the lights were supposed to be out. When I was eight or nine, I went to a small private school in New York City with a very comfortable library, with lots and lots of books. There I stumbled upon Ruth Stiles Gannett's *My Father's Dragon*. I was delighted by the ingenuity of the protagonist Elmer Elevator. Having been given guidance by the cat about which items to take to the Island of Tangerina (chewing gum, rubber bands, a toothbrush, a jackknife, seven hair ribbons), he had to use these strategically as he worked his way through various challenges. I was also mesmerized by the art: There are wonderful images of the rhinoceros brushing its tusk, the lion with his marvelous mane braided with bows, and Elmer walking along a bridge of crocodiles. The illustrations are absolutely delicious and really take the text into another dimension, graphically extending it.

Books are so important in conveying messages to children. We may not fully appreciate the impact of a book until we are older, but there are things that we learn from our reading. From *My Father's Dragon* I learned that you have to use your noodle—and that the underdog can triumph in the end.

Babar, the young king of the elephants, and his wife, Queen Celeste, have just left for their wedding trip in a balloon.

"Good-by! See you soon!" cry the elephants as they watch the balloon rise and drift away.

Arthur, Babar's little cousin, still waves his beret. Old Cornelius, who is chief over all the elephants when the King is away, anxiously sighs: "I do hope they won't have any accidents!"

The country of the elephants is now far away. The balloon glides noiselessly in the sky. Babar and Celeste admire the landscape below.

What a beautiful journey! The air is balmy, the wind is gentle. There is the ocean, the big blue ocean.

Blown out over the sea by the wind, the balloon is suddenly caught by a violent storm. Babar and Celeste tremble with fear and cling with all their might to the basket of the balloon.

By extraordinary good fortune, just as the balloon is about to fall into the sea, a final puff of wind blows it on an island where it flattens out and collapses.

"You aren't hurt, Celeste, are you?" Babar inquires anxiously. "No! Well then look, we are saved!"

THE TRAVELS OF BABAR by Jean de Brunhoff

Vocation

The wagon lurched; there was a sudden heavy splash beside it. Laura sat straight up and clawed the blanket from her head.

Pa was gone. Ma sat alone, holding tight to the reins with both hands. Mary hid her face in the blanket again, but Laura rose up farther. She couldn't see the creek bank. She couldn't see anything in front of the wagon but water rushing at it. And in the water, three heads; Pet's head and Patty's head and Pa's small, wet head. Pa's fist in the water was holding tight to Pet's bridle.

Laura could faintly hear Pa's voice through the rushing of the water. It sounded calm and cheerful, but she couldn't hear what he said. He was talking to the horses. Ma's face was white and scared.

"Lie down, Laura," Ma said.

Laura lay down. She felt cold and sick. Her eyes were shut tight, but she could still see the terrible water and Pa's brown beard drowning in it.

For a long, long time the wagon swayed and swung, and Mary cried without making a sound, and Laura's stomach felt sicker and sicker. Then the front wheels struck and grated, and Pa shouted. The whole wagon jerked and jolted and tipped backward, but the wheels were turning on the ground. Laura was up again, holding to the seat; she saw Pet's and Patty's scrambling wet backs climbing a steep bank, and Pa running beside them, shouting, "Hi, Patty! Hi, Pet! Get up! Get up! Whoopsy-daisy! Good girls!"

At the top of the bank they stood still, panting and dripping. And the wagon stood still, safely out of that creek.

Pa stood panting and dripping, too, and Ma said, "Oh, Charles!"

"There, there, Caroline," said Pa. "We're all safe, thanks to a good tight wagon-box well fastened to the running-gear. I never saw a creek rise so fast in my life. Pet and Patty are good swimmers, but I guess they wouldn't have made it if I hadn't helped them."

LITTLE HOUSE ON THE PRAIRIE by Laura Ingalls Wilder, illustrated by Garth Williams

THE LITTLE HOUSE BOOKS

by Laura Ingalls Wilder,
illustrated by Garth Williams

Called "that miracle book that no depression could stop," Laura Ingalls Wilder's saga about her life on the American prairie reminded its first readers in 1932 that times could be hard but you could still get through them. One of the few books that actually sold through the Depression years, *Little House in the Big Woods* focuses on a family living in the woods of Wisconsin in 1870—self-sustaining in their efforts, living off the land. They hunt and trap, make cheese and maple sugar; but they also sing, dance, and enjoy what they have in life. This message proved irresistible for American children even as the Depression turned into the war years. By the 1950s, when Garth Williams re-illustrated the series, the stories fascinated young readers, now living in cities, who had never known what it was like to be part of a small community.

Over a series of nine books, the Wilder family moves from Lake Pepin, Wisconsin, to De Smet, South Dakota, and Laura grows up to have children of her own. When scholars go back to manuscripts of these books, it is clear that Wilder collaborated with her daughter Rose Wilder Lane, a ghostwriter by trade, to achieve a finished manuscript. Although we may never know what one wrote and the other changed, these books stand as one of the greatest mother/daughter collaborations of all times. In the 1930s, however, dual author books were considered substandard—hence only Laura's name graces the title page. Even more popular today than when first published, the Little House series imparts many messages to eager readers. Emily Bazelon, senior editor of *Slate*, loved how every item mattered in the pioneer economy. Eden Ross Lipson, *New York Times* book critic, was guided by its wisdom since childhood.

Eden Ross Lipson
There is dignity, honor, and pleasure in work well done.

When I was nine, I encountered a series of books that I have loved all my life. The stories about Laura Ingalls Wilder and her family as they progress from Wisconsin to South Dakota, through good times and bad, unself-consciously recall the expansionist era in American history. The books describe a self-sufficient, brave, and proud family. They give precise, accurate details of the changing American life that shifted quickly from rural to agricultural on its way to industrial.

There is no magic in the Little House books—no invisible railway platform leading to a fantastic place, no wizards at all. This plain account focuses on ordinary lives, but that is why it is so thrilling and engrossing. The family's ordinary lives are so far from our own, unimaginably remote to today's children. But the lesson the books taught me, and still teach without comment, is that there is dignity, honor, and pleasure in work well done.

As soon as the hog was dead Pa and Uncle Henry lifted it up and down in the boiling water until it was well scalded. Then they laid it on a board and scraped it with their knives, and all the bristles came off. After that they hung the hog in a tree, took out the insides, and left it hanging to cool.

When it was cool they took it down and cut it up. There were hams and shoulders, side meat and spare-ribs and belly. There was the heart and the liver and the tongue, and the head to be made into headcheese, and the dish-pan full of bits to be made into sausage.

The meat was laid on a board in the backdoor shed, and every piece was sprinkled with salt. The hams and the shoulders were put to pickle in brine, for they would be smoked, like the venison, in the hollow log.

"You can't beat hickory-cured ham," Pa said.

He was blowing up the bladder. It made a little white balloon, and he tied the end tight with a string and gave it to Mary and Laura to play with. They could throw it into the air and spat it back and forth with their hands. Or it would bounce along the ground and they could kick it. But even better fun than a balloon was the pig's tail.

Pa skinned it for them carefully, and into the large end he thrust a sharpened stick. Ma opened the front end of the cookstove and raked hot coals, out into the iron hearth. Then Laura and Mary took turns holding the pig's tail over the coals.

It sizzled and fried, and drops of fat dripped off it and blazed on the coals. Ma sprinkled it with salt. Their hands and their faces got very hot, and Laura burned her finger, but she was so excited she did not care. Roasting the pig's tail was such fun that it was hard to play fair, taking turns.

At last it was done. It was nicely browned all over, and how good it smelled! They carried it into the yard to cool it, and even before it was cool enough they began tasting it and burned their tongues.

They ate every little bit of meat off the bones, and then they gave the bones to Jack. And that was the end of the pig's tail. There would not be another one till next year.

LITTLE HOUSE IN THE BIG WOODS by Laura Ingalls Wilder, illustrated by Garth Williams

Emily Bazelon

To marvel at the wonder of the ordinary

The first book I read to myself was *Little House in the Big Woods* by Laura Ingalls Wilder. Threaded through it, and the series that follows, is a tactile and fervent appreciation of the objects the Ingalls family needs to survive, and the children's few cherished playthings. When they have no nails or hinges for the door to their new prairie home, Laura's father bores holes through cross-pieces, drives a wooden peg into each one, and cuts three long straps for hinges. When the family slaughters a pig, they blow the bladder into a white balloon that Laura and her sister bat back and forth. Then they fry the pig's tail over the coals and relish the brown cracklings. The attention to detail, the precision and care with which each description is rendered, conveys the objects' importance. To this family, everything had a potential use. Every scrap mattered. That seemed enviable to me, somehow, as a child—it made the ease and carelessness of our throwaway culture seem dull and thoughtless by comparison. (And that was in the 1970s!)

Laura's family is a model of makeshift entrepreneurship, of course, because they are constantly on the move. Pioneers run out of nails. There's no corner store. When I read the series as a child, it was the romance of the family's wanderlust and their almost unflagging good spirits that shone from the pages. When I reread the books to my own children recently, I couldn't help realizing that the wanderlust really belongs to Laura's father, and that he practically destroys his family with it. They learn to make do, yes. But they also lose a home they have built in a dispute over Indian Territory, crops they have carefully sown to a plague of locust, and the eyesight of Laura's sister, Mary, in a scarlet fever outbreak. Behind all the enterprising pioneer doings, and even the gleeful moments of tossing a pig's bladder, is real suffering. But the beauty of the books is that child readers don't have to experience the upheaval on this level. They can learn from Laura to marvel at the wonder of the ordinary. That is the gift her parents' hard life gave her, and she has passed it on.

Her spy clothes consisted first of all of an ancient pair of blue jeans, so old that her mother had forbidden her to wear them, but which Harriet loved because she had fixed up the belt with hooks to carry her spy tools. Her tools were a flashlight, in case she were ever out at night, which she never was, a leather pouch for her notebook, another leather case for extra pens, a water canteen, and a boy scout knife which had, among other features, a screwdriver and a knife and fork which collapsed. She had never had occasion to eat anywhere, but someday it might come in handy.

She attached everything to the belt, and it all worked fine except that she rattled a little. Next she put on an old dark-blue sweatshirt with a hood which she wore at the beach house in the summer so that it still smelled of salt air in a comforting way. Then she put on an old pair of blue sneakers with holes over each of her little toes. Her mother had actually gone so far as to throw these out, but Harriet had rescued them from the garbage when the cook wasn't looking.

She finished by donning a pair of black-rimmed spectacles wth no glass in them.

She had found these once in her father's desk and now sometimes wore them even to school, because she thought they made her look smarter.

She stood back and looked at herself in the full-length mirror which hung on her bathroom door. She was very pleased. Then she ran quickly down the steps and out, banging the front door behind her.

HARRIET THE SPY by Louise Fitzhugh

HARRIET THE SPY

by Louise Fitzhugh

Published in 1964, *Harriet the Spy* shocked many adult critics of children's books. Harriet broke the law—she entered people's homes and hid while observing them; she wrote truthful but unpleasant and unkind details about the people she encountered, even her classmates. Obsessive and compulsive, she had to carry a notebook around with her at all times and write, just as she had to eat the same lunch every day. She was wise cracking and cynical—in fact, she looks much like many contemporary heroes and heroines of children's books. But in the early 1960s Harriet seemed strange indeed to those who expected protagonists of books to be mild mannered and plucky. "I doubt its appeal" to children, one of the book's detractors wrote.

However, in Harriet young readers found someone they could identify with, a flawed but believable protagonist. Harriet M. Welsch lives with two utterly feckless parents and her nurse, Ole Golly, on the Upper East Side of New York. In the first part of the story, Harriet dresses in her spy uniform—sweatshirt, blue jeans, pens, flashlight, and knife—and travels on a route with her notebook, writing down her thoughts and observations. But in the second part of the book, her world begins to spin out of control. Ole Golly gets married, leaving Harriet to fend for herself when her classmates seize her notebook and start to read it. Then, they make Harriet even more of an outsider than she has ever been.

Any child who has ever felt a victim of cruelty can identify with Harriet. The appeal of this book over the years has been wide ranging. Dr. Perri Klass, who teaches both pediatrics and journalism at New York University, believes that Harriet provides invaluable insight into the issues that writers face.

Perri Klass
The intoxicating and addictive joy of observation

I went through a very long phase—in fact I am still not out of it—of carrying a spy notebook. From *Harriet the Spy* I discovered the pleasure, even the addictive pleasure, of having a notebook and writing things down. Harriet is going to be a writer, but she is not particularly introspective. She is interested in herself, but much more interested in the mysteries of other people. Her method is observation, reporting, figuring out people's stories, and understanding the complicated world in which she lives. She shows us one of the most important pleasures of a writer: trying to imagine other circumstances and other points of view.

When Harriet's notebook is read by her classmates, who are angered and offended by what she has written about them, her nurse Ole Golly does not reproach Harriet and advise her to try thinking nice thoughts about people for a change. "Harriet, you are going to have to do two things, and you don't like either one of them: 1) You have to apologize. 2) You have to lie." And she goes on to say, "But to yourself you must always tell the truth." I look at this statement as a lesson about the impact of the written word, and a caution that if you are going to give offense, you should do so deliberately. Words are powerful, and you should choose them and use them with care.

The most important lesson of *Harriet the Spy*, however, is a message about the intoxicating and addictive joys of observation, of looking at the people across from you on the bus, or sitting next to you at the coffee shop counter, or ahead of you in line, and noting down the details of appearance and clothing and gesture—of listening in on their conversations (of course)—of trying to figure out their family dynamics and their back story. That's what Harriet did with her spy route and her spy notebook—she worked on figuring out the world and its stories. She did it because she was driven to do it; she did it because she had figured out how much fun it was; she did it because it was her way of operating in the world and making it her own.

Both boys looked like well-padded fullbacks with oversized helmets. Inside their flight gear, however, they were quite different. Tom, lean, tall, and with a blond crew cut, had a serious look in his deep-set blue eyes as he scanned the horizon. Bud, a skilled pilot himself, was not as tall as Tom, but he had shoulders like a hammer thrower and the open, frank face of an athlete who liked to play for fun.

"The worst is over," Tom called through his mike, "But keep buckled in tight. I'm making another dive before I take her in. But I warn you, next time we're going higher, where we'll get hit harder by cosmic rays. It'll be a better test of the effect of radiation on the relotrol."

Tom glanced at a black metal box with three dials resting in his lap. It contained the receiver of a control instrument to be used in connection with the giant robot he was building. Tom had partially completed the mechanical giant to be used for repairs and maintenance in a new atomic energy plant which his father was building. The relotrol would relay radio impulses needed to guide the robot working in areas of the plant where the radiation would be fatal to human beings.

"How did your gimmick react, Tom?" Bud asked.

"Not good, I'll have to make some changes. Under really stiff radiation this relotrol would foul up the radio orders to the robot."

Bud grinned. "You mean Mr. Robot wouldn't know what to do? He'd sort of go berserk?"

"Right."

"Well, what's next on the program, inventor boy?"

"To work on the relotrol some more," Tom replied. He clamped his invention under the instrument panel to keep it from being jarred, then nosed the plane down in the direction of the Swift Enterprises airfield.

Below was the town of Shopton, with the old Swift Construction Company buildings on one side and the new experimental group on the other. The shiny rooftops of the laboratories reflected the morning sun.

"Swift Enterprises looks mighty enterprising!" Bud said. "Do you feel enterprising enough to work the bugs out of the relotrol right now?"

"As soon as we land, Bud," Tom said, looking down.

But Bud's eyes were not on the airfield. They were following a black dot that had suddenly appeared against the horizon.

"Something's coming at us from three o'clock," he said. "It's too small to be a plane."

The speck quickly increased in size.

"It's a bird," said Bud in amazement. "A large black crow."

Tom climbed a few hundred feet to avoid hitting it, then cut the jet's speed. As the bird winged below him, he said, "That's too big for a crow. It's larger than an eagle."

Steve Wozniak

Inventing things might bring many kinds of rewards.

TOM SWIFT

by Victor Appleton II

The Stratemeyer Syndicate—built by Edward Stratemeyer, a ghostwriter for Horatio Alger, and then run by his daughter Harriett—turned out sixty-five highly successful series for young readers in the early 1900s, including such staples of childhood reading as the Bobbsey Twins, Tom Swift, the Hardy Boys, and Nancy Drew. The Syndicate developed the model for each series, outlined plots, hired ghostwriters, and then placed a fictitious author's name on each series. For the Tom Swift books they used "Victor Appleton II" as the name of the author.

In 1910 the Syndicate introduced a genius inventor who made tremendous breakthroughs in technology, Tom Swift. Rather than update the volumes in this saga, which ran for 30 years, it launched a new series about his son, Tom Swift Jr., published from 1954 to 1971. For these books, Tom Jr., always eighteen, helps his father run Swift Enterprises. They have an invention factory, private airport and airplane, and untold amounts of cash. The young Swift involves himself in all of the science and technology explorations of the day—space travel, robots, and teleconferencing by video cameras. The Swifts even communicate with extraterrestrials.

With all of his technology savvy, Tom Swift never imagines or comes near a computer. However, inspired by these books, Steve Wozniak, cofounder of Apple Inc., invented both Apple I and Apple II.

Around fourth grade, I started reading the Tom Swift Jr. series. As a young engineer, Tom Swift could design anything. He and his father owned their own company; he entrapped aliens, built submarines, and pursued projects all over the globe. I found his entire world incredibly intriguing.

To me Tom Swift represented the epitome of creative freedom, scientific knowledge, and the ability to find solutions to problems. Tom Swift showed me that inventing things might bring many kinds of rewards. Also I admired his utilitarian and humanitarian attitude. To this day, I return to the Tom Swift books, and I have read them to my own children as a form of inspiration.

Now the girl who answers
the telephone called up the next towns
of Bangerville and Bopperville and
Kipperville and Kopperville and told them
what was happening in Popperville.
All the people came over to see
if Mike Mulligan and his steam shovel
could dig the cellar in just one day.
The more people came, the faster
Mike Mulligan and Mary Anne dug.
But they would have to hurry.
They were only halfway through
and the sun was beginning to go down.
They finished the third corner . . . neat and square.

MIKE MULLIGAN AND HIS STEAM SHOVEL by Virginia Lee Burton

**MIKE MULLIGAN AND HIS
STEAM SHOVEL**

by Virginia Lee Burton

All of Virginia Lee Burton's books revolve around the problems created by change: The old order must make way for the new and survive in different circumstances. In *Mike Mulligan and His Steam Shovel*, she explored this theme in the saga of Mike Mulligan and his steam shovel Mary Anne, who "could dig as much in a day as a hundred men could dig in a week." But when gasoline, electric, and the new diesel motor shovels come along, they take all the jobs away. Eventually Mary Anne finds work; however, after she digs the cellar of a new town hall, no one can figure out how to get her out of the hole she has created.

After getting the story to this point, Burton, always a perfectionist, didn't know how to resolve it. But one day, after she read it to a young boy, he provided a very satisfactory ending. Many children have helped authors in similar ways over the years, but Burton's response to that aid was extraordinary—she credited Dickie Berkenbush in an asterisk on the appropriate page. Consequently, for his entire life Richard Berkenbush could enjoy the fame that this classic children's book bestowed on him.

The book stands as a testament to the genius of Burton as a graphic artist. Every page has been designed to achieve a perfect combination of text and art; and the plot, about a boy and his steam shovel, is naturally compelling for young readers. Television talk show host Jay Leno not only cherished the book for its story, but he also found insight into his own character as well.

Jay Leno
The more of an audience I had, the more I'd act up.

Mike Mulligan and His Steam Shovel is the first book I remember reading as a child, and I still have it. The people who lived across the street from us had a coal cellar. Once a month when the delivery guy came, I'd run over there and watch them dump the coal and read my book. There was a line in the book that I have always remembered: "The more people came, the faster Mike Mulligan and Mary Anne dug." That line made sense to me. I was always a show-off. The more of an audience I had, the more I'd act up.

Of course during these stirring times I came in contact with all the great men of the Colonies. The one who impressed me most was, naturally, General George Washington.

Not only was he a magnificent figure of a man and soldier, but the wheat grown at Mount Vernon was of a superb quality. There were always a few grains to be found in his boot-tops and pocket flaps. Quite a few crumbs too, so I always looked forward to seeing him.

On one of his visits to Ben, however, he appeared greatly cast down.

"The situation of our Colonies, Dr. Franklin," he said, "is becoming desperate. Our brave soldiers lack shoes and uniforms, powder and arms. I fear that we must appeal to some foreign power for aid. But to what country shall we appeal? That seems to be the question. Of course there is Spain."

"French pastry," I whispered in Ben's ear.

"And of course France," said Ben.

"There is Russia," suggested the General.

"French wines," I hissed.

"And France," said Ben.

"There are Denmark and Sweden," the General said.

"Beautiful ladies," I whispered.

"France," said Ben. "Undoubtedly France!"

"Very well," said General Washington, "France it seems to be. Dr. Franklin, will you go to the Court of France to plead our cause? It is a heavy responsibility for on your success depends our whole hope of victory."

Ben rose. "We will, General, we will," he said determinedly.

"We?" asked the General.

"I mean I—of course—I will," replied Ben. "When do we—I mean I—sail?"

"At once," said the General, rising and looking very noble. "The armed sloop *Reprisal* is ready to sail. With you, Dr. Franklin, will go the hopes and prayers of a new Nation, the ideals, the aspirations—"

"AND Amos," I added, but he didn't hear me.

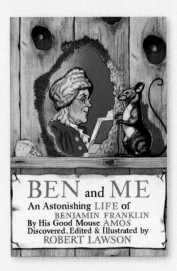

BEN AND ME

by Robert Lawson

In *Ben and Me: An Astonishing Life of Benjamin Franklin as Written by His Good Mouse Amos*, author Robert Lawson claims to discover a manuscript in Philadelphia, lodged in an old secretary desk. Written by Benjamin Franklin's sidekick Amos, Franklin's mouse friend—with "pen in paw"—strives to set the record straight about the great man who was overenthusiastic about himself." In slightly over a hundred pages Amos, with tongue-in-cheek humor, explores the scientific achievements of Franklin as well as his efforts on behalf of General George Washington, a man who always had a few grains of the magnificent wheat of Mount Vernon on his boot-tops. The grand world of Revolutionary War America has been reduced to a mouse-eyed view, presenting insights into Franklin's irresistible charm with the ladies of Paris and the tendency of the founding fathers to spend excessive time in committees.

After the success of Lawson's artwork for *Mr. Popper's Penguins*, his publisher Little, Brown asked him to suggest a subject that he would like to illustrate, preferably a biography, so that they could find an author for it. Lawson sent them the basic outline; they loved the idea but felt that they could not possibly find an author willing to write such a cockeyed story and asked Lawson to do so himself. The book has imparted its humor, history, and wisdom to succeeding generations of American children. Pulitzer Prize–winning historian David McCullough discovered *Ben and Me* as a boy.

David McCullough

In the writing of history and biography, one has to call on imagination.

I met my first revisionist historian when I was six. His name was Amos, and he was a mouse, an eighteenth-century church mouse to be exact, one of twenty-six children who with their mother and father lived in old Christ Church in Philadelphia. Amos, who took up lodging in Benjamin Franklin's fur hat, is the narrator of the delightful *Ben and Me* by Robert Lawson, first published in 1939 and still very much in print.

Most so-called historians have had Franklin all wrong, according to Amos. "Ben was undoubtedly a splendid fellow, a great man, a patriot and all that," he writes, "but he *was* undeniably stupid at times and had it not been for me— well, here's the true story."

I was instantly hooked. I learned all about Philadelphia, printing presses, electricity, Franklin stoves, and the Palace of Versailles. I got to know Benjamin Franklin and, like Amos, relished his company.

Robert Lawson knew his subject. In one particularly enjoyable incident George Washington tells Ben Franklin they need money to fight the Revolutionary War and that Franklin should go to another country to borrow some. Franklin can't decide. Should he go to Spain, Russia, Denmark, Sweden, or France? Amos wants Franklin to select France because the food is so very good there. After Franklin reaches France, his adventures are set in a knowing rendition of the real events. Lawson understood the details of Franklin's life and the world of Franklin's travels and work, which gives the book its great charm.

In the writing of history and biography, one has to call on imagination— in the sense of transporting oneself into that other time and the lives of those other people, all vanished, distant, and different. That takes research and analysis, to be sure. But it also demands imagination. This I learned early from *Ben and Me*, a book I still read for my grandchildren and for its enduring pleasure.

The night Max wore his wolf suit and made mischief of one kind
and another
his mother called him "WILD THING!"
and Max said "I'LL EAT YOU UP!"
so he was sent to bed without eating anything.
That very night in Max's room a forest grew
and grew—
and grew until his ceiling hung with vines
and the walls became the world all around
and an ocean tumbled by with a private boat for Max
and he sailed off through night and day
and in and out of weeks
and almost over a year
to where the wild things are.

WHERE THE WILD THINGS ARE by Maurice Sendak

WHERE THE WILD THINGS ARE

by Maurice Sendak

Maurice Sendak worked for a period of time on a manuscript called "Where the Wild Horses Are" before abandoning it because he could not draw horses. But since he still liked the book's concept, he hunted for an appropriate character to substitute. When the word *things* came to mind, he remembered all his relatives who used to pinch his cheeks and say, "You're so cute, I could eat you up." As Sendak drew these wild things they changed from skinny, undernourished creatures to fantastic animals with considerable weight and density. The resulting book, *Where the Wild Things Are*, seems anything but a family tribute.

In this groundbreaking picture book, Sendak delves into the psyche of his hero Max. Raging against his mother because he is sent to bed without supper, Max wills his bedroom to change into a forest. There he locates the motley group of wild things. Taming them, becoming their king, and engaging in a wild rumpus, Max returns home to find his own bedroom and his supper still hot. Through his dreams and fantasies, Max deals with his anger against his mother, becomes empowered, and can fall asleep at peace.

In 1963, when the book was published, rage against a mother was considered radical content for a children's book. Although some adults took an immediate dislike to the book, it won the Caldecott Medal and the hearts of children everywhere. They understood Sendak's emotional truth and also longed themselves to tame a group of wild things. As one fan wrote to the author, "How much does it cost to get where the Wild Things are? If it is not expensive, my sister and I would like to spend the summer there." Now part of the American canon of children's books, *Where the Wild Things Are* continues to inspire other children's book creators to experiment with the picture book. In the case of Marc Brown, author of the series of books about Arthur the Aardvark, it gave him an ambition for his life.

Marc Brown
In the blank after the word ambition, I wrote illustrator.

Three very important things happened to me in high school. Through art books I discovered the work of Marc Chagall; I was so impressed that I changed my name from Mark to Marc. My favorite teacher, my high school art teacher, gave me the best advice I ever got. She told me that if I wanted to be successful, I should do what I really loved doing and execute it as well as I could.

I also read the book that made a huge difference in my life, Maurice Sendak's *Where the Wild Things Are*. I was so moved by what Sendak was able to accomplish in that book with a minimum of words. It was as if a light bulb went off in my head. I had no idea about the potential that the field of children's books held until I looked at *Where the Wild Things Are*, a book that determined the course of my life. Recently I was perusing my high school yearbook and noticed that under my picture, in the blank after the word *ambition*, I wrote *illustrator*. That was definitely a "post-Sendak" ambition.

My curiosity, in a sense, was stronger than my fear; for I could not remain where I was, but crept back to the bank again, whence, sheltering my head behind a bush of broom, I might command the road before our door. I was scarcely in position ere my enemies began to arrive, seven or eight of them, running hard, their feet beating out of time along the road, and the man with the lantern some paces in front. Three men ran together, hand in hand; and I made out, even through the mist, that the middle man of this trio was the blind beggar. The next moment his voice showed me I was right.

"Down with the door!" he cried.

"Ay, ay, sir!" answered two or three; and a rush was made upon the "Admiral Benbow," the lantern-bearer following; and then I could see them pause, and hear speeches passed in a lower key, as if they were surprised to find the door open. But the pause was brief, for the blind man again issued his command. His voice sounded louder and higher, as if he were afire with eagerness and rage.

"In, in, in!" he shouted, and cursed them for their delay. Four or five of them obeyed at once, two remaining on the road with the formidable beggar. There was a pause, then a cry of surprise, and then a voice shouting from the house:

"Bill's dead."

But the blind man swore at them again for their delay.

"Search him, some of you shirking lubbers, and the rest of you aloft and get the chest," he cried.

I could hear their feet rattling up our old stairs, so that the house must have shook with it. Promptly afterwards, fresh sounds of astonishment arose; the window of the captain's room was thrown open with a slam and a jingle of broken glass; and a man leaned out into the moonlight, head and shoulders, and addressed the blind beggar on the road below him.

"Pew," he cried, "they've been before us. Some one's turned the chest out alow and aloft."

"Is it there?" roared Pew.

"The money's there."

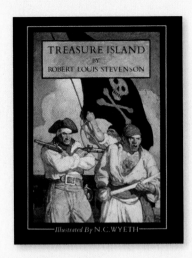

TREASURE ISLAND

by Robert Louis Stevenson

Treasure Island began as a drawing of an island, executed in watercolors by the stepson of Robert Louis Stevenson. As Stevenson helped complete the work of art, he drew in three red crosses, added Spyglass Hill, and named the location *Treasure Island*. When his stepson asked for a story to accompany the map, Stevenson obliged, becoming one of a legion of adults who craft their best children's book initially for a single child. The first of Stevenson's successful works of fiction, *Treasure Island* has enthralled young readers since 1881 when it appeared as a serialized story.

Treasure Island contains a wonderful sense of place and fully realized characters; Long John Silver, the arch-villain of the piece, emerges as larger than life. A good tale well told, the story moves from one exciting adventure to another—from the moment that a mysterious seaman, Billy Bones, arrives at the Admiral Benbow Inn to the denouement as a band of heroes escapes the island with treasure, foiling pirates in the process.

The edition of *Treasure Island* most frequently praised by adults who encountered it as a child is the one created by N. C. Wyeth in 1911 for Charles Scribner's Sons. In eighteen pieces of art, Wyeth deftly sets character, setting, and ambiance for the story. According to Andrew Wyeth, Charlton Heston and his son, who were making a movie from the book, hunted all over England for an inn that looked like the Admiral Benbow Inn in the Wyeth illustration; only later did they discover that they should have been filming Wyeth's own childhood home in Needham, Massachusetts, the inspiration for the art. These illustrations, created on large

(continued on page 135)

Wendell Minor

Study from life, study the natural landscape, paint outdoors, soak up the atmospheric light. Aim for simplicity.

When I was a young boy in middle school, *Treasure Island* was one of my favorite books, the Scribner Classic edition, illustrated by N. C. Wyeth. Suffering from dyslexia, I was starved for visual information. The pictures in that book allowed me to create my own visual realm. What incredible illustrations Wyeth painted for this title, one of fifteen books he created for the Scribner Classic series. His illustrations in this volume—like "Blind Pew"—are so dynamic and exciting.

Wyeth was the star pupil of Howard Pyle. Pyle taught his students many things: Study from life, study the natural landscape, paint outdoors, and soak up the atmospheric light. And he trained his students to aim for simplicity. The dynamic quality of simplification was really the genius behind Wyeth's art in *Treasure Island*. What resulted were images of immense power, images burned forever in my memory and those of so many other children.

Wyeth was superhuman in his abilities. He could paint thirty or forty large canvasses in a day. He needed the elbow room of these immense canvases to create the energy in his paintings. Although he always lamented that he was not considered a fine artist, his work has had lasting influence. Children are more affected by the art in their books than is any adult by fine art in a gallery. More people saw and responded to N. C. Wyeth's work in his lifetime than reacted to the work of Edward Hopper in his.

When I came from the Midwest to the East Coast, the first place I headed was Chadds Ford, Pennsylvania, and the Brandywine River. I just wanted to understand the landscape Wyeth viewed every day. One painting in the Brandywine Museum particularly fascinated me—a still life of an old bottle in which Wyeth brilliantly captured the dust. In the lower corner he indicated that he had painted this piece in forty-five minutes. Larger than life, he would forever intimidate future artists.

Ultimately, Wyeth influenced my decision to become a book illustrator, rather than a gallery artist. At one point I was selected to illustrate one of the first Scribner Classics to be released in over fifty years: Jack London's *The Call of the Wild*. On the back jacket, my name is listed between N. C. Wyeth and Maxfield Parrish. In my mind, the back jacket of that book is more important than the front jacket.

I believe that children's books are the last pond in the Serengeti. They are the one place we go to drink for inspiration. All of us can still go—and do—to those amazing books by N. C. Wyeth.

TREASURE ISLAND illustrated by N. C. Wyeth

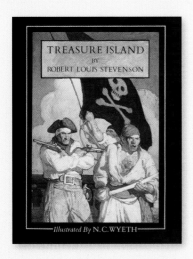

canvasses almost as tall as Wyeth himself, were in Wyeth's own estimation "better in every quality than anything I ever did." He had striven to keep his paintings fresh, brilliant, dramatic, striking in the composition and color, and with a great deal of emotional content. He succeeded brilliantly at what he set out to do.

Both Wendell Minor, one of the premier children's book and jacket illustrators in the country, and Andrew Wyeth, America's most renowned painter, selected *Treasure Island* as a key influence on their own lives and careers.

Andrew Wyeth

My father's visual interpretation fired my imagination and sent me on the path to become an artist.

I didn't learn to read until quite late in life. When I was about nine years old, my father read *Treasure Island* to me and my sister. Every night he would read a chapter, and we would sit there enthralled because he would impersonate the characters: Billy Bones, Blind Pew, Long John Silver, or Jim Hawkins. He would act it out. He read from his own book, the one he had illustrated in 1911 for Scribner's. I remember very clearly every detail of that story.

While writing the book, Robert Louis Stevenson read a chapter to his family every night, just like my father did. Stevenson broke away from a very proper family. To get to know the characters, he explored London's low life. That helped him make the characters in *Treasure Island* vital and alive.

Not only did I love the story, but the paintings really interested me. My father brought Stevenson's text to life in those illustrations. Many remember the image "Blind Pew tapping up and down the road in a frenzy" from this book. I had always loved that image—the moonlight on the Admiral Benbow Inn, the characterization of Blind Pew with his cape. When Betsy and I first got married, we didn't have much money but we heard it was up for sale and bought it for $1,000. It seemed like an enormous amount of money then. We first hung the painting over our living room fireplace. My own children grew up with it. Robert Montgomery, the actor, came to our house one day. He looked over at the mantle and said, "You know that picture influenced me to become an actor."

The model for the Benbow Inn was my father's childhood home in Needham, Massachusetts—located on South Street and still standing. Another image in the book, Ben Gunn behind the oak tree, was based on a tree that stood right across from that house. My father, a great reader, drew on his childhood memories for the artwork in this book.

Blind Pew and other paintings of my father's that Betsy and I have gathered over the years now hang in the Brandywine Museum in Chadds Ford, Pennsylvania. In the heavy timbers of the mill that the Brandywine Museum is built on, you feel you are on the deck of the *Hispaniola*; the paintings just fit perfectly into the museum.

Stevenson's text and my father's visual interpretation fired my imagination and sent me on the path to become an artist. His illustrations have influenced untold others as well. Recently one of his paintings, *Indian Love Call*, sold for $1.8 million. My father would truly have been shocked by that figure—and by the lasting effect of his art almost a hundred years after it was created.

I jumped to the ledge below, found it was really quite wide, slid on the seat of my pants to the next ledge, and stopped. The hawk apparently couldn't count. She did not know I had a youngster, for she checked her nest, saw the open mouths, and then she forgot me.

I scrambled to the riverbed somehow, being very careful not to hurt the hot fuzzy body that was against my own. However, Frightful, as I called her right then and there because of the difficulties we had had in getting together, did not think so gently of me. She dug her talons into my skin to brace herself during the bumpy ride to the ground.

I stumbled to the stream, placed her in a nest of buttercups, and dropped beside her. I fell asleep.

When I awoke my eyes opened on two gray eyes in a white stroobly head. Small pinfeathers were sticking out of the stroobly down, like feathers in an Indian quiver. The big blue beak curled down in a snarl and up in a smile.

"Oh, Frightful," I said, "you are a raving beauty." Frightful fluffed her nubby feathers and shook. I picked her up in the cup of my hands and held her under my chin. I stuck my nose in the deep warm fuzz. It smelled dusty dusty and sweet.

I liked that bird. Oh, how I liked that bird from that smelly minute. It was so pleasant to feel the beating life and see the funny little awkward movements of a young thing.

MY SIDE OF THE MOUNTAIN by Jean Craighead George

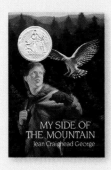

MY SIDE OF THE MOUNTAIN

by Jean Craighead George

As the daughter of a naturalist, and sister to the Craighead brothers known for their research on grizzly bears, Jean Craighead George grew up exploring the natural world and raising wild creatures. One day she announced that she was running away from home; forty minutes later she returned. As an adult, she decided to write about a boy who actually managed to accomplish what she had failed to do, testing his survival skills while living in a hemlock tree hollow in the Catskill Mountains. Although at first her publisher balked at the idea of releasing the book—fearing that it might encourage children to run away—they decided in 1959 to issue *My Side of the Mountain*.

The reader first meets Sam Gribley nestled in his tree home in the middle of a December snowstorm. Then in his simple but lyrical first-person account, Sam tells how he chose the location, once owned by an ancestor, and how he slowly developed his survival skills—fishing, hunting, finding a water source, making clothing, and even developing acorn flour for pancakes. For a companion Sam captures and trains a peregrine falcon, Frightful. As he makes astute and precise observations about the plants and animals around him, Sam creates a life of freedom and joy for himself. In fact he brilliantly fulfills the childhood dream of running away—even if only in a book.

Robert F. Kennedy Jr., who has been named by *Time* magazine as one of the "Heroes for the Planet," was captivated by *My Side of the Mountain* and the idea of raising a falcon. This book led him, as well as many others, into a career of environmental activism.

Robert F. Kennedy Jr.
To take up ecological stewardship

In 1986 I met Jean Craighead George at a friend's home in upstate New York. I grew up admiring the Craigheads, a family of naturalists whose adventures I followed in *National Geographic*, where they always seemed to be attaching transmitters to grizzly bears, banding bald eagles, or paddling canoes and fiberglass kayaks on descents down Western white waters. Always there were flocks of children participating in every adventure and experiment. I thought the Craigheads might be the only family in America having more fun than the Kennedys. Obsessed with falcons as I was from birth, I first read *My Side of the Mountain* in 1964. When I met Jean Craighead George that day in New York, she reminded me about the letter I had written her, at age eleven, politely inquiring if she knew where I could find an occupied kestrel nest.

As a student at Millbrook School, just across the Hudson from Delhi—where Sam and Frightful had had their adventures—I belonged to a small cadre of students who not only shared my devotion to the birds but who also had mastered the sport of falconry. We captured and trained red-tails and kestrels, immature birds on their first migration. We talked about hawks every spare moment—at meals, between classes, and after chapel. We marked in our memories the raptor nests we found during our daily winter hunting excursions. In the spring we climbed up to those nests to band baby red-tails, crows, and owls. We learned to use ropes and climbing spurs to scale the tall oak and ash trees where the large raptors nested. We even began a raptor breeding project, one of the first in history, and were partially successful, persuading a golden eagle and a red-tailed hawk to lay eggs in captivity.

My experience as a young falconer accounts in large part for my lifelong devotion to raptors and my continued interest in natural history. Our time as falconers left a mark on my schoolmates as well. All of them have chosen careers in the natural sciences or as environmental advocates with exceptional records. For each one of them, reading *My Side of the Mountain* was the formative inspiration of their falconry experience. My years as a falconer informed my own career choice as an environmental lawyer and advocate. *My Side of the Mountain* has inspired countless children, as it did me, to take up ecological stewardship in our adult years.

It was about dark now; so I dropped the canoe down the river under some willows that hung over the bank, and waited for the moon to rise. I made fast to a willow; then I took a bite to eat, and by-and-by laid down in the canoe to smoke a pipe and lay out a plan. I says to myself, they'll follow the track of that sackful of rocks to the shore and then drag the river for me. And they'll follow that meal track to the lake and go browsing down the creek that leads out of it to find the robbers that killed me and took the things. They won't ever hunt the river for anything but my dead carcass. They'll soon get tired of that, and won't bother no more about me. All right; I can stop anywhere I want to. Jackson's Island is good enough for me; I know that island pretty well, and nobody ever comes there. And then I can paddle over to town nights, and slink around and pick up things I want. Jackson's Island's the place.

I was pretty tired, and the first thing I knowed I was asleep. When I woke up I didn't know where I was, for a minute. I set up and looked around, a little scared. Then I remembered. The river looked miles and miles across. The moon was so bright I could a counted the drift logs that went a-slipping along, black and still, hundreds of yards out from shore. Everything was dead quiet, and it looked late, and *smelt* late. You know what I mean—I don't know the words to put it in.

I took a good gap and a stretch, and was just going to unhitch and start when I heard a sound away over the water. I listened. Pretty soon I made it out. It was that dull kind of a regular sound that comes from oars working in rowlocks when it's a still night. I peeped out through the willow branches, and there it was—a skiff, away across the water. I couldn't tell how many was in it. It kept a-coming, and when it was abreast of me I see there warn't but one man in it. Thinks I, maybe it's pap, though I warn't expecting him. He dropped below me, with the current, and by-and-by he came a-swinging up shore in the easy water, and he went by so close I could a reached out the gun and touched him. Well, it *was* pap, sure enough—and sober, too, by the way he laid to his oars.

I didn't lose no time. The next minute I was a-spinning down stream soft but quick in the shade of the bank. I made two mile and a half, and then struck out a quarter of a mile or more towards the middle of the river, because pretty soon I would be passing the ferry landing, and people might see me and hail me. I got out amongst the driftwood, and then laid down in the bottom of the canoe and let her float. I laid there, and had a good rest and a smoke out of my pipe, looking away into the sky; not a cloud in it. The sky looks ever so deep when you lay down on your back in the moonshine; I never knowed it before. And how far a body can hear on the water such nights!

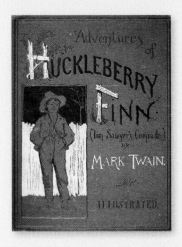

THE ADVENTURES OF HUCKLEBERRY FINN

THE ADVENTURES OF TOM SAWYER

by Mark Twain

"[I]f I'd 'a' knowed what a trouble it was to make a book I wouldn't 'a' tackled it, and ain't a-going to no more." So Huckleberry Finn ended the book his author, Mark Twain, called "Huck's autobiography." Huck Finn made his first appearance as Tom Sawyer's sidekick in *The Adventures of Tom Sawyer*. In this book published in 1876, filled with boyhood pranks and escapades, Tom and Huck get to live in the wild on Jackson's Island, defeat the ominous Indian Joe, and discover a treasure in gold. In the fictional Mississippi river town of St. Petersburg, based on Hannibal, Missouri, they struggle against the restrictions imposed by the adult community and yearn for the freedom offered by the Mississippi River.

In 1884, eight years and many manuscripts later—Twain considered pigeonholing or even burning the book— Huck debuted in his own novel, one of the most controversial ones ever published in the United States. For more than 125 years, one group or another has tried to deprive young readers of *The Adventures of Huckleberry Finn*. The public library in Concord, Massachusetts, initially banned the book for being "trash and only suitable for the slums." In recent years the portrayal of the runaway slave Jim has brought the book back under attack, making it one of the most challenged books of our time.

Of all its readers, young people seem to have been the most enthusiastic, reveling in an adventure story that personifies personal freedom. Told in the first-person voice of fourteen-year-old Huck, the saga begins with Huck under the guardianship of the

(continued on page 141)

Jean Craighead George

I write about what I know.

My mother read *The Adventures of Huckleberry Finn* to my brothers and me in the evening while we gathered around her chair. As I listened with my eyes closed, in my mind I created the raft, the Mississippi River, and Huckleberry and his friends. It was easy. Mark Twain was an on-scene writer.

The Adventures of Huckleberry Finn is unforgettable because Mark Twain knew what he was writing about—the Mississippi and its people and ecology. Having learned that lesson, when I began my writing career, I wrote about what I knew. Or, if the environment was strange to me, I traveled there to live for a while. I learned about the plants and animals and climate, and interacted with the people. When I returned home to write, I would then close my eyes, return to the locale, open my eyes, and write.

Brad Paisley

The power of the pen to change people's lives

The Adventures of Huckleberry Finn is my favorite book, and Mark Twain is one of my favorite authors. Recently, my wife and I had our first child, a boy, and discussed his name for a long time. We could have named him William Warren Paisley, but that sounded like a Supreme Court judge. We both loved the ring and the uniqueness of William Huckleberry Paisley.

This name, like the character in the book, indicates a spirit of adventure that I hope he embodies. I can see him now—out playing in the woods, taking chances. His name represents the free-thinking ideas of Mark Twain that I have always embraced.

But I had second thoughts about making the unusual name official. In the hospital we were getting ready to leave, and I was sitting there with the pen. I asked myself if I really was going to name my child Huckleberry. As I wrote the name on that sheet, I said to Kim, "Keep this pen. This is a reminder to him of the power of the pen. With that pen I changed his life—when I wrote his name down."

That is what writers like Mark Twain do; they change people's lives with the power of the pen.

Tom went on whitewashing—paid no attention to the steamboat. Ben stared a moment and then said:

"Hi-*yi! You're* up a stump, ain't you!"

No answer. Tom surveyed his last touch with the eye of an artist, then he gave his brush another gentle sweep and surveyed the result, as before. Ben ranged up alongside of him. Tom's mouth watered for the apple, but he stuck to his work. Ben said:

"Hello, old chap, you got to work, hey?"

Tom wheeled suddenly and said:

"Why, it's you, Ben! I warn't noticing."

"*Say—I'm* going in a-swimming, *I* am. Don't you wish you could? But of course you'd druther *work*—wouldn't you? Course you would!"

Tom contemplated the boy a bit, and said:

"What do you call work?"

"Why, ain't *that* work?"

Tom resumed his whitewashing, and answered carelessly:

"Well, maybe it is, and maybe it ain't. All I know, is, it suits Tom Sawyer."

"Oh come, now, you don't mean to let on that you *like* it?"

The brush continued to move.

"Like it? Well, I don't see why I oughtn't to like it. Does a boy get a chance to whitewash a fence every day?"

That put the thing in a new light. Ben stopped nibbling his apple. Tom swept his brush daintily back and forth—stepped back to note the effect—added a touch here and there—criticized the effect again—Ben watching every move and getting more and more interested, more and more absorbed. Presently he said:

"Say, Tom, let *me* whitewash a little."

Tom considered, was about to consent; but he altered his mind:

"No—no—I reckon it wouldn't hardly do, Ben. You see, Aunt Polly's awful particular about this fence—right here on the street, you know—but if it was the back fence I wouldn't mind and *she* wouldn't. Yes, she's awful particular about this fence; it's got to be done very careful; I reckon there ain't one boy in a thousand, maybe two thousand, that can do it the way it's got to be done."

"No—is that so? Oh come, now—lemme just try. Only just a little—I'd let *you*, if you was me, Tom."

"Ben, I'd like to, honest injun; but Aunt Polly—well, Jim wanted to do it, but she wouldn't let him; Sid wanted to do it, and she wouldn't let Sid. Now don't you see how I'm fixed? If you was to tackle this fence and anything was to happen to it—"

"Oh, shucks, I'll be just as careful. Now lemme try. Say—I'll give you the core of my apple."

"Well, here—No, Ben, now don't. I'm afeard—"

"I'll give you *all* of it!"

Tom gave up the brush with reluctance in his face, but alacrity in his heart. And while the late steamer *Big Missouri* worked and sweated in the sun, the retired artist sat on a barrel in the shade close by, dangled his legs, munched his apple, and planned the slaughter of more innocents.

Widow Douglas. Then his alcoholic father reappears, kidnaps his son, and locks Huck in a backwoods cabin. Faking his own death, Huck boards a raft headed down the Mississippi River and links up with Jim, a runaway slave trying to get to freedom in Cairo, Illinois, a free state. On their journey down the Mississippi they encounter, as Russell Baker has written, "murderers, bullies, swindlers, lynchers, thieves, liars, frauds . . . hypocrites, windbags, and traders in human flesh." In the end, Huck heads out west; if these people represent civilization, Huck understandably wants little part of it.

Along with its detractors, the book has also garnered a multitude of defenders over the years. T. S. Eliot, Ralph Ellison, William Faulkner, F. Scott Fitzgerald, and J. D. Salinger are among the writers who have sung its praises. Ernest Hemingway claimed that "[a]ll modern American literature comes from one book by Mark Twain called *Huckleberry Finn*." Although Twain wrote at the beginning of the book, "persons attempting to find a moral in it will be banished," many readers have responded to the serious underpinnings of these sagas. Newbery Award winner Jean Craighead George and Grammy Award winner Brad Paisley drew inspiration from Huck Finn's escapades. Robert S. Pirie, former CEO of Rothschild, Inc., enjoyed both of Twain's masterpieces.

Robert S. Pirie
How to get others to do what I hoped they would do

My father was in the army for many years and died when I was very young. I really don't remember him reading to me, nor did my mother. But I remember very well reading under the covers with a flashlight after I went to bed, something which I hope children still do today.

I particularly look back with pleasure on *The Adventures of Tom Sawyer* and *The Adventures of Huckleberry Finn*. There are so many scenes from those two books that have stayed with me: Tom Sawyer as he hoodwinks others into doing his work, whitewashing the fence, and Huck Finn posing successfully as a girl—until he catches a ball of lead the wrong way. As a lawyer and investment banker for over fifty years, the Tom Sawyer approach shaped my career. It was my early introduction into how to get others to do what I hoped they would do.

"It is my honor," continued the professor, loud enough to be heard above Dulcy's interruption, "to bring to you this fabulously amazing and most phenomenal product, and its name is"—he paused dramatically, snapping free the fastenings of the case and throwing up the cover—"its name is EVERSOMUCH MORE-SO!"

The judge, the sheriff, Uncle Ulysses, Dulcy, and Homer all stared at the cans displayed so suddenly before their eyes.

"What—?" Uncle Ulysses started to ask.

"Ah-h, *what?*" echoed the stranger. "Ah-h, yes, my good friends, I can see the question in your friendly faces. *What* is this remarkable EVERSOMUCH MORE-SO, and *what* can this phenomenal EVERSOMUCH MORE-SO do for me? In just one minute, just thirty short seconds, I am going to demonstrate to you and to prove to you without the shadow of a doubt that this product can accomplish wondrous things.

"Each and every can," said the professor, picking up a can and continuing without a pause, "yes, *each* and *every* can comes complete with a handy adjustable top. A slight twist to either left or right opens the tiny holes in the cap, making EVERSOMUCH MORE-SO readily accessible for instantaneous application.

"Now for the purposes of demonstration," the professor continued quickly, "we shall use these delicious-looking doughnuts. Young man," he said to Homer, "if you will be so kind as to pass the tray, and if you gentlemen," he requested, bowing low, "would be so kind as to take two doughnuts. . ."

While Homer passed the tray and everyone took two doughnuts, one in each hand, the professor said, "Now, my friends, we are ready to—uht, uht, sonny, don't forget me!" And before Homer could pass the tray the professor speared two doughnuts on the other end of his cane.

The judge and Uncle Ulysses exchanged looks, and the sheriff was about to ask, "When—?"

"*Now,*" said the professor loudly, banging on his case for undivided attention, "now we are ready to proceed with our demonstration. Yes, in just one minute, only sixty seconds— but first," said the professor, picking up a can of EVERSOMUCH MORE-SO, "I shall acquaint you with this wondrous product."

CENTERBURG TALES: MORE ADVENTURES OF HOMER PRICE by Robert McCloskey

**CENTERBURG TALES: MORE
ADVENTURES OF HOMER PRICE**

by Robert McCloskey

Robert McClosky excelled both in writing and art, and his picture books—*Make Way for Ducklings, Blueberries for Sal,* and *Time of Wonder*—have been a staple of childhood since the 1940s. Switching to the novel format, McCloskey returned to his Ohio roots to create the setting for an episodic narrative about Homer Price, a boy growing up in Centerburg, Ohio. Based on the American tall-tale tradition, *Homer Price* features a great cast of characters placed in small-town America. In the most famous story, Homer struggles with an automatic doughnut machine that won't shut off. *Centerburg Tales: More Adventures of Homer Price*, published in 1951, continues Homer's madcap adventures in a town where "nothing ever happens here anymore."

McCloskey once said that he had one foot firmly planted mid-air and the other on a banana peel, and the combination no doubt led to madcap humor in the story "Ever So Much More So." In it a traveling salesman pawns off a magic elixir that will make everything seem better. When Dr. David Linden, Professor of Neuroscience at Johns Hopkins University, discovered this story as a boy, he began to explore the relationship between what happens in the mind and in someone's personality.

David Linden
How mental function confers humanity

Although Robert McCloskey is best known for *Make Way for Ducklings*, he wrote another book that had a profound effect on my life: *Centerburg Tales: More Adventures of Homer Price*, which I read in elementary school. My favorite story in this collection was "Ever So Much More So," which told about a magical chemical that increased the intensity of all sensations and actions: "It will make a rose smell ever so much more lovely, curly hair ever so much more curly, beautiful music ever so much more beautiful." When the residents of Centerburg begin eating "EVERSOMUCH MORE-SO," it causes their personality traits to become much more exaggerated; each person becomes a more pronounced version of himself— "more like himself than he is already."

I have spent a lifetime studying the biology of mental function, trying to examine brain evolution, memory, and how neuronal function confers our humanity. This story sparked my nascent interest in mental function and sent me on that path.

He slept in the stable that night and on the next day did find a sea captain who would—in spite of the bad hand—take him on as a cabin boy. Johnny did not like the captain, the ship, nor the voyage. It was going to Halifax and the cold turn the weather had taken and his insufficient clothing made him desire a trip to the tropic Sugar Isles above all else. But all seemed settled until the shipmaster casually told him he must furnish his own blankets, oilskins, sea boots, warm pea jacket. Johnny had no money to buy such things.

Having no safe place now to leave his cup, he had tied the strings of a flannel bag to his belt. It struck at him as he walked. The luckiest thing he had ever done was to disobey his mother and show this cup to Cilla last July. Now he would disobey her again and sell it.

There were many silversmiths who would have bought it, but the cup was so old-fashioned he could not expect from them more than its value in old silver. However, Mr. Lyte, owning the matching cups, would pay a very good price. So once more he went to that merchant's counting house on Long Wharf.

It was the same as before, except "Cousin Sewall" was not there. The grasshoppery old clerks were bent over their ledgers. Neither moved as Johnny slipped quietly past them and entered the inner office.

Mr. Lyte looked up from his papers. There was a glimmer almost of hatred in the sliding black eyes as he recognized Johnny. Mr. Justice had humiliated him publicly, and the story had gone quickly around the wharves, among his friends.

He spoke very quietly. "Well?"

"Look. I have no money. No food. Only the clothes I stand in. I've no choice. This cup is worth about four pounds if I sold it for old silver. I'm a silversmith and I know. But to you, because it matches your others, it is worth about four times as much. Give me twenty pounds and you can have it."

Through the melted tallow on his face there was a faint flush of blood. Although his voice was suave enough, Johnny knew he was furious.

"I've never yet bought stolen goods. I'm not going to begin now—not even with my own."

Johnny put the cup back in its bag, but before he could tie the strings to his belt Mr. Lyte's long fingers had reached out and taken it.

"If you will give me back my property," Johnny said politely, "I'll take it to Mr. Revere or Mr. Burt. Four pounds is all I really need."

JOHNNY TREMAIN by Esther Forbes, illustrated by Lynd Ward

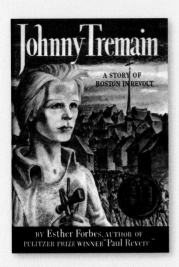

JOHNNY TREMAIN

by Esther Forbes,
illustrated by Lynd Ward

After Esther Forbes had won a Pulitzer Prize for *Paul Revere and the World He Lived In*, she turned her attention to writing about a silversmith's fourteen-year-old apprentice during the Revolutionary War. In *Johnny Tremain*, published during World War II, Forbes wanted to explore the idea of how in peacetime societies look on those under twenty as children—but in wartime those same boys are expected to become men and defend the country.

The story spans two years in the life of Johnny Tremain. After he badly burns his hand, he must search for a new trade. As a delivery boy for the Patriot's newspaper, the *Boston Observer*, he becomes involved with the Sons of Liberty and the growing conflict with the British. The novel conveys a detailed account of the Revolution but does so through an exciting story. As the *New York Times* said of Forbes, she was a "novelist who wrote like a historian and a historian who wrote like a novelist."

However, by all accounts, Forbes faced some serious handicaps as an author. She suffered from terrible handwriting, atrocious spelling, and had no idea how to use any punctuation mark except for the dash. Forbes counted on her editors to take her eccentric, but absolutely brilliant, manuscript and transform it into a readable book. Winner of the Newbery Award and quickly hailed as a masterpiece, *Johnny Tremain* has been teaching young readers about the Revolutionary War for more than sixty-five years. Jack Pikulski, a member of the Reading Hall of Fame, found that it also taught him a lot about reading when he first shared the book with his daughter.

Jack Pikulski

I reoriented my career to work on the prevention of reading problems.

It seems quite ironic that I didn't discover the power of children's literature until I was well into adulthood—not until after earning a doctorate in, of all areas, *reading*!

Books were for school. We read basal readers, which I actually enjoyed; we used books to memorize "facts" like the leading imports and exports of European countries. However, I do remember my fourth-grade teacher, Mrs. Morgan, reading several pages of *Heidi* to us daily. That was wonderful, but something was lacking because I associated the magic of that reading only with Mrs. Morgan, not with the book. Maybe it just wasn't a boys' book.

No one in my family expected me to attend, let alone graduate from, college, but I graduated three times, majoring each time in psychology. In my doctoral program I concentrated on the psychology of reading, which included the diagnosis and treatment of reading problems. Later, at the University of Delaware, I headed the reading clinic. I loved what I did. I grew profoundly aware of the central role of reading in the lives of children and their parents. The gratification that comes with helping a struggling reader is incomparable.

It took Esther Forbes and *Johnny Tremain* to introduce me to dimensions of children's books that I had not yet discovered. When my daughter, Beth, was in third grade, I somehow (maybe divine inspiration!) decided to read that book to her—a bit every night—just the way Mrs. Morgan read *Heidi*. The book is too challenging for third graders, but not if a parent who loves Boston, and history, and learning, reads it to a third grader whom he loves. What an experience! The power of that story of heroism, dedication, patriotism; the brilliant, vivid descriptions of colonial Boston; the resurrection of personages like John Hancock and Paul Revere made us feel like we were walking the streets of Boston and helping to plot the defeat of the Red Coats!

While not the whole reason, I think that the reading of that book to Beth helped me reorient my career so that I now concentrate on preventing reading problems and introducing children to the treasure of children's literature. I cherish the work I did early in my career; it's critical work that still needs to be done. But Beth and Johnny (both Tremain and my son, Johnny) helped lead me to a new world of reading. I learned from *Johnny Tremain* that children's books not only inform and entertain, but they make lasting impressions and add richness to our lives and the lives of those we love. While I am definitely into my mature years, I still read children's books; I always will. And that worn copy of *Johnny Tremain* sits above my desk ready for me to read to my first grandchild. I'll try to wait until he or she is in third grade.

"It is good I have some one
To help me," he said.
"Right here in my hat
On the top of my head!"
It is good that I have him
Here with me today.
He helps me a lot.
This is Little Cat A."

And then Little Cat A
Took the hat off HIS head.
"It is good I have some one
To help ME," he said.
"This is Little Cat B.
And I keep him about,
And when I need help
Then I let him come out."

And then B said,
"I think we need Little Cat C.
That spot is too much
For the A cat and me.
But now, have no fear!
We will clean it away!
The three of us! Little Cats B, C and A!"

THE CAT IN THE HAT COMES BACK by Dr. Seuss

THE CAT IN THE HAT COMES BACK

by Dr. Seuss

Dr. Seuss's *The Cat in the Hat*, published in 1957, began its journey as part of the "reading wars" of the 1950s. William Spaulding, head of Houghton Mifflin's Educational Division, had been searching for a way to upstage the leading reading textbook publisher, Scott Foresman. This competitor had a lock on reading education with its stories about Dick, Jane, and Spot. Spaulding suggested to Theodore Geisel, who wrote as Dr. Seuss, a friend from World War II army days, that he create a story, with a limited vocabulary of around 300 words, which would actually encourage children to read. Although it was one of the hardest tasks he ever undertook, eventually he crafted *The Cat in the Hat* in 236 well-chosen words. Many felt that this slim volume appeared to be a solution for the problem of the day, "Why Johnny Can't Read."

Seuss followed his success with a sequel in 1958, *The Cat in the Hat Comes Back*. He found it easier to write because he had already established his characters and setting. Also he allowed himself the grand total of 290 words to complete the task. In the book the Cat enters their house to soak in the bathtub and eat cake. When he attempts to clean off the pink ring of color that has accumulated around the tub, the Cat reveals his secret team, a small Cat A in his hat, who has a Cat B in his hat, with a Cat C in his hat. Finally Cat Z arrives, too small to see but in possession of a magical substance "Voom" that finally clears away the mess.

As cultural critic Louis Menard has noted, a subtle political message underscores this McCarthy-era book—remaking the pink stain of communism with atomic power. Harvard scientist Steven Pinker believes that the book alludes to some very sophisticated mathematic concepts.

Steven Pinker

It forced me to think about nested sets, infinitesimals, Zeno's paradox, and other concepts in mathematics.

As a young child my first book was Dr. Seuss's *The Cat in the Hat Comes Back*, which I remember fondly to this day. It provided much needed relief from those dull, dull, Dick-and-Jane readers that were forced on me in the first grade at school! I still remember the series of little cats each nested in a bigger cat's hat—Cats A, B, and C down to Z. That image forced me to think about nested sets, infinitesimals, Zeno's paradox, and other concepts that I studied much later in mathematics.

Dogs in cars again.
Going away.
Going away fast.

Look at those dogs go.
Go, dogs. Go!

"Stop, dogs. Stop!
The light is red now."

"Go, dogs. Go!"
The light is green now."

GO, DOG. GO! by P. D. Eastman

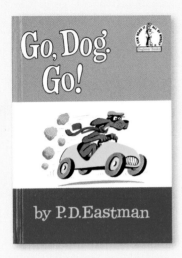

GO, DOG. GO!

by P. D. Eastman

The incredible success of Dr. Seuss's *Cat in the Hat* inspired Random House to establish a new series, Beginner Books, which proudly announced "I Can Read It All by Myself." Seuss, his wife Helen Geisel, and Phyllis Cerf served as the initial editorial board to locate and shape material suitable for children learning to read. Although none of the books ever achieved the fame of Seuss's best work for the series—he also wrote *Green Eggs and Ham* and *One Fish Two Fish Red Fish Blue Fish* as Beginner Books—many classic titles appeared as Beginner Books, including P. D. Eastman's *Are You My Mother?* and Mike McClintock's *A Fly Went By*.

In 1961 Philip Dey Eastman followed up *Are You My Mother?* with a story destined to become even more successful, *Go, Dog. Go!*. In a book that beguiled readers while using only seventy-five words, anthropomorphic dogs engage in a variety of activities, all executed with a great deal of energy.

Author Jon Scieszka, the first National Ambassador for Children's Books, found relief from Dick and Jane in Eastman's masterpiece.

Jon Scieszka

To build a world as funny and as purpose-driven as a bunch of dogs in cars speeding toward a party in a tree

Go, Dog. Go! by P. D. Eastman is the truest book I have ever read. It is the book that got me started as a reader and a writer. It is a story clear as a spring day, funny as a dressed-up monkey, wise as the most gnarly Zen koan.

And like most great truths, it is right there in plain sight . . . and it seems so simple. The entire text of the first page is all of one word: *Dog*. And so it is.

The next page spread expands on the truth: "Big dog. Little dog." These dogs are followed by black dogs and white dogs, dogs at work, dogs at play, a red dog on a blue tree, a blue dog on a red tree, two dogs in a house on a boat in the water. All with illustrations showing oh so satisfyingly just exactly that.

Go, Dog. Go! rocked my first-grade world.

At school I had been trying to learn to read by deciphering stories featuring two lame kids named Dick and Jane. They never did much of anything exciting. And they talked funny. If this was reading, I wondered why anyone would bother.

Then I found *Go, Dog. Go!* Here was a book about dogs driving around in cars who finally meet up in a tree for a party. But this book seemed so much more real to me (so much more like my family of five brothers) than the books about those strange kids with the funny speech patterns.

And the hat. The hat may mean more than we can ever know.

Three times throughout the book—interwoven in the onrushing description of dogs in boats, dogs in bed, dogs in cars—a pink poodle asks a yellow dog, "Do you like my hat?"

Three times the yellow dog answers, "I do not."

After the two-page all out dog party in the tree, the pink poodle, now in the most outrageous party hat, asks the yellow dog one more time, "And now do you like my hat?"

And of course he does. And of course they drive off into the sunset together.

Go, Dog. Go! made me want to be a reader, to read aloud those truths that were right there to see, and to knowingly revisit the question of the hat. *Go, Dog. Go!* made me start thinking about being a writer—to build a world as funny and as purpose-driven as a bunch of dogs in cars speeding toward a party in a tree.

And that title. That might be the best koan of all. Three words. Three different punctuation marks. A description? A challenge? A cheering on of every dog and every beginning reader?

Yes. Yes. And yes.

Thank you, P. D. Eastman.

Go, Dog. Go!

For the fourth time
he called in his wise men.
"Again you must help me,"
begged the king.

Once again the wise men
said it would be easy.

Elephants!
The wise men brought in elephants
to chase the lions away.

The lion-chasing elephants
did a wonderful job.

Soon every last lion was gone.

The elephants were very, very happy
living with the king.
But the king was most unhappy
living with elephants.

"How do you get rid
of elephants?" yelled the king.

"We can do it," said the wise men.
"We will do it right away."

They brought back all the mice.

THE KING, THE MICE AND THE CHEESE by Nancy and Eric Gurney

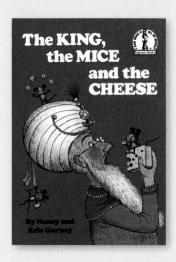

THE KING, THE MICE AND THE CHEESE

by Nancy and Eric Gurney

By 1965, when Nancy and Eric Gurney's *The King, the Mice and the Cheese* was published, all of the characteristic qualities of the series had been firmly put in place—64 pages, controlled vocabulary of under 400 words, simple yet compelling texts, and repetition. This small gem, a story of logic run amuck, features a king who loves his cheese, but its smell attracts mice. To get rid of the mice, the wise men bring in a series of animals, only to invite the mice back again in the end. Finally the king says to the mice, "I'll learn how to get along with you. You'll learn how to get along with me."

Andrew Weaver, a Canadian climate scientist, believes the message of the Gurneys' story should be taken to heart as we discuss our problems with the environment.

Andrew Weaver

Pause before taking extreme measures.

As a climate scientist, when I consider the idea of tinkering with Earth's air, water, or sunlight to fight global warming, I remember the lessons in one of my favorite children's books.

In *The King, the Mice and the Cheese* by Nancy and Eric Gurney, the castle of a cheese-loving king is infested with mice. Consequently, the king brings in cats to get rid of the mice. Then when the castle is overrun with cats, he brings in dogs to get rid of them. Then he resorts to lions to get rid of the dogs; elephants, to get rid of the lions; and, finally, mice to get rid of the elephants.

That scenario should give all scientists pause before taking extreme measures to mess with Mother Nature.

motivation

The very little engine looked up and saw the tears in the dolls' eyes. And she thought of the good little boys and girls on the other side of the mountain who would not have any toys or good food unless she helped.

Then she said, "I think I can. I think I can. I think I can." And she hitched herself to the little train.

She tugged and pulled and pulled and tugged and slowly, slowly, slowly they started off.

The toy clown jumped aboard and all the dolls and the toy animals began to smile and cheer.

Puff, puff, chug, chug, went the Little Blue Engine. "I think I can—I think I can—I think I can—I think I can—I think I can—I think I can—I think I can—I think I can."

Up, up, up. Faster and faster and faster and faster the little engine climbed, until at last they reached the top of the mountain.

THE LITTLE ENGINE THAT COULD retold by Watty Piper, illustrated by Loren Long

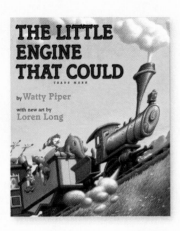

THE LITTLE ENGINE THAT COULD

retold by Watty Piper

The phrase, "I think I can. I think I can. I think I can," has become part of the American lexicon, much like other familiar statements— "one small step for man" or "ask not what your country can do for you." But although we know that Neil Armstrong and John F. Kennedy spoke the latter two statements, the authorship of the first remains in question. The writer of *The Little Engine That Could*, a story about an anthropomorphic train, has long been in question. Lawsuits, contests, and scholarly research have never determined the exact origin of the story, but many versions of this piece of American folklore appeared in Sunday school publications and school readers around the turn of the twentieth century.

Within a year of the 1929 stock market crash, the publisher Platt & Munk released the best-known version of the tale, a picture book that has sold millions of copies. Attributed to Watty Piper, the pseudonym used for all titles written by the staff, the first edition featured the art of Lois Lenski and was reissued in 1954 with art by Doris and George Hauman. The Piper version of the story provided genders for the trains and a purpose for the trip. A female train going over the mountains with toys and food for boys and girls breaks down, and a toy clown tries to attract other engines to pull them to their destination. All the male engines refuse to help, but The Little Blue Engine, another female, takes them up the mountain saying, "I think I can," and down it with the refrain, "I thought I could. I thought I could." Recently the illustrator Loren Long has created a magnificent new edition of this classic tale.

The Little Engine That Could provides for children a narrative example of the power of positive thinking. Sportscaster Tiki Barber took its message to heart as a child. Former U.S. Secretary of Health and Human Services Donna E. Shalala has thought about the book's message throughout her career. Director of the Miami Ballet Edward Villella has vividly remembered the book for decades.

Tiki Barber
The power of a positive attitude, determination, desire, and never giving up

My mom always kept books around the house, so I was drawn to them. She also instilled the importance of academics. She wouldn't let my brother and me go to practice until we did our homework.

I read all the time. One of my earliest memories is of my mother, my brother, and me sitting in our living room, with the television off, music playing, and the back door open. We were all reading something. One of my favorite books was *The Little Engine That Could*. Of course, now that choice makes sense to me. My twin brother and I were premature babies and suffered with seizures as small children. "They'll probably never play contact sports," the doctor told my mother. Growing up in a predominantly white neighborhood, I faced racial stereotypes.

As someone who has now played football and written books myself, I think *The Little Engine That Could* still contains an important message for young readers. It taught me about the power of a positive attitude, determination, desire, and never giving up.

Donna E. Shalala

Spunk—tempered by focus, patience, and a commitment to the long haul

I have always loved *The Little Engine That Could*. Of course, the story is a metaphor about the power of optimism and determination in the face of seemingly insurmountable obstacles; but, for me, it is more about the spirit of stepping up to the plate when you're needed and helping others for the greater good.

I found a kindred spirit in the little engine whose "I think I can, I think I can, I think I can," attitude resembles many of my own experiences. For most of my professional career in academia and public service, I have taken on positions for which the general consensus has been that I was not qualified, so uphill climbs have been the norm for me. Where some would say I had overreached, I saw each of these challenges as opportunities to watch, listen, learn, and, ultimately, grow both as a person and a leader.

The little engine had spunk, but it was tempered by focus, patience, and a commitment to the long haul. She knew that there were children waiting on the other side of the mountain, and someone needed to step in. That's a characteristic I've always looked for in a prospective employee. Big shiny engines with all the bells and whistles might look like the best candidates for a job, but if they are not willing to roll up their sleeves and share the load, then I don't think they will be a good fit for my organization.

What if the little engine hadn't succeeded? To me, that wasn't the point. She put her heart and soul into her work, and that made all the difference.

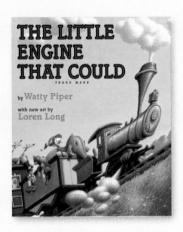

Edward Villella
A positive attitude and point of view

My parents, who lived through the Depression and World War II, came from a tough, blue-collar background. My mother was an orphan; my father, a high school graduate. Although they were good people, it simply was not in their culture to read to us or tell us stories. But my mother did bring us to the library.

I remember vividly one book from my childhood, *The Little Engine That Could*. The little engine uses the power of positive thinking and action. As a child, I had a lot of energy and a great need for guidance and direction; I was hunting for a way to look at life. In that book I discovered that there might be many challenges for me to overcome. But those challenges could be faced with positive thinking. I have used this concept throughout my professional career.

The world that I am in is not all beauty. Our responsibility is to make the difficult look easy. But it is a very complicated, complex, and competitive life. Both your body and mind are your instruments. We are physical, but we have very sophisticated ways to approach movement. We bring structured forms to it and work within guidelines. You have to commit to this life—and you also have to deal with injuries, personalities, and politics.

In 1986 I was able to build my own dance company, the Miami City Ballet, from the ground up. I didn't inherit old-fashioned ideas or personnel; I could use my experience as a dancer to form a unique company for other dancers. In the company there is close communication between me and the people who work here. I have to gain their respect every day, but there is a bond between us. Everyone calls me by my first name; anyone can talk to me at any time. I have been able to face the challenges of building something different and unique with a positive attitude and point of view. I first encountered that philosophy in *The Little Engine That Could*.

On and on went
CHOO CHOO
out of the city
through the suburbs
and into the country.
It was getting dark! . . .
She had lost her way! . . . .
She did not have much
coal or water left as she
had lost her tender. . . . . . .
Finally she came to where
the tracks divided.
One track went one
way and the other
track the other way.
She did not know
which track to take
so she took the
track that went
the other way.

It was an old old track that
Hadn't been used for years.
Bushes and weeds had grown
Between the ties. The trees
Had spread their branches
Over it. It was up hill and
Almost dark now…
And this is how
The poor tired
Little engine
Went.......

CHOOO choo choo choo ch
ch CHOOoo. . . . choo . . . . . . choo
choooo . . . . . choo . . . . . . ch . . . . . ch
ch . . . . ch . . . . ch . . . . ch
a   a   a   a   a   AH CHOO! And there she sat!

CHOO CHOO by Virginia Lee Burton

CHOO CHOO

by Virginia Lee Burton

Virginia Lee Burton tried unsuccessfully to interest thirteen publishers in her first manuscript, "Jonnifer Lint." One of them, Lovell Thompson of Houghton Mifflin, encouraged Burton to come up with a different book idea. Although he loved her strength as a draftsperson, he thought she needed to develop a story that children would want to hear. So Burton went home, read her text to her son Aris, and he promptly fell asleep. Asking herself what might keep Aris awake, Burton began to draft a philosophy of children's books that would make her the greatest American female picture book artist of the twentieth century. After she figured out how to wed her artistic talents and the sensibilities of children, she crafted one classic picture book after another—including *Mike Mulligan and His Steam Shovel* and *The Little House*.

Her first book, *Choo Choo*, appeared in 1937. The dedication page—"to my son Aris"—features an illustration of a young boy playing with a train set. Created in black and white because of the expense of full-color books at this time and Burton's neophyte status, *Choo Choo* immediately established Burton's competence as a picture book creator. Choo Choo, a train, carries people everywhere, but at some point she decides that she would rather go off by herself. Eventually she travels down an old track where she must halt in a dark and isolated spot. But those who care for her come and find her, pulling her back to usefulness and a community. The book contains all the classic Burton trademarks—a female inanimate object as the protagonist, type set to mirror or extend the illustrations, and strong graphic images.

Aris Demetrios—today a distinguished sculptor whose acrobat series immediately reminds viewers of Burton—watched his mother create *Choo Choo* and all her subsequent books. In the process she taught him about art and life.

Aris Demetrios
No matter what is thrown at you, you deal with it and keep going.

When I was a child, the trains came from Boston, went around a loop in Rockport, Massachusetts, and then headed the other way. So while my mother was working on *Choo Choo*, she went to Rockport to draw the cabs of the steam engines. It was amazing how thorough she was in her research.

A wonderful artist in her own right, Jinnee as we know her, wrote children's books to support our family. In *Choo Choo*, the train runs away. I believe some part of my mother just wanted to pursue her fine art. But Choo Choo comes back and gets on the tracks. So did my mother; she stayed on the tracks, creating books, supporting us.

She read every one of her books to me, my brother Michael, and our friends. She'd read the same saga for a month and would change a word here or there, watching to see if we'd go to sleep. If her stories worked over this period of time, she knew she had found something universal that would engage other children.

Very focused, my mother got up at four in the morning, prepared us for school, and then returned to work. When we came back from school, we were always welcome in her studio. There on the surfaces or the walls would be all her drawings. She'd create a quick dummy of the book sequentially. Then she would draw each piece, over and over, until she got it exactly right. *Life Story* took her ten years to finish. She'd have a version, and then she'd tear it up and do it again. A picture book was always fluid, never finished. She never fell into formulas. Every single book was a unique artistic statement; she was a true artist in every sense of the word

She was amazingly aware of her surroundings. In the middle of the winter, she worked in a barn with a coal stove providing heat. While drawing she saw a little mouse walk across her board. Over a few days the mouse grew tamer. Finally my mother would put out her left hand, and the mouse would curl up in it and sleep. Then she would draw the mouse with her right hand. That drawing still makes me weep when I see it.

My mother taught me so many important lessons. Personally she praised me for everything that I did and constantly supported me. I also learned from her what an artist does, the continual rethinking and redoing. From her books I learned that no matter what is thrown at you, you deal with it and keep going. That theme ties all her work together.

As her son, I have heard from so many people whose lives have been changed by her books. The minute people think of them, their faces light up. Her books are some of our most cherished cultural icons.

After a tasty lunch of blackeye peas—with huckleberry muffins for dessert—it was time to pole back home.

"Liza Lou," said Auntie Jane, "if you will take this soiled Sunday-go-to-meeting finery, and boil it up, and scrub it all real clean for me by next Friday, I'll bake you a pecan pie of your very own.

"But get on home real quick now, so as you won't be out in that Yeller Belly Swamp after dark."

Liza Lou didn't have to be told twice. She knew all about the wicked swamp witch lurking out there in the reeds. If ever she caught you, there was no telling what she'd do.

LIZA LOU AND THE YELLER BELLY SWAMP by Mercer Mayer

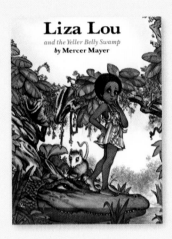

**LIZA LOU AND THE
YELLER BELLY SWAMP**

by Mercer Mayer

Mercer Mayer, who would become an incredibly prolific artist and writer, began publishing children's books in 1967 with a small wordless title, ideal for preschool readers, called *A Boy, a Dog, and a Frog*. As Mayer evolved as an illustrator he moved from tight, controlled, black-and-white scratchboard illustrations to lush, full-color art bursting off the page. His most successful books, among the more than three hundred he has produced, delve into the realm of childhood fears, nightmares, and hidden monsters in titles such as *There's a Nightmare in My Closet*.

In 1976 he published *Liza Lou and the Yeller Belly Swamp*, which initially attracted only a small amount of attention, although it did win the California Young Reader Medal. But Liza Lou, one of the most resourceful of the Mayer heroines, has become one of his best-loved protagonists over time. Liza Lou lives at the edge of the Yeller Belly Swamp, and her mother sends her through the dreaded area each day with a new errand. As someone with a lot of pluck and incredible wit, Liza outsmarts not just one but four monsters—the swamp haunt, witch, gobblygook, and devil—in a totally satisfying manner for the readers. As the book ends, we learn that no one has seen these monsters since Liza Lou encountered them, and no one misses them either.

Massachusetts Governor Deval Patrick first read *Liza Lou and the Yeller Belly Swamp* to his two daughters.

Deval Patrick

With courage, perseverance, intelligence, and a little wit, no task is too difficult.

As the father of daughters, I realized from the time my two girls were very young how important it was for them to be exposed to books about strong, bright females. *Liza Lou and the Yeller Belly Swamp* by Mercer Mayer is just such a book. This little girl's can-do spirit is an inspiration to us all. As she encounters frightening creatures on her errands through the swamp, it never occurs to Liza Lou that she can't accomplish her task. Like the challenges of life, the swamp's witches, haunts, gobblygooks, and even the devil can be vanquished with courage and wit.

My daughters are young adults now, and I am proud to say they have learned to meet challenges with the confidence and humor of Liza Lou. We can all learn a lesson from this plucky little girl. With courage, perseverance, intelligence, and a little wit, no task is too difficult.

In the capital of one of the large and rich provinces of the kingdom of China there lived a tailor, named Mustapha, who was so poor that he could hardly, by his daily labour, maintain himself and his family, which consisted of a wife and son.

His son, who was called Aladdin, had been brought up in a very careless and idle manner, and by that means had contracted many vicious habits. He was obstinate, and disobedient to his father and mother, who, when he grew up, could not keep him within doors. He was in the habit of going out early in the morning, and would stay out all day, playing in the streets with idle children of his own age.

When he was old enough to learn a trade, his father, not being able to put him out to any other, took him into his own shop, and taught him how to use his needle: but neither fair words nor the fear of chastisement were capable of fixing his lively genius. All his father's endeavours to keep him to his work were in vain; for no sooner was his back turned, than he was gone for that day. Mustapha chastised him, but Aladdin was incorrigible, and his father, to his great grief, was forced to abandon him to his idleness: and was so much troubled at not being able to reclaim him, that it threw him into a fit of sickness, of which he died in a few months.

The mother, finding that her son would not follow his father's business, shut up the shop, sold off the implements of trade, and with the money she received for them, and what she could get by spinning cotton, thought to maintain herself and her son.

Aladdin, who was now no longer restrained by the fear of a father, and who cared so little for his mother that whenever she chid him he would abuse her, gave himself entirely over to his idle habits, and was never out of the streets from his companions. This course he followed till he was fifteen years old, without giving his mind any useful pursuit, or the least reflection on what would become of him.

THE ARABIAN NIGHTS

Somewhere around 800–900 AD, the first manuscript appeared featuring a collection of stories from ancient Arabia—including Yemen, India, Persia, Pakistan, Afghanistan, Egypt, and Syria. All revolved around the framing tale of a despotic ruler, who wed a new bride each night only to have her killed in the morning. To save the women of the kingdom, the young Scheherazade married him and held him captivated by her stories. Each night he postponed her execution, so that he could hear the end of another tale.

The first European version of *The Thousand and One Nights*, also called *The Arabian Nights*, was translated into French by Antoine Galland in the early eighteenth century. Sir Richard Francis Burton created a ten-volume English translation in 1885. Since many of the stories seemed totally appropriate for children—"Ali Baba and the Forty Thieves," "The Voyages of Sinbad the Sailor," and "Aladdin's Lamp"—Andrew Lang published a book for young readers, *The Arabian Nights Entertainments*. He shortened the stories and left out material best suited for, as he said, "old gentlemen." Geraldine McCaughrean in *One Thousand and One Arabian Nights* created a modern classic edition for those who want to share the tales with children. Much like Grimm's fairy tales—never intended for a young audience—the stories have always had a profound effect on the children who encounter them.

"*The Arabian Nights* is more generally loved than Shakespeare," wrote Robert Louis Stevenson. Because it celebrates the power of story, this epic has appealed to writers for centuries. Contemporary advocates include writers Julia Alvarez, who read the stories while growing up in the Dominican Republic, and Azar Nafisi, who first encountered the book as a child in Iran.

Julia Alvarez
A way to escape

Perhaps you think that because I became a writer, I was one of those born bookworms who despite lack of encouragement kept a diary and read Cervantes by the time she was nine. I'm afraid I was definitely in the nonreading tradition of my family. I didn't care much for books. In part it was because I was surrounded by nonreaders; there weren't many books around. At the American school where I was sent in hopes that it might turn me into a well-behaved young lady who spoke English, I was introduced to books: Dick and Jane, and their tame little pets Spot and Puff. Just that morning we had trapped tarantulas in the yard and witnessed Iluminada receiving a spirit. Believe me, the Dick-and-Jane readers seemed bland in contrast to the world I was living in. Besides, these books were written in that impossible marbles-in-your-mouth language of English. In my first self-motivated piece of writing, I scratched out a note for my teacher, a note that eventually found its way home to my mother. "Dear Mrs. Brown," my note read, "I love you very much. But why should I read when I can have fun?"

But then I read my first book, read in the sense of being carried away by a narrative to a world I had not known before. It was *The Thousand and One Nights*, and it was given to me by my maiden aunt who read books and knew Latin and had not married by the time she was an old lady of twenty-six. *The Thousand and One Nights* was the story of a young girl who lived in a kingdom where the sultan was killing all the women. This young girl's father kept her hidden away in his library. There, she spent the day reading books and learning all the stories in the world. Finally, this young girl volunteered to go to the sultan and try to save all the women in her kingdom. For 1,001 nights, she told the sultan story after story she had read in the books in her father's library. Wonderful stories that mesmerized me as well as the sultan. In fact, he was so happy with this young storyteller that he spared her life and stopped killing women altogether. He also made her the queen of his kingdom.

Wow! I was impressed. I hadn't known stories had this kind of power. They could save lives. Reading could lead to becoming a queen. I became curious about books, books with bright, colorful pictures that were not part of school, books that began with a smart girl about to do something exciting—like Scheherazade in *The Thousand and One Nights*.

Looking back, it strikes me as curious that this was the book that made the biggest impression on me as a young child. Here we were living in a dictatorship, surrounded by secret police and disappearances. It makes me wonder if part of my affection for the young girl was that she had found a way to escape a situation not unlike the one we were in.

THE ARABIAN NIGHTS illustrated by Maxfield Parrish

Azar Nafisi

To see and envision the world and ourselves through fresh and new eyes

I first heard about *The Thousand and One Nights* when I was about four, and my father each night would choose to tell me a story from the treasure trove of Persian classical literature. The last time I read it was for a private class I had with seven of my female students in 1995.

I love Scheherazade's tale; like all great works of imagination, it is simple and yet profound, opening so many windows to the luminous worlds hidden in the depth of what we call everyday reality. To me this story contains a hidden theme—old and timeless—about the power of stories to reshape and redefine reality. It reminds me of what Vladimir Nabokov called the "third eye of imagination," helping us to see and envision the world and ourselves through fresh and new eyes.

Every morning—Monday to Friday—Lucinda skated to school. School was private and belonged to Anna C. Brackett, a person both terrible and wonderful and always to be reckoned with. Lucinda had much the same feeling about Miss Brackett as she had about God. She was everywhere; she knew everything; and she couldn't be fooled.

Miss Peters taught in the school, and every morning that was fair or tolerable she and Lucinda started out together. They arrived together, but the distance between they took each at her own pace. At the end of the first block on the cross-street, Lucinda would take the curb at a jump, wave a farewell hand, shout: "See you there, Miss Peters," and away she would go. Chug—clump—chirr—clump! That was the last Miss Peters would hear of her. The last she would see was a swaying figure in a pongee pinafore, buttoned up the back, a navy-blue sailor, sailing off her head but anchored to her by a stout elastic band under her chin. Arms would be waving like the churning paddles of a side-wheeler.

But the first thing Patrolman M'Gonegal would see was a half-squatting figure, hands on knees, skates close together, coasting through the entrance to Bryant Park; taking the curves westward without a stumble and coming to a final stop with a very unladylike: "Whoop!" It was at the corner of Fortieth Street that Lucinda would pick up Miss Peters again, and they would take the final block in company;

Lucinda moderating, Miss Peters accelerating, and both making the most of equality. The equality vanished, once inside the door on Thirty-Ninth Street.

Patrolman M'Gonegal's beat was Bryant Park, and that stretch of Fifth Avenue that bound it. He had marked Lucinda long before, and without interest, as a child of society, going down the avenue, pulling at the hand of a rigid Frenchwoman like a puppy on a leash. But the leash had been slipped; the puppy was free, and he watched for her every morning with a sense of deep satisfaction. Young things shouldn't be tied up. Didn't he know it—he had three of his own. A city like New York wasn't too big to turn them loose in—barring a few corners of it. He had been waiting for a week to pick Lucinda's acquaintance when she gave him the chance by catching her skate on the curb and plunging headlong into the traffic of the street.

ROLLER SKATES by Ruth Sawyer, illustrated by Valenti Angelo

ROLLER SKATES

ROLLER SKATES

by Ruth Sawyer,
illustrated by Valenti Angelo

Ruth Sawyer, who started the first storytelling program at the New York Public Library, is better known today as the mother-in-law of the beloved children's book author, Robert McCloskey. But during her lifetime her own books attracted many readers, and *Roller Skates* won the Newbery Award in 1937. For this book, she drew heavily on childhood memories. At age ten, she herself had been left for a year in New York City, while her family traveled abroad. In the novel set in the 1890s, Sawyer created the character of ten-year-old Lucinda Wyman, whose mother has to go to Italy for her health. Lucinda's normal regimen now abandoned, she explores the city on roller skates, loving both the freedom and the speed that they provide. Because she pays no attention to social, economic, or class distinctions, she develops friendship with a diverse group of people. Lucinda dines with those who know Andrew Carnegie and with a fruit seller and rag picker.

As readers follow Lucinda during this unusual year—where she teaches English and walks dogs to earn extra money—they grow to love some of these offbeat characters just as much as Lucinda does. Hence the death of one of her young friends, Trinket, seems particularly devastating. Many of Sawyer's views about childhood inform the philosophy of the book; she felt children needed to escape rules and regulations—"a free child is a happy child"—and find a way to belong to themselves, to follow their own path. Journalist Karen MacPherson identified with Lucinda, because she shared the character's love of roller skating.

Karen MacPherson

Live life to the hilt because death can claim us at any moment.

When I was ten, roller skating was my passion. Each day, I would fasten those old-fashioned metal skates onto my shoes, tighten them with a special key that I kept on a string around my neck, and set off in high spirits to explore my world. So it's no wonder that I was thrilled by the story of Lucinda in *Roller Skates*, Ruth Sawyer's Newbery Medal–winning novel. Here was a girl who also understood the joy of seeing the world on wheels, "Clug—clump—chirr—clump!"

But that was just the beginning of my bond with Lucinda. A shy, introspective child, I saw Lucinda (so lively, open-hearted, and self-confident) as the girl I longed to be. I envied her bobbed hairstyle—so much less troublesome than my long, often-tangled curls—as well as the ease with which she cultivated friendships with everyone, from the local policeman to the boy who ran a fruit stand. It was Lucinda who introduced me to *The Peterkin Papers*, Irish fairy tales, and Shakespeare. From her, I learned such useful exclamations as "Jumping Jehoshaphat" and "Glory be to God." But most important, she taught me something so valuable that it has become an integral component of my emotional core: Live life to the hilt because death can claim us at any moment.

Gideon was a boy of seven with brown eyes and curly hair. When he laughed his nose had small wrinkles at the sides, and when he was very pleased—or frightened or ashamed—his cheeks grew red.

From the first moment he came into the nursery he was interested in the doll's house. "Let me play with it," he said, and he bent down and looked into the rooms.

"You can move the furniture about and put out the cups and saucers, as long as you put them all back," said Ellen.

"That's not playing!" said Gideon. "Can't we put the doll's house up a tree?"

"A tree? Why the birds might nest in it!" said Ellen.

"Do you think they would?" asked Gideon, and he laughed with pleasure. "Think of robins and wrens sitting on the tables and chairs!"

Impunity Jane laughed too.

"Let's put it on a raft and float it on the river," said Gideon.

"Don't be silly," said Ellen. "It might be swept away and go right out to sea."

"Then fishes could come into it," said Gideon.

"Fishes!"

Impunity Jane became excited, but Ellen still said, "No."

IMPUNITY JANE by Rumer Godden, illustrated by Adrienne Adams

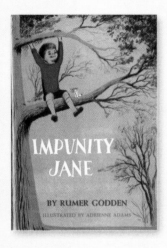

IMPUNITY JANE

by Rumer Godden,
illustrated by Adrienne Adams

Rumer Godden was one of the rare individuals who could write as eloquently for children as she could for adults. Even in her eighties, she retained a remarkably childlike spirit and could relate vivid stories about her early years in India. Godden herself once said, "I rank writing books for children next to poetry in difficulty. In each discipline every word must do its task. . . . When writing books for children you can't bend down to them—you must get down to a child's horizon, become a child." For all her novels, including *Black Narcissus, The River,* and *The Greengage Summer,* Godden was appointed Order of the British Empire in 1993.

In 1947 Godden created her first children's book, *The Dolls' House;* her lifelong fascination with dolls led to other books including *Impunity Jane: The Story of a Pocket Doll,* published in 1954. Impunity Jane, a four-inch-high china doll, was purchased in London and then placed in a dollhouse for more than fifty years. Fortunately a little boy saves her, adopts her as his mascot, and presents her with the kind of adventures she has always desired. Filled with Godden's lyrical and yet simple language, the book speaks to every child who longs to be outside the confines of his or her own home and see the world. As a child, actress Kathy Bates discovered *Impunity Jane* along with many other books.

Kathy Bates

I didn't want to live like a doll in a dollhouse.

Books have been an essential part of my life for as long as I can remember. I loved hearing my mother's voice as she read to me. Her sister, my Aunt Lee, worked for Cokesbury Bookstore in Tennessee and sent us books for birthdays and Christmas. She'd wrap them individually, so there were always lots of presents: *Charlotte's Web, Eloise, Madeline, A Little Princess, Winnie-the-Pooh, The Wind in the Willows, A Child's Garden of Verses, Alice's Adventures in Wonderland,* and *Through the Looking-Glass.* As I got older, there were poetry books and a scarlet leather-bound edition of the complete works of Shakespeare.

In one of my favorite books, Rumer Godden's *Impunity Jane,* a little doll is bought and taken home to sit on a pincushion in a dollhouse. She calls herself Impunity, which means, "escaping without hurt." She sits in the dollhouse for more than fifty years, longing to live in a pocket and see the world. When finally a seven-year-old boy named Gideon reaches into the dollhouse and steals her, she has all kinds of adventures. "I'm Imp-imp-impunity," she cries.

As I was growing up and feminism was spreading throughout America, I often thought of Impunity Jane. Like her, I wanted the whole world to be open to me—I didn't want to live like a doll in a dollhouse.

"What in the world are you going to do now, Jo?" asked Meg, one snowy afternoon as her sister came tramping through the hall, in rubber boots, old sack and hood, with a broom in one hand and a shovel in the other.

"Going out for exercise," answered Jo, with a mischievous twinkle in her eyes.

"I should think two long walks this morning would have been enough! It's cold and dull out; and I advise you to stay warm and dry, by the fire, as I do," said Meg, with a shiver.

"Never take advice! Can't keep still all day, and, not being a pussy-cat, I don't like to doze by the fire. I like adventures, and I'm going to find some."

Meg went back to toast her feet and read *Ivanhoe*; and Jo began to dig paths with great energy. The snow was light, and with her broom she soon swept a path all around the garden, for Beth to walk in when the sun came out; and the invalid dolls needed air. Now the garden separated the Marches' house from that of Mr Laurence. Both stood in a suburb of the city, which was still country-like, with groves and lawns, large gardens, and quiet streets. A low hedge parted the two estates. On one side was an old, brown house, looking rather bare and shabby, robbed of the vines that in summer covered its walls, and the flowers which then surrounded it. On the other side was a stately stone mansion, plainly betokening every sort of comfort and luxury, from the big coach-house and well-kept grounds to the conservatory and the glimpses of lovely things one caught between the rich curtains. Yet it seemed a lonely, lifeless sort of house; for no children frolicked on the lawn, no motherly face ever smiled at the windows, and few people went in and out, except the old gentleman and his grandson.

To Jo's lively fancy, this fine house seemed a kind of enchanted palace, full of splendours and delights, which no one enjoyed. She had long wanted to behold these hidden glories, and to know the "Laurence boy," who looked as if he would like to be known, if he only knew how to begin. Since the party, she had been more eager than ever, and had planned many ways of making friends with him; but he had not been seen lately, and Jo began to think he had gone away, when she one day spied a brown face at an upper window, looking wistfully down into their garden, where Beth and Amy were snowballing one another.

"That boy is suffering for society and fun," she said to herself. "His grandpa does not know what's good for him, and keeps him shut up all alone. He needs a party of jolly boys to play with, or somebody young and lively. I've a great mind to go over and tell the old gentleman so!"

The idea amused Jo, who liked to do daring things, and was always scandalizing Meg by her queer performances. The plan of "going over" was not forgotten; and when the snowy afternoon came, Jo resolved to try what could be done. She saw Mr. Laurence drive off, and then sallied out to dig her way down to the hedge, where she paused and took a survey. All quiet—curtains down at the lower windows; servants out of sight, and nothing human visible but a curly black head leaning on a thin hand at the upper window.

"There he is," thought Jo, "poor boy! All alone and sick this dismal day. It's a shame! I'll toss up a snowball, and make him look out, and then say a kind word to him."

LITTLE WOMEN by Louisa May Alcott

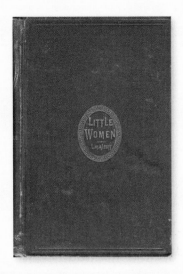

LITTLE WOMEN

by Louisa May Alcott

It seems perfectly appropriate that Louisa May Alcott, a radical abolitionist and suffragette, would continue to inspire other women to think outside the box. For Alcott, writing came as a solution to her family's poverty; at first she penned potboilers that she later regretted. But it was a request from her publisher for a story for girls that sent her on to fame and fortune. She wrote about what she knew, or a much idealized version of what she knew— herself and her sisters. It took Alcott a mere ten weeks to craft *Little Women*, the first true classic for children in the United States. When released in the fall of 1868, right after the Civil War, the book sold 2,000 copies immediately. Alcott's fans clamored for more; they particularly begged her to marry Jo March to the wealthy Laurie, her best friend who obviously loved her. Six months later Part II appeared, this time selling 13,000 copies immediately and around 30,000 in the first fourteen months. By 1880 both volumes were combined together in the book now titled *Little Women*.

The four March girls—determined Jo, beautiful Meg, saintly Beth, and artistic Amy—experience first the problems of the Civil War years and then the period after the war. All struggle with character defects (Meg vanity; Jo temper; Beth shyness; and Amy selfishness); all deal with the problems created by their family's poverty. Without question one of the saddest moments universally acknowledged in children's fiction comes when Beth dies. And that, of course, underscores the great strength of Alcott's work; she brings these characters to life. But Jo carries the story. She refuses

(continued on page 173)

Bobbie Ann Mason
The first writer who became real to me

Louisa May Alcott, author of *Little Women*, was the only female face in the Authors card game. Her countenance is a cameo carved on my brain during childhood. I was a country girl, in Kentucky, attending a rural school, where there was no library. My reading was limited to the popular series books—the Bobbsey Twins, Nancy Drew, Judy Bolton—books my mother bought for me at the wallpaper store, which had a small book nook. I read them over and over, for there was nothing else to read.

In the summer of my tenth year, when my mother was working at a clothing factory, she sent me to the factory library, full of dusty discards from the state library system. On a dark shelf in the shadows I found *Little Women*. I plunged into Alcott's story of the four March sisters. This portrait of family life in New England during the Civil War era was strange and inviting, with quaint words I didn't understand—lots of Latin and Greek mythology—and mysterious home remedies like arnica and blancmange. The characters even play a game of Authors.

Jo carries the book. Jo is a bookworm who uses slang, whistles, and wants to go to war. Jo hides in her garret, eating apples and reading a book, with a pet rat called Scrabble. (I loved the word *garret*.) Jo writes plays: Roderigo in his russet-leather boots and red cloak, strumming a guitar. A hundred and forty years later, young girls are still idolizing guys with guitars. Louisa May Alcott had her finger on the pulse.

Jo was always scribbling. I was determined to be like Jo, who went to New York to seek her fortune as a writer. I began writing Nancy Drew–like stories in blue Double Q notebooks. Then I transferred my admiration from Jo to Louisa May Alcott herself, for she was the writer who had imagined Jo. And she was Jo, I felt sure. She was the first writer who became real to me—a woman famous enough to get into the Authors card game!

I answered an ad in the back of a magazine. The Famous Writers School sent me its aptitude test, then a barrage of offers for writing lessons, costing giant sums of money. I had to tell them that I didn't have money for lessons—I was only eleven years old. But after college I went to New York to be a writer, just as Jo March had, and as Louisa May Alcott once had.

Judy Woodruff

Anything could be possible in my life.

When I was nine or ten years old, I fell in love with *Little Women*. Jo March jumped off the pages as an outspoken and funny tomboy who chafed under the expectations of young women during Civil War–era America. She was one of the reasons I dreamed anything could be possible in my life.

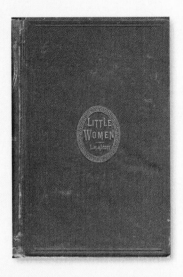

to accept what society tells her to be. She is generous and loving, cutting off her own hair to provide money for the family, but she is never a victim. She finds her own path and becomes what she wants to be, a writer. Jo may have inspired more women over the years—including Hilary Clinton and philosopher Simone de Beauvoir—than any other figure in children's literature. In three separate essays writer Bobbie Ann Mason, actress Julianne Moore, and television journalist Judy Woodruff all talk about the lasting effect that Jo March had on their lives.

Julianne Moore
A woman could choose.

The one thing I know about myself is that I am a reader. I remember the first sentence that I ever read from a book on science, "'Mother, mother,' said Bob, 'I see a robin.'" I loved to read; reading shaped me and led me to acting.

But the most important books of my childhood were Louisa May Alcott's *Little Women* and Laura Ingalls Wilder's Little House series. I read everything that either one of these authors ever wrote, including Wilder's diary, *On the Way Home*. These books were childhood narratives, little girl narratives, about childhood experience. They explored being in new places, struggling with really big feelings, finding a way in the family, finding your way in the world, and determining who you wanted to be. I never liked *Treasure Island* or any boy adventure stories. I liked emotional female narratives in which characters struggled with how they felt and how they were going to behave, as children and as emerging adults.

All of these books deal with choice and personal responsibility. The Alcott books are quite emotional; I cried and cried when I read about Beth dying. Alcott's novels are not condescending or sentimental and explore moral issues and the conflicts that arise when Jo tries to be a good person. When Jo writes pulp fiction, she is ashamed, and she has to learn how to write something meaningful. From Jo I learned that a woman could choose—Jo realizes that she can turn away from pulp fiction, that she has a choice about her career as a writer.

With the Wilder books you are following one character, Laura, who grew up and became a schoolteacher and then married. She was enormously self-directed. In *The First Four Years*, you read about Wilder's incredible struggle just to get started. Then she matured and wrote this series of books.

Both these authors were reflecting in their books on who they were and what they were able to accomplish. I understood the relationship between the author and the books that they had chosen to write when I was a ten-, eleven-, and twelve-year-old girl.

Then when I was in junior high, I tried out for a couple of plays. I realized that reading scenes was just like reading aloud, the exact same thing. I could always hear a story and hear a voice. Acting became an extension of reading the books and the authors that I loved.

Storytelling

One winter morning Peter woke up and looked out the window. Snow had fallen during the night. It covered everything as far as he could see.

After breakfast he put on his snowsuit and ran outside. The snow was piled up very high along the street to make a path for walking.

Crunch, crunch, crunch, his feet sank into the snow.

THE SNOWY DAY by Ezra Jack Keats

THE SNOWY DAY

by Ezra Jack Keats

Ezra Jack Keats had spent many years illustrating the children's books of other writers, an uninspired career devoid of passion. But then he realized that the children in his Brooklyn neighborhood were not featured in books for children. For in "the all white world of children's books" those from other ethnic backgrounds received scant notice. Consequently, in the first book that he both wrote and illustrated, Keats chose to show the children he saw daily, playing in their urban landscape.

In *The Snowy Day,* published in 1962, Peter dons a red snow suit and discovers the joy of playing in the snow. Illustrated with bold collages in bright colors, the universal story speaks to all children who delight in a wintry world. After the book won the Caldecott Medal, it was for a period of time in the 1960s the only book on the shelves of school and public libraries to feature a black protagonist. Keats went on to craft other titles with a multiethnic cast of characters, and he inspired black authors and illustrators in the 1960s to create their own children's books. In *The Snowy Day* National Book Award winner Sherman Alexie was able to see himself for the first time in a book.

Sherman Alexie
People might want to listen to me, too.

When I was growing up—a registered member of the Spokane and Coeur d'Alene tribes—*The Snowy Day* by Ezra Jack Keats was pretty much the only children's book that featured a protagonist with dark skin. I vividly remember the first day I pulled that book off the shelf. It was the first time I looked at a book and saw a brown, black, beige character—a character who resembled me physically and spiritually, in all his gorgeous loneliness and splendid isolation. I was somewhat of a hermit, even at a very young age.

The Snowy Day transformed me from someone who read regularly into a true book hound. I really think the age at which you find the book with which you truly identify determines the rest of your reading life. The younger you are when you do that, the more likely you're going to be a serious reader. Reading centers on finding yourself in a book.

Later I was handed a collection of Native American poetry by a writing teacher. Until then I had never read any works by other Native Americans. I was struck by a line from Paiute poet Adrian Lewis: "Oh, Uncle Adrian, I'm in the reservation of my mind." I knew right then that I wanted to be a writer. It has been a gorgeous, lonely, magical, and terrifying journey.

Ezra Jack Keats and Adrian Lewis wrote stories and poems that made me realize that people might want to listen to me, too.

This is a fierce bad Rabbit; look at his savage whiskers, and his claws and his turned-up tail.

This is a nice gentle Rabbit. His mother has given him a carrot.

The bad Rabbit would like some carrot.

He doesn't say "Please." He takes it!

And he scratches the good Rabbit very badly.

The good Rabbit creeps away, and hides in a hole. It feels sad.

This is a man with a gun.

He sees something sitting on a bench. He thinks it is a very funny bird!

He comes creeping up behind the trees.

And then he shoots—Bang!

This is what happens—

But this is all he finds on the bench, when he rushes up with his gun.

The good Rabbit peeps out of its hole,

And it sees the bad Rabbit tearing past—without any tail or whiskers!

THE STORY OF A FIERCE BAD RABBIT by Beatrix Potter

For the poor old tailor was very ill with a fever, tossing and turning in his four-post bed; and still in his dreams he mumbled—"No more twist! no more twist!"

All that day he was ill, and the next day, and the next, and what should become of the cherry-coloured coat? In the tailor's shop in Westgate Street the embroidered silk and satin lay cut out upon the table—one-and-twenty button-holes—and who should come to sew them, when the window was barred, and the door was fast locked?

But that does not hinder the little brown mice; they run in and out without keys through all the old houses in Gloucester!

THE TAILOR OF GLOUCESTER by Beatrix Potter

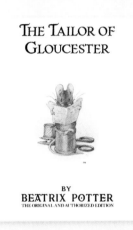

THE TALES OF BEATRIX POTTER

When a young English artist and storyteller, Beatrix Potter, presented a rabbit story to several British publishers, they resolutely turned her work down. So in December of 1901, she printed and privately published 250 copies of *The Tale of Peter Rabbit*, a book that she had initially created as a letter to a sick child. Its popularity caused one of the publishers who had formerly rejected her book to reconsider. Although they asked her to make a major change—all the art had to be executed in full color—Frederick Warne issued the same story in the fall of 1902.

The success of this small book, today the best-selling children's picture book in the world, led Potter to a series of small books with fabulous stories—and sometimes very big words. The vocabulary of Potter's titles often amazes modern readers; Peter found the lettuce "soporific." Potter was a brilliant naturalist and crafted intricate watercolors true in their scientific details. She took great delight in all of the aspects of book making,

(continued on page 181)

Ken Follett
How to write

The Story of a Fierce Bad Rabbit by Beatrix Potter is the shortest thriller ever written. In just 141 words it presents suspense, crime, gunplay, and retributive justice. I read it to my children when they were small, and now I read it to my grandchildren. It still teaches me how to write.

Beverly Cleary
To write the stories I wanted to read

As a child, I owned only two books: *The Story of the Three Bears* and the *Volland Mother Goose*. But because of my mother's efforts to organize a local library above a bank, crates of books began to arrive from the Oregon State Library for the children of Yamhill. What good books they were! Those crates included fairy tales by Joseph Jacobs and lots of small picture storybooks by Beatrix Potter.

My favorite was *The Tailor of Gloucester*. Not only did I love the story, but I was entranced by the picture of the waistcoat so beautifully embroidered by mice. I studied that picture and knew that someday I, too, wanted to sew beautifully.

For many years, I have patterned stories instead. My first ideas grew out of my own work with children as a librarian. The books that I write are the stories I wanted to read as a child. Decades have passed since I first encountered books, but even as a child I recognized that reading gave people power.

One autumn when the nuts were ripe, and the leaves on the hazel bushes were golden and green—Nutkin and Twinkleberry and all the other little squirrels came out of the wood, and down to the edge of the lake.

They made little rafts out of twigs, and they paddled away over the water to Owl Island to gather nuts.

Each squirrel had a little sack and a large oar, and spread out his tail for a sail.

They also took with them an offering of three fat mice as a present for Old Brown, and put them down upon his doorstep.

Then Twinkleberry and the other little squirrels each made a low bow, and said politely—

"Old Mr. Brown, will you favour us with permission to gather nuts upon your island?"

THE TALE OF SQUIRREL NUTKIN by Beatrix Potter

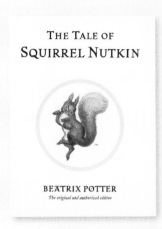

THE TALE OF
SQUIRREL NUTKIN

BEATRIX POTTER
The original and authorized edition

using the text, art, and paper to make the book pleasing to both parents and children.

Potter created more than twenty small books for children, each with its own unique stories. In *The Tailor of Gloucester*—in a time "when gentlemen wore ruffles, and gold-laced waistcoats of paduasoy and taffeta"— an impoverished tailor works on fine clothes for others. But when he becomes ill, the mice of his home sew together an important piece of clothing. In an extremely short text, *The Story of a Fierce Bad Rabbit*, a bad rabbit that steals and scratches other bunnies gets his comeuppance. In *The Tale of Squirrel Nutkin* an impudent squirrel loses part of his tail to an old wise owl.

Potter's many adult fans are legion, and a whole book could be filled with tributes to her. Internationally renowned author Ken Follett discovered ideas about writing in *The Story of a Fierce Bad Rabbit*. Beloved children's author Beverly Cleary wanted to master sewing after picking up *The Tailor of Gloucester*. I myself gained more of an understanding about squirrel behavior from *The Tale of Squirrel Nutkin* than I did from any science book.

Anita Silvey

Books provide lessons so subtle and varied that it may take years before we use everything we absorb.

One summer weekend while staying in a Vermont cottage, I walked toward the front porch and stopped abruptly. A group of squirrels, one adult and six babies, had commandeered this space for their classroom. The mother ran across the porch, holding her tail at a particular angle; the little squirrels followed, mimicking every step she took, their tails curved exactly like hers. Then she leapt to a nearby tree; one after another they took the same jump. Heading down the tree, she ran around the porch, came up the other side, and pranced across it again to execute another perfect tree leap. The entire exercise resembled a small ballet—with squirrel tails perfectly curled at each step.

I stood mesmerized as I gained an appreciation into squirrel behavior, training, and schooling. Then I laughed—because I had seen it all before. I knew about squirrels from Beatrix Potter's *The Tale of Squirrel Nutkin*. One of the greatest naturalists ever to craft books for children, Potter lived with a squirrel and studied it. One of her drawings shows these creatures using their tails as sails, gliding across a lake, as if they were performing a ballet. Before I had even had the words to describe squirrel school, I had been given a perfect image of it.

As children, in our own school of life, we soak up clues about our world just as eagerly as small squirrels. Exposure to children's books provides verbal and visual material to help us along the way. So subtle and varied can the lessons be that it may take years before we use everything we absorbed. So forty years after I first read *The Tale of Squirrel Nutkin*, I finally understood one small detail that the author had shown me as a child.

Wilbur's new home was in the lower part of the barn, directly underneath the cows. Mr. Zuckerman knew that a manure pile is a good place to keep a young pig. Pigs need warmth, and it was warm and comfortable down there in the barn cellar on the south side.

Fern came almost every day to visit him. She found an old milking stool that had been discarded, and she placed the stool in the sheepfold next to Wilbur's pen. Here she sat quietly during the long afternoons, thinking and listening and watching Wilbur. The sheep soon got to know her and trust her. So did the geese, who lived with the sheep. All the animals trusted her, she was so quiet and friendly. Mr. Zuckerman did not allow her to take Wilbur out, and he did not allow her to get into the pigpen. But he told Fern that she could sit on the stool and watch Wilbur as long as she wanted to. It made her happy just to be near the pig, and it made Wilbur happy to know that she was sitting there, right outside his pen. But he never had any fun—no walks, no rides, no swims.

One afternoon in June, when Wilbur was almost two months old, he wandered out into his small yard outside the barn. Fern had not arrived for her usual visit. Wilbur stood in the sun feeling lonely and bored.

"There's never anything to do around here," he thought. He walked slowly to his food trough and sniffed to see if anything had been overlooked at lunch. He found a small strip of potato skin and ate it. His back itched, so he leaned against the fence and rubbed against the boards. When he tired of this, he walked indoors, climbed to the top of the manure pile, and sat down. He didn't feel like going to sleep, he didn't feel like digging, he was tired of standing still, tired of lying down. "I'm less than two months old and I'm tired of living," he said. He walked out to the yard again.

"When I'm out here," he said, "there's no place to go but in. When I'm indoors, there's no place to go but out in the yard."

"That's where you're wrong, my friend, my friend," said a voice.

Wilbur looked through the fence and saw the goose standing there.

"You don't have to stay in that dirty-little dirty-little dirty-little yard," said the goose, who talked rather fast. "One of the boards is loose. Push on it, push-push-push on it, and come on out!"

CHARLOTTE'S WEB by E. B. White, illustrated by Garth Williams

CHARLOTTE'S WEB

by E. B. White,
illustrated by Garth Williams

New Yorker writer E. B. White produced hundreds of essays for adults, but only three children's books, each of them gems. Considered the greatest American children's novel of the twentieth century, *Charlotte's Web* grew out of one of White's adult essays. He had written about the death of a pig and was musing about how he might keep such a pig alive in a book for children. As he walked down to his barn, carrying some slops for his pig, he saw a spider spinning a web.

In *Charlotte's Web*, Charlotte, a spider, serves as the main protagonist; Fern, a young girl, plays a supporting role. Both females work to save the life of Wilbur, the runt pig of the litter. In fact, the reader learns to appreciate an entire group of talking animals and watch their interactions in the barn. Then at the state fair, Charlotte asserts the power of the pen—in this case the words she weaves in her web. With just seven words, she convinces everyone that Wilbur, "some pig," is truly something special and must be kept alive.

A consummate craftsman, White brings precision and genius to each part of the story. He opens the book with an immediately compelling sentence, "Where's Pa going with that ax?" He excels in character descriptions, "Charlotte is fierce, brutal, scheming, bloodthirsty—everything I don't like," Wilbur declares. And the lyrical language of the descriptive passages takes your breath away: "The barn was very large. It was very old. It smelled of hay and it smelled of manure." Because of the writing and storytelling, *Charlotte's Web* has remained a staple of classrooms across the country, a teacher's favorite to read aloud.

Like most American children, Newbery Award winner Louis Sachar was introduced to the book by a teacher. Caldecott Award winner Eric Rohmann, in his third-grade class, found himself swept up for the first time by the words and pictures in a book.

Louis Sachar

If you see something in writing, then it must be true, even if it is written by a spider on a web.

My fourth-grade teacher read a chapter of *Charlotte's Web* every day after lunch; her reading out loud surprised me because a teacher hadn't done this since we were in kindergarten or maybe first grade. I remember very little about fourth grade except the teacher reading us that book. I liked the way E. B. White wrote. I thought the book was funny, tender, full of charm, and drew readers in. You really care about Wilbur. White never condescends to his readers; he also includes satirical comments on society. If you see something in writing, then it must be true, even if it is written by a spider on a web.

The impact of this book on me shows the importance of reading aloud to students. The memory of my teacher and that book has stuck with me for more than forty years.

After all, Wilbur was a very young pig—
not much more than a baby, really. He wished
Fern were there to take him in her arms and
comfort him. When he looked up and saw Mr.
Zuckerman standing quite close to him, holding
a pail of warm slops, he felt relieved. He lifted
his nose and sniffed. The smell was delicious—
warm milk, potato skins, wheat middlings,
Kellogg's Corn Flakes, and a popover left from
the Zuckerman's breakfast.

"Come, pig!" said Mr. Zuckerman, tapping
the pail. "Come, pig!"

Wilbur took a step forward toward the pail.

"No-no-no!" said the goose. "It's the old pail
trick, Wilbur. Don't fall for it, don't fall for it!
He's trying to lure you back into captivity-ivity.
He's appealing to your stomach."

Wilbur didn't care. The food smelled
appetizing. He took another step toward the
pail.

"Pig, pig!" said Mr. Zuckerman in a kind
voice, and began walking slowly toward the
barnyard, looking all about him innocently, as
if he didn't know that a little white pig was
following along behind him.

"You'll be sorry-sorry-sorry," called the
goose.

Wilbur didn't care. He kept walking toward
the pail of slops.

"You'll miss your freedom," honked the
goose. "An hour of freedom is worth a barrel of
slops."

Wilbur didn't care.

When Mr. Zuckerman reached the pigpen,
he climbed over the fence and poured the slops
into the trough. Then he pulled the loose board
away from the fence, so that there was a wide
hole for Wilbur to walk through.

"Reconsider, reconsider!" cried the goose.

Wilbur paid no attention. He stepped
through the fence into his yard. He walked
to the trough and took a long drink of slops,
sucking in the milk hungrily and chewing the
popover. It was good to be home again.

While Wilbur ate, Lurvy fetched a hammer
and some 8-penny nails and nailed the board
in place. Then he and Mr. Zuckerman leaned
lazily on the fence and Mr. Zuckerman scratched
Wilbur's back with a stick.

"He's quite a pig," said Lurvy.

"Yes, he'll make a good pig," said Mr.
Zuckerman.

Wilbur heard the words of praise. He felt
the warm milk inside his stomach. He felt the
pleasant rubbing of the stick along his itchy
back. he felt peaceful and happy and sleepy.
This had been a tiring afternoon. It was still only
about four o'clock but Wilbur was ready for bed.

"I'm really too young to go out into the
world alone," he thought as he lay down.

CHARLOTTE'S WEB by E. B. White, illustrated by Garth Williams

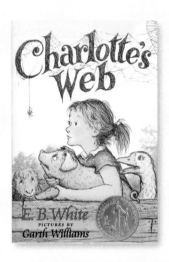

Eric Rohmann

Reading is magnanimous; a book becomes the person who is reading it.

Growing up I was not much of a reader, but eventually reading found its way. I began with DC Comic books—Superman and Batman—a few picture books, and the occasional true-nature tale. And then there was my third-grade teacher, Ms. Cerny, who at the end of each week brought us stories.

On Friday afternoon she would take the last hour of class to read to us. I can still close my eyes and remember the details: the pale yellow classroom, her precise pronunciation, the sunlight drifting in, the row of primers on the counter along the windows. And on that very first Friday, the book in her hands was *Charlotte's Web*. The experience of being in that classroom, listening along with my friends who were also caught up in the story, was the first time I'd ever really fallen into a book, moved by the emotion of the reading of a story. When early in the book an apprehensive Wilbur says, "I'm really too young to go out into the world alone," I was suddenly within the story. Wilbur was talking to me.

Now, reading the book as an adult, I'm not surprised this story captured me. There's simplicity and clarity to E. B. White's writing. His simple sentences, lucid and direct, add up to whole worlds when strung together. E. B. White's writing is visual. I could imagine—make a visual image in my mind—what he was saying. Because he used a spider and a pig as protagonists, creatures familiar to me, I could envision Charlotte and Wilbur. The book is made even richer by Garth Williams' spare and exuberant illustrations. They expand the story—the words and art giving to one another to create a unique whole.

But on its deepest level *Charlotte's Web* demonstrates how words, with their power, create reality. Of course, everyone sees Charlotte's words—they are displayed in her spider webs. Wilbur's life is saved by what he and everyone else sees. It was the same with me. In that classroom I learned that a book isn't just words and pictures. I learned that reading is magnanimous; that a book becomes the person who is reading it. *Charlotte's Web*, for me, has Ms. Cerny's face on it.

Today when I read *Charlotte's Web* I am a boy again—a boy who is delighted and surprised to discover the way in which a story, honestly told, can soak in, find its way deep inside. Reading the book, I'm transported to that classroom, the richness of it all. Now, when I work on each of my books, I do my best to give some of that same feeling to my own readers.

THE STORY OF MANKIND by Hendrik Willem Van Loon

THE STORY OF MANKIND

by Hendrik Willem Van Loon

In 1922 the first Newbery Medal was awarded to a sprawling (over 600 pages) work of information designated as the "most distinguished contribution" to books for children. The scope of Hendrik Willem Van Loon's *The Story of Mankind* is daunting; he tackles the entire history of life on Earth—from the biological beginning of man to the Sumerian, Phoenician, Indo-European, Greek, Roman, English, French, and American civilizations. Moses, Jesus, Mohammed, Buddha, and Confucius all receive chapters as well.

Obviously, this approach to history meant that only scant attention could be paid to any period of time. Early response to the book, in articles in the *Horn Book* magazine, suggested that "most readers will want to follow up the reading of that book with more profound treatment of world history . . . But *The Story of Mankind* affords the kind of first sight that we get when we reach the top of high mountains." Of course, all such encyclopedic approaches to history naturally reflect the biases of the author and time.

For something so ambitious in its undertaking, the text remains light and breezy: "Constantine, sometimes (Heaven knows why) called Constantine the Great, was emperor. He was a terrible ruffian." Throughout the book Van Loon treated historical figures as flesh-and-blood human beings. That storytelling quality attracted Newbery Award–winning author Russell Freedman.

Russell Freedman
The dramatic storytelling possibilities of history

When I was growing up in San Francisco, my father was the manager of Macmillan's West Coast office. He often invited authors home for dinner. John Steinbeck, Margaret Mitchell, William Saroyan, and John Masefield, England's poet laureate, all came to dinner at our house when I was a boy. Their books didn't mean much to me at the time, so I wasn't impressed. My literary hero was Howard Pease, who wrote exciting stories about boys who ran away from home and sailed all over the world in the merchant marine. Sure, some famous men and women sat at my family's dinner table, but Howard Pease—he was a real *writer*! I wanted my father to invite him to dinner, but no luck. I guess he wasn't a Macmillan author.

Another "real writer" in my estimation was the author of a book my father gave me when I was in the fifth grade. It immediately became one of my favorites, and I have kept my copy to this day. It was a book packed with exciting stories—with incredible tales of great men and women, battles fought, daring adventures, and heroic deeds. But the best thing about it, the very best thing, was that every story in the book was true.

The Story of Mankind by Hendrik Willem Van Loon was a history book, a book of nonfiction. Yet I read it as a boy not to fulfill a school assignment, not to write a report, but because I was swept along by the stories it told. I read it for pleasure, for the thrill of discovery. History, according to Hendrik Van Loon, wasn't just a bunch of dry facts and dates; it was the stirring stories of real people leading meaningful lives.

After I won the Newbery Medal for my biography of Lincoln in 1988, I took my boyhood copy of *The Story of Mankind* down from the shelf and discovered that it was the first book to win the Newbery when the award was introduced in 1922 (before I was born). As I thumbed through the pages, I remembered my excitement while reading it so many years ago.

As an adult, I've found that if you know little about a subject, and are curious, the best way to introduce yourself to that subject is to pick up a good children's book. Often the author didn't know much about the subject either and had to go through a patient learning process in order to write with integrity—with clarity and understanding. Thanks to that learning process, the author will have insights that a specialist in the field might not have. The skill of a children's nonfiction writer resides not in being an expert in the subject but in being able to convey the essence of that subject in an accessible and compelling way.

The Story of Mankind opened my eyes to the dramatic storytelling possibilities of history. That was one of my first lessons as a writer.

At that moment something hit the saucepan with a loud ping, and ashes flew up out of the fire. A long arrow with a green feather stuck, quivering, among the embers.

The four explorers started to their feet.

"It's begun," said Titty.

Roger grabbed at the arrow and pulled it out of the fire.

Titty took it from him at once. "It may be poisoned," she said. "Don't touch the point of it."

"Listen," said Captain John.

They listened. There was not a sound to be heard but the quiet lapping of the water against the western shore of the island.

"It's him," said Titty. "He's winged his arrow with a feather from his green parrot."

"Listen," said Captain John again.

"Shut up, just for a minute," said Mate Susan.

There was the sharp crack of a dead stick breaking somewhere in the middle of the island.

"We must scout," said Captain John. "I'll take one end of the line, the mate the other. Titty and Roger go in the middle. Spread out. As soon as one of us sees him, the others close in to help."

They spread out across the island, and began to move forward. But they had not gone ten yards when John gave a shout.

"Swallow has gone," he shouted. He was on the left of the line, and as soon as he came out of the camping ground he saw the landing-place where he had left Swallow when he came

back with the milk. No Swallow was there. The others ran together to the landing-place. There was not a sign of Swallow. She had simply disappeared.

"Spread out again. Spread out again," said John. "We'll comb the whole island. Keep a look-out, Mister Mate, from your shore. She can't have drifted away. He's taken her, but he's still on the island. We heard him."

"Roger and I pulled her right up," said Titty. "She couldn't have drifted off."

"Spread out again," said Captain John. "Then listen. Advance as soon as the mate blows her whistle. A hoot like an owl means all right. Three hoots means something's up. Blow as soon as you're ready, Mister Mate."

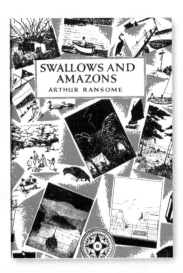

SWALLOWS AND AMAZONS

by Arthur Ransome

If any series of books conjures up endless summer vacation, it would be Arthur Ransome's Swallows and Amazons. Set in the English Lake District, the first title, *Swallows and Amazons*, published in 1930, follows the Walker children—Ship's Master John, First Mate Susan, Able Seaman Titty, and Ship's Boy Roger—as they sail their boat *Swallow* to a small lake island and camp on it. Although their mother makes arrangements for them to pick up milk every day and encourages them to eat green vegetables to avoid scurvy, she allows them the luxury of being on their own, away from adult supervision. In a book filled with nautical terminology and details about sailing, the Walkers immediately encounter two girls and their dinghy *Amazon*, which flies a pirate flag. They all have a great deal of fun sailing, camping, fishing, seeking treasure, and solving small mysteries. Not only do the children frequently engage in fantasy play in the book, they enjoy freedom from the restrictions of the adult world, in itself a childhood fantasy.

Arthur Ransome drew on his own childhood memories of summer vacations in the Lake District for his series of twelve books. Although as a journalist Ransome would travel to Revolutionary Russia and marry Trotsky's secretary, he eventually settled in the Lake District. Extremely successful during Ransome's lifetime, the books went out of print for a period of time in the United States, but they have been reissued with Ransome's own illustrations by David R. Godine. These books, exotic in their setting and nautical terminology, kept Pulitzer Prize winner Anthony Lewis enthralled.

Anthony Lewis
To tell stories in my own writing

How I got into Arthur Ransome's Swallows and Amazons books I cannot imagine. I knew nothing about sailing and could not understand some of the references. Moreover, the books were set in England, and I was ignorant of the places and some of the language. I even remember feeling at sea as I read— pun intended. But the books had a charm and fascination that captured me despite my lack of acquaintance with many of the subjects.

I have spent my life as a journalist and writer; the books I read as a child moved me in that direction. But there was something more. I loved stories, and the stories in those books led me to tell stories in my writing, even about the law.

Once upon a time in Paris there lived a little boy whose name was Pascal. He had no brothers or sisters, and he was very sad and lonely at home.

Once he brought home a lost cat, and some time later a stray puppy. But his mother said animals brought dirt into the house, and so Pascal was soon alone again in his mother's clean well-kept rooms.

Then one day, on his way to school, he caught sight of a fine red balloon, tied to a street lamp. Pascal laid his school bag on the ground. He climbed up the lamppost, untied the balloon, and ran off with it to the bus stop.

THE RED BALLOON by Albert Lamorisse

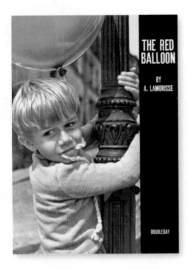

THE RED BALLOON

by Albert Lamorisse

Usually books derived from movies tend to have the shelf life of fresh produce; serving only as a memento of the film, they fade and vanish in a few weeks and are quickly remaindered and forgotten. However, Albert Lamorisse's *The Red Balloon*—created from photographs taken during the filming of the Oscar-winning movie—remains a classic more than fifty years after its 1956 release. One of the rare photographic books of the 1950s still in print, *The Red Balloon* features Pascal, a sad and lonely boy portrayed by the filmmaker's son, who finds a red balloon one morning on his way to school. Taking it throughout the Ménilmontant section of Paris, Pascal soon discovers that the balloon can respond to commands, and it begins to follow him around like a playful pet. Illustrated with both black-and-white and color photographs, the story, which takes place over three days, ends with a magical scene: The balloons of Paris arrive to attach themselves to Pascal— "that was how Pascal took a wonderful trip all around the world."

Although the film is basically wordless, the book contains a lengthy text. The pictures seem familiar but show the same scenes from slightly different angles. Mysterious and powerful, as either metaphor or story, *The Red Balloon* remains one of those cultural artifacts remembered for years by those who encounter it—either as a book or as a movie. In the case of bookseller Mitchell Kaplan, this story became one of the cornerstones of his literary foundation.

Mitchell Kaplan
Through books, I could experience other worlds.

The Red Balloon simply came alive for me. Everything in the story seemed animated. I learned later that the book had been adapted from a film; but I never saw it as a child. *The Red Balloon* was the first book that I remember illustrated with photographs. I believed that everything in the book was a character, including the balloon; there was nothing metaphoric about the story for me. During that time I was able to encounter books without any kind of critical overlay or adult cynicism.

Looking back now, I can understand a bit about why that book was so vivid to me. I knew the world of Miami Beach, but it was so different from the streets of Paris. Paris seemed so exotic—the cobblestoned streets, narrow alleyways. The book totally transported me into another world. It taught me that through books I could experience other worlds and feel a strong sense of empathy; these two lessons have informed my reading even until today.

In the rest of my life I have built on the legacy of those early books. Today I organize my day around reading. On our bookmark for the store, we feature a quote that I love from Jorge Luis Borges, "I cannot sleep unless I'm surrounded by books." I may never have gone to sleep without being read to or reading myself. And when I had my own children, I read them children's books at night, including one that they also loved, *The Red Balloon*.

Unhappy Birthday Party

I've sent out invitations,
To each and every friend.
I've even asked relations,
But no one can attend.

The badger's very busy,
It seems his mother's ill.
The goat is feeling dizzy,
The bush pig has a chill.

The antelope has been mislaid,
The mouse is visiting a rat.
It couldn't be that they're afraid
Of one poor tiger cat!

THE ANIMAL BOOK by Alice and Martin Provensen

THE ANIMAL BOOK

by Alice and Martin Provensen

Golden Books, a bold new publishing experiment, began in 1942 as a partnership between Simon & Schuster and Western Printing and Lithograph Company, whose giant presses needed to be kept running during World War II. They set out to make high-quality children's books affordable to the average American family. In 1942 a typical picture book cost $1.75, with 5,000 to 10,000 copies printed. Golden Books published editions of 50,000 copies, with the low price of 25 cents. Sold in supermarkets, these pleasing volumes found their way into homes in record numbers. Over time, during the baby boom years of the 1950s, entire home libraries often consisted only of Golden Books.

The key to the success of this series came not only from its affordable price but from the very talented writers and artists who contributed stories and illustrations: Margaret Wise Brown, Edith Thacher Hurd, Ruth Krauss, Garth Williams, Feodor Rojankovsky, Alice and Martin Provensen, and Richard Scarry, among others. Some of the most popular children's books of the era appeared first as Golden Books: *The Poky Little Puppy*, one of the best-selling picture books of all time; Margaret Wise Brown's *Sailor Dog*, illustrated by Garth Williams; and *The Color Kittens*, illustrated by Alice and Martin Provensen. Three-time Caldecott Medal winner David Wiesner still owns another Provensen title, *The Animal Book*, which first appeared in 1952.

David Wiesner

The emotional power that can be created by a combination of stories and pictures

As a kid, I didn't have a lot of picture books. But one was always in the house, *The Animal Book* by Alice and Martin Provensen. It contains short stories, single-page poems, music, and animal stories—some serious, some funny. Both the stories and the pictures lingered in my memory for years. When I saw some of the Provensens' artwork as an adult, I remembered this book and discovered that my sister had kept our copy. She then gave it to me.

The book includes a poem about a birthday party for a tiger, "Unhappy Birthday Party." The tiger has sent out all these invitations for his party, but everyone is too busy to come. Of course, no one wants to attend the event because he is a tiger. As a child, I found this poem and the picture of the tiger heartbreaking; it was crushing. In this poem I encountered the emotional power that can be created by a combination of stories and pictures. I realized what words and pictures could do—and how much feeling they could engender.

I may have used some of the Provensens' color palette in my early picture books. Later when I saw their artwork in a gallery in New York, I got to meet Alice Provensen and asked her to sign my book. It is one of the few signed books that I own, but I treasure it.

If I've told you these details about Asteroid B-612 and if I've given you its number, it is on account of the grown-ups. Grown-ups like numbers. When you tell them about a new friend, they never ask questions about what really matters. They never ask: "What does his voice sound like?" "What games does he like best?" "Does he collect butterflies?" They ask: "How old is he?" "How many brothers does he have?" "How much does he weigh?" "How much money does his father make?" Only then do they think they know him. If you tell grown-ups, "I saw a beautiful red brick house, with geraniums at the windows and doves on the roof . . . ," they won't be able to imagine such a house. You have to tell them, "I saw a house worth a hundred thousand francs." Then they exclaim, "What a pretty house!"

So if you tell them: "The proof of the little prince's existence is that he was delightful, that he laughed, and that he wanted a sheep. When someone wants a sheep, that proves he exists," they shrug their shoulders and treat you like a child! But if you tell them, "The planet he came from is Asteroid B-612," then they'll be convinced, and they won't bother you with their questions. That's the way they are. You must not hold it against them. Children should be very understanding of grown-ups.

THE LITTLE PRINCE by Antoine de Saint-Exupéry

THE LITTLE PRINCE

by Antoine de Saint-Exupéry

One of the most eccentric and memorable characters to invade a children's book, The Little Prince from planet B-612 encounters a stranded aviator in the Sahara Desert. While the pilot works to repair his engine, for he has a supply of water that will last him only eight days, the Prince shares his vision of Earth, the universe, relationships, and life. Part story, part philosophy, the book, which works equally well with children and college students, ends with the space traveler returning to his planet and the rose he left there.

The quirky, autobiographical tale, written while the French aviator Antoine de Saint-Exupéry lived on Long Island, appeared in 1943 only a year before his death flying a mission in World War II. Drawing on his own experience in 1935 when his plane crash-landed in the Libyan desert, and his tumultuous relationship with his wife Consuelo (the inspiration for the rose on the Little Prince's planet), he transformed personal experience into the universal search for life's meaning. Richard Howard's superb translation from the French, published in 2000, corrects some of the errors of the first American version and provides a fresh interpretation of the classic.

Having sold more than 50 million copies worldwide, and having been translated into 160 languages, The Little Prince has achieved the status of one of the fifty best-selling books of all times.

Television's beloved Fred Rogers kept its most famous quote on the wall of his office, "L'essential est invisible pour les yeux." ("What is essential is invisible to the eye.") It helped remind him on a daily basis how much there was to appreciate in each person, beyond what meets the eye. MacArthur Fellow Peter Sís, growing up in Czechoslovakia during the Communist regime, discovered the book in time to inspire his own career as a filmmaker and artist.

Peter Sís

Individual and personal feelings could be communicated in a story.

The book that most influenced my life—perhaps even my entire career—is *The Little Prince* by Antoine de Saint-Exupéry, which I discovered sometime between the ages of twelve and fourteen. My father had told me about it, and I was afraid I might not be up to understanding it. Since my father had a very vivid imagination, it was sometimes difficult for me to live up to his expectations. But *The Little Prince* turned out to be just perfect for my age and my state of mind. It was completely different from anything I had known up to this point in my life.

I believe that I cried when I read the book. *The Little Prince* showed me that very individual and personal feelings could be communicated in a story. But it also showed me that an artist could incorporate these feelings and emotions in the drawings. It alerted me to the potential of art and guided me to a career as an illustrator.

He skirted the carcass and parted the grass at the place where he had seen the fawn. It did not seem possible that it was only yesterday. The fawn was not there. He circled the clearing. There was no sound, no sign. The buzzards clacked their wings, impatient to return to their business. He returned to the spot where the fawn had emerged and dropped to all fours, studying the sand for the small hoof-prints. The night's rain had washed away all tracks except those of cat and buzzards. But the cat-sign had not been made in this direction. Under a scrub palmetto he was able to make out a track, pointed and dainty as the mark of a ground-dove. He crawled past the palmetto.

Movement directly in front of him startled him so that he tumbled backward. The fawn lifted its face to his. It turned its head with a wide, wondering motion and shook him through with the stare of its liquid eyes. It was quivering. It made no effort to rise or run. Jody could not trust himself to move.

He whispered, "It's me."

THE YEARLING by Marjorie Kinnan Rawlings, illustrated by N. C. Wyeth

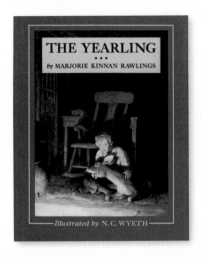

THE YEARLING

by Marjorie Kinnan Rawlings

In *The Yearling* by Marjorie Kinnan Rawlings, the Baxter family struggles to survive in the scrub country of Florida, often with barely enough to eat. All of their children have died, except Jody, who hunts, fishes, and rambles through the natural world under the watchful eye of his father. Jody finds an orphaned fawn, Flag, and manages to convince his parents to keep it. The deer follows him everywhere, becoming the one true companion of this lonely child. In the end, after the death of Flag, Jody stoically faces his life as an adult. "He did not believe he should ever again love anything, man or woman or his own child, as he had loved the yearling. He would be lonely all his life. But a man took it for his share and went on."

In 1876 Reuben and Sara Long created a frontier homestead on Pat's Island in Florida, now part of Florida's Ocala National Forest. Their son Melvin found and adopted a fawn. Rawlings used this actual setting and a few facts about the Longs, her neighbors in North Florida, to craft her novel. Today those who want to see the remains of the homestead and magnificent setting for the book can take "The Yearling" trail over that land. Excelling in its loving detail of the natural world and its regional dialect, *The Yearling* won the Pulitzer Prize for literature in 1939. The next year a beautifully illustrated edition by N. C. Wyeth helped make the book popular for family reading. For Newbery Medal winner Lois Lowry, the book remains the most memorable reading experience of her childhood.

Lois Lowry
What fiction could accomplish

For me the book that profoundly affected my life was *The Yearling*. My mother read it to me when I was eight years old. I still remember the sound of her voice, the shape of her shoulders as she held the thick hard-cover book, and the hall light illuminating her as she sat in the hallway and read to me and my sister, each in our bedrooms.

It was the first book that allowed me to see how the writer could elicit an emotional reaction—she made my mother cry. I saw what an enormous power the writer had. That book transported me into the life of that little boy and that family. It took me to another place and helped me understand their lives. I had never experienced that with other books. It was the right book for me at the right time. Although I could not have articulated what I experienced at the time, I now realize that *The Yearling* made me understand what fiction could accomplish and what a writer could do with words.

I watched Little Man as he scooted into his seat beside two other little boys. He sat for a while with a stony face looking out the window; then, evidently accepting the fact that the book in front of him was the best that he could expect, he turned and opened it. But as he stared at the book's inside cover, his face clouded, changing from sulky acceptance to puzzlement. His brows furrowed. Then his eyes grew wide, and suddenly he sucked in his breath and sprang from his chair like a wounded animal, flinging the book onto the floor and stomping madly upon it.

Miss Crocker rushed to Little Man and grabbed him up in powerful hands. She shook him vigorously, then set him on the floor again. "Now, just what's gotten into you, Clayton Chester?"

But Little Man said nothing. He just stood staring down at the open book, shivering with indignant anger.

"Pick it up," she ordered.

"No!" defied Little Man.

"No? I'll give you ten seconds to pick up that book, boy, or I'm going to get my switch."

Little Man bit his lower lip, and I knew that he was not going to pick up the book. Rapidly, I turned to the inside cover of my own book and saw immediately what had made Little Man so furious. Stamped on the inside cover was a chart which read:

The blank lines continued down to line 20 and I knew that they had all been reserved for black students. A knot of anger swelled in my throat and held there. But as Miss Crocker directed Little Man to bend over the "whipping" chair, I put aside my anger and jumped up.

"Miz Crocker, don't, please!" I cried. Miss Crocker's dark eyes warned me not to say another word. "I know why he done it!"

"You want part of this switch, Cassie?"

"No'm," I said hastily. "I just wanna tell you how come Little Man done what he done."

"Sit down!" she ordered as I hurried toward her with the open book in my hand.

Holding the book up to her, I said, "See, Miz Crocker, see what it says. They give us these ole books when they didn't want 'em no more."

PROPERTY OF THE BOARD OF EDUCATION			
Spokane County, Mississippi			
September, 1922			
CHRONOLOGICAL ISSUANCE	DATE OF ISSUANCE	CONDITION OF BOOK	RACE OF STUDENT
1	September 1922	New	White
2	September 1923	Excellent	White
3	September 1924	Excellent	White
4	September 1925	Very Good	White
5	September 1926	Good	White
6	September 1927	Good	White
7	September 1928	Average	White
8	September 1929	Average	White
9	September 1930	Average	White
10	September 1931	Poor	White
11	September 1932	Poor	White
12	September 1933	Very Poor	nigra
13			
14			
15			

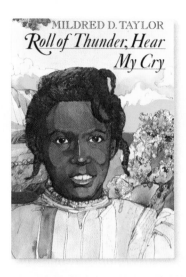

ROLL OF THUNDER, HEAR MY CRY

by Mildred D. Taylor

Mildred Taylor's *Roll of Thunder, Hear My Cry* is considered by many critics the finest piece of historical fiction in the last half of the twentieth century. Like Laura Ingalls Wilder, Taylor drew on family history for her saga of the Logans, a proud black family living in rural Mississippi in the 1930s. They witness the nightriders, intent on terrorizing blacks and destroying property; they fight to save their own land. Because the Logans are such wonderful people, the reader becomes their ally and rejoices in their triumphs.

Taylor began the Logan saga in her first book, *Song of the Trees*, and has written many fine volumes about them—*Let the Circle Be Unbroken*, *The Gold Cadillac*, and *The Land*. So those who find themselves enchanted by Cassie, Stacy, Little Man, and David can follow their adventures in subsequent books. Published in 1976, *Roll of Thunder, Hear My Cry* mirrors contemporary concerns—but it also recreates in detail another period, place, and time.

When I ask my graduate students what books have had a profound effect on their lives, they often respond by mentioning *Roll of Thunder, Hear My Cry*. More than one of them has said that this book allowed them to understand how prejudice feels—to the person on the other side of that hatred. *New York Times* best-selling author Ann M. Martin discovered the book as an adult and examined how Taylor communicates the nature of racism to young readers.

Ann M. Martin

A powerful way to communicate racism to young readers

As a child, I was immersed in books. My sister and I were lucky enough to grow up in a household full of books. We were given books as gifts for holidays and on our birthdays. And we went to the library every week. Much of my childhood was spent reading. Both my mother, a preschool teacher, and my father, a cartoonist, read to us. My father was a storyteller as well, and for years he amused my sister and me with tales about a tiny man named Mr. Pieball.

I was exposed to, and distinctly remember, many classic picture books. But the most moving children's book I've read was one I encountered as an adult, Mildred Taylor's *Roll of Thunder, Hear My Cry*. I read it for the first time around 1980, and then I was struck by the story itself, by its messages. Rereading it twenty-five years later, I was able to look at it with a writer's eye, and I was struck anew.

With incredible grace, honesty, and energy, Taylor tells a gripping story so heartbreaking that at times it's difficult to read, yet she makes it appealing to adults and young readers alike. She conveys the story from the point of view of fourth-grader Cassie. Through Cassie's nine-year-old eyes the issue of race relations is explored: Perhaps the most appalling concept being that this story of inequality, injustice, and violence takes place in the early 1930s—scarcely fifty years before it was published.

Taylor makes her points by relating details that are often excruciating. Near the beginning of the story, for instance, Cassie is looking through her school textbook and finds a chart, which is reproduced for the reader, chronicling the condition of the book. When the book is brand new and in excellent condition, it is given to a white child. Over the years the condition of the book deteriorates, and by the time it's deemed "very poor" (and of course out of date), it's issued to an African American student—or "nigra" (as opposed to "White"). Even the use of upper- and lowercase letters is telling. What a powerful way to communicate racism to young readers.

Taylor's masterful portrayal of prejudice—as well as of a strong and loving family—and of life in rural Mississippi during the Depression will stay with readers of any age for a long, long time.

Jim, Who ran away from his Nurse,
and was eaten by a Lion.

There was a Boy whose name was Jim;
His Friends were very good to him.
They gave him Tea, and Cakes, and Jam,
And slices of delicious Ham,
And Chocolate with pink inside,
And little Tricycles to ride,
And read him Stories through and through,
And even took him to the Zoo—
But there it was the dreadful Fate
Befel him, which I now relate.

You know—at least you ought to know,
For I have often told you so—
That Children never are allowed
To leave their Nurses in a Crowd;
Now this was Jim's especial Foible,
He ran away when he was able,
And on this inauspicious day
He slipped his hand and ran away!
He hadn't gone a yard when—Bang!

With opens jaws, a Lion sprang,
And hungrily began to eat
The Boy: beginning at his feet.

Now, just imagine how it feels
When first your toes and then your heels,
And then by gradual degrees,
Your shins and ankles, calves and knees,
Are slowly eaten, bit by bit.
No wonder Jim detested it!
No wonder that he shouted, "Hi!"
The Honest Keeper heard his cry,
Though very fat he almost ran
To help the little gentleman.

"Ponto!" he ordered as he came
(For Ponto was the Lion's name),
"Ponto!" he cried, with angry Frown.
"Let go, Sir! Down, Sir! Put it down!"

CAUTIONARY TALES FOR CHILDREN by H. Belloc, illustrated by B. T. B.

CAUTIONARY TALES FOR CHILDREN

Designed for the Admonition of Children between the ages of eight and fourteen years.

Verses by
H. BELLOC

Pictures by
B. T. B.

THE BAD CHILD'S BOOK OF BEASTS

CAUTIONARY TALES FOR CHILDREN

by H. Belloc,
illustrated by B. T. B.

In a lifetime of amazing accomplishments Hilaire Belloc produced around 150 works of history, biography, and verse, served in the British House of Commons, and lectured on military history at Cambridge. Today he is remembered for his humorous books for children, highly original works that can be compared to Lewis Carroll's *Alice's Adventures in Wonderland* and Edward Lear's nonsense verse.

In 1895 Belloc graduated from Oxford with a degree in history. His first children's book, *The Bad Child's Book of Beasts*, appeared in 1896 and contained the illustrations of his Oxford friend, Lord Basil Blackwood (B. T. B.). Together the two comic geniuses presented a variety of characters—the Yak, the Rhinoceros, the Dromedary—in text and art. "Then tell your papa where the Yak can be got / And if he is awfully rich / He will buy you the creature— / or else / he will not. / (I cannot be positive which.)" Blackwood also illustrated Belloc's 1907 volume of *Cautionary Tales for Children*, a darker and more satiric volume. In it Belloc presents the terrible fates that befall bad children: Jim, "Who ran away from his Nurse, and was eaten by a Lion"; Matilda, who "told such Dreadful Lies / It made one Gasp and Stretch one's Eyes"; and Rebecca, a door slammer, "was not really bad at heart, / But only rather rude and wild: / She was an aggravating child." At the end comes Charles Augustus Fortescue, who did what was right and accumulated an immense fortune.

For more than a century both books have delighted children. From them Caldecott Medal winner Mordicai Gerstein grew to understand the power of satire and parody.

Mordicai Gerstein

A way to change the world—by making fun of it

When I was seven—every few weeks after a movie or a lunch out—I went with my parents to the old Pickwick Book Shop on Hollywood Boulevard in Los Angeles. While Mom and Dad browsed for Thomas Mann and the latest Hemingway, I went directly to a shelf where I had discovered a book that fascinated me. I spent my entire time there studying its hilarious pictures, strange rhymed stories, and exotic vocabulary. Each time, as we were leaving, I begged my parents to buy it; each time—maybe because it was too expensive or they thought it somehow inappropriate—they refused. Finally, after what seemed to me years, they relented, and I joyfully brought home my very own copy of Hilaire Belloc's *The Bad Child's Book of Beasts* and *Cautionary Tales for Children* in one volume.

The book was funny in a way I hadn't experienced before. It was funny in a sneaky way. It pretended to be a book of deadpan Victorian moral fables but was really something else—a book that made fun of the very thing it appeared to be. It conspired with me, the child, to undermine adult pomposity, rules, and authority. The marvelous drawings by B. T. B. were not afraid to be grotesque. I loved all things grotesque. The drawing of a portly old zookeeper, tearfully poking with his cane at all that was left of young Jim after being eaten by a lion—his head—was grisly, sentimental, and very funny. The picture was a wonder of mixed messages. Jim was later reincarnated by Maurice Sendak as Pierre, the fearless insurgent whose motto was "I don't care!"

Belloc, and later Lewis Carroll, P. L. Travers, and others introduced me to the deliciously subversive realm of parody and satire. They showed me a way one could respond to the world, and maybe change it, by making fun of it.

We were approaching the lighted square of the opening when the roar began. The blast of air came like a sudden whistling gale; it took my breath and flattened my ears against my head, and I closed my eyes instinctively. I was still in the rear, and when I opened my eyes again I saw one of the mice sliding past me, clawing uselessly with his small nails at the smooth metal beneath him. Another followed him, and still another, as one by one they were blown backward into the dark maze of tunnels we had just left. I braced myself in the corner of the shaft and grabbed at one as he slid by. It was the white mouse. I caught him by one leg, pulled him around behind me and held on. Another blew face-on into the rat ahead of me and stopped there—it was Jonathan, who had been near the lead. But the rest were lost, six in all. They were simply too light; they blew away like dead leaves, and we never saw them again.

In another minute the roar stopped, the rush of air slowed from a gale to a breeze, and we were able to go forward again.

I said to the white mouse: "You'd better hold on to me. That might happen again."

He looked at me in dismay. "But what about the others? Six are lost! I've got to go back and look for them."

Jonathan quickly joined him: "I'll go with you."

"No," I said. "That would be useless and foolish. You have no idea which shaft they were blown into, nor even if they all went the same way. And if you should find them—how would you find your way out again? And suppose the wind comes again? Then there would be eight lost instead of six."

The wind did come again, half a dozen times more, while we worked with the screwdriver to pry open the screen. Each time we had to stop work and hang on. The two mice clung to the screen itself, some of us braced ourselves behind them, in case they should slip. And Justin, taking the thread with him as a guideline, went back to search for the other six. He explored shaft after shaft to the end of the spool, calling softly as he went—but it was futile. To this day we don't know what became of those six mice. They may have found their way out eventually, or they may have died in there. We left an opening in the screen for them, just in case.

MRS. FRISBY AND THE RATS OF NIMH by Robert C. O'Brien, illustrated by Zena Bernstein

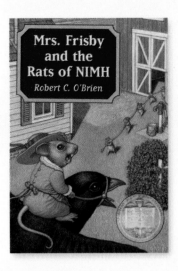

MRS. FRISBY AND THE RATS OF NIMH

by Robert C. O'Brien,
illustrated by Zena Bernstein

In a novel that combines talking animals with scientific exploration, Mrs. Frisby, a widowed field mouse with four small children, faces the demolition of her winter home. But her youngest son Timothy, ill from pneumonia, cannot be moved. When she seeks a solution for her problem she encounters Nicodemus and the rats of NIMH, rodents who have undergone scientific experiments at the National Institute of Mental Health and received mind-enhancing drugs. But as Nicodemus explains, "By teaching us how to read, they taught us how to get away." After fleeing from the institute, they have been evolving a plan to create a totally self-sustaining, utopian rat community.

In a media-crazed age, when every outlet promotes some author or another, Robert C. O'Brien's personal story is completely refreshing. He wrote *Mrs. Frisby and the Rats of NIMH* while on staff at *National Geographic.* Since the magazine frowned on their writers developing projects for others, Robert Leslie Conly adopted a pseudonym based on his mother's name and published this novel covertly. Hence the book developed a devoted audience without a book tour or media appearances. When it won the Newbery Medal in 1972, Conly was required to appear and make a speech, but he sent his editor in his stead. Consequently only at his death did the world learn that the mild-mannered reporter just happened to be an accomplished children's book author as well.

One of those books that pulls children in and keeps them enthralled, *Mrs. Frisby and the Rats of NIMH* gave British journalist Lucy Mangan a whole new way to look at the world.

Lucy Mangan

Children should be encouraged to read anything and everything because you never know what they will get out of a book.

In Robert C. O'Brien's *Mrs. Frisby and the Rats of NIMH*, the wise Nicodemus describes the world rats might have created: "A rat civilization would probably never have built skyscrapers, since rats prefer to live underground. But think of the endless subways-below-subways-below-subways they would have had."

I read that when I was nine, and it rocked my world. Everything I took for granted only existed because it was built or organized by us, because we were here first. And it could all have been so different. It wasn't preordained, immutable, or even anything special. Just ours, developed to serve our needs. I was just about catatonic with the shock of this revelation, but at this point Darren Ford started throwing Legos at my head—so my immediate mental crisis was averted.

Children should be encouraged to read anything and everything because you never know what they will get out of a book.

The Bobbsey twins were very busy that morning. They were all seated around the dining-room table, making houses and furnishing them. The houses were being made out of pasteboard shoe boxes, and had square holes cut in them for doors, and other long holes for windows, and had pasteboard chairs and tables, and bits of dress goods for carpets and rugs, and bits of tissue paper stuck up to the windows for lace curtains. Three of the houses were long and low, but Bert had placed his box on one end and divided it into five stories, and Flossie said it looked exactly like a "department" house in New York.

There were four of the twins. Now that sounds funny, doesn't it? But, you see, there were two sets. Bert and Nan, age eight, and Freddie and Flossie, age four.

Nan was a tall and slender girl, with a dark face and red cheeks. Her eyes were a deep brown and so were the curls that clustered around her head.

Bert was indeed a twin, not only because he was the same age as Nan, but because he looked so very much like her. To be sure, he looked like a boy, while she looked like a girl, but he had the same dark complexion, the same brown eyes and hair, and his voice was very much the same, only stronger.

THE BOBBSEY TWINS, OR MERRY DAYS INDOORS AND OUT by Laura Lee Hope

THE BOBBSEY TWINS, OR MERRY DAYS INDOORS AND OUT

by Laura Lee Hope

In 1904 one of the most successful children's book series of all times was launched with *The Bobbsey Twins, Or Merry Days Indoors and Out*; the book introduced an idyllic town, Lakeport on the shore of Lake Metoka, and two sets of fraternal twins, Nan and Bert and Flossie and Freddie. The first book in the Bobbsey Twins series, which would be published for over seventy years, was written by the founder of the Stratemeyer Syndicate, Edward Stratemeyer, who wanted to test the series' potential. All the books appeared under the pseudonym of Laura Lee Hope. Initially they were more episodic and less plot- or action-driven than other Syndicate staples: the Bobbsey twins experienced fabulous outings together: sleigh rides, train journeys, and seaside vacations. Various Stratemeyer Syndicate writers over the years paid scant attention to series consistency; Snoop the cat even changes genders from book to book. But Nan, Bert, Flossie, and Freddie always display an innocent charm, enthusiasm, curiosity, and basic decency.

Actor Kirk Douglas, one of the greatest male screen legends of all time, was born in 1916 and became part of the first generation of children to discover the joys of the Bobbsey Twins. Looking at the role of reading in his life, he fervently believes in the importance of books for children.

Kirk Douglas
Reading makes a child's mind sharper.

Betty, the oldest of my six sisters, first read the Bobbsey Twins books to me when I was young, and then I was finally able to read them for myself. In my many years as an actor, I have found the ability to read one of my most important assets.

Today, in this age of technology, we don't read to children enough, and they suffer because of it. We can't allow reading to become a lost art; young people must be encouraged to be readers. In my last book, *Let's Face It: 90 Years of Living, Loving, and Learning*, I acknowledge that we have made a mess of this world: "We must leave our homes—our planet—in good order for our grandchildren to inherit. We cannot leave a legacy of incompetence. We have made a mess, we must clean it up." The younger generation will inherit what we have created. So we must do everything we can to help them deal with the future.

Reading books of any kind simply makes a child's mind sharper. I have seven grandchildren, and I always give them books as presents. It is so important for parents and grandparents to do everything they can to get children to read. Being read to, by anyone, helps a child develop the habit of reading. Children's books are more important now than they have ever been in our society.

In a hole in the ground there lived a hobbit. Not a nasty, dirty, wet hole, filled with the ends of worms and an oozy smell, nor yet a dry, bare, sandy hole with nothing in it to sit down on or to eat: it was a hobbit-hole, and that means comfort.

It had a perfectly round door like a porthole, painted green, with a shiny yellow brass knob in the exact middle. The door opened on to a tube-shaped hall like a tunnel: a very comfortable tunnel without smoke, with paneled walls, and floors tiled and carpeted, provided with polished chairs, and lots and lots of pegs for hats and coats—the hobbit was fond of visitors. The tunnel wound on and on, going fairly but not quite straight into the side of the hill—The Hill, as all the people for many miles round called it—and many little round doors opened out of it, first on one side and then on another. No going upstairs for the hobbit: bedrooms, bathrooms, cellars, pantries (lots of these), wardrobes (he had whole rooms devoted to clothes), kitchens, dining-rooms, all were on the same floor, and indeed on the same passage. The best rooms were all on the left-hand side (going in), for these were the only ones to have windows, deep-set round windows looking over his garden, and meadows beyond, sloping down to the river.

This hobbit was a very well-to-do hobbit, and his name was Baggins. The Bagginses have lived in the neighbourhood of The Hill for time out of mind, and people considered them very respectable, not only because most of them were rich, but also because they never had any adventures or did anything unexpected: you could tell what a Baggins would say on any question without the bother of asking him. This is a story of how a Baggins had an adventure, and found himself doing and saying things altogether unexpected. He may have lost the neighbours' respect, but he gained— well, you will see whether he gained anything in the end.

THE HOBBIT by J. R. R. Tolkien

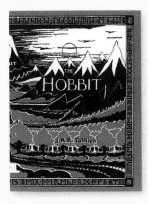

THE HOBBIT

by J. R. R. Tolkien

The standard bearer for all fantasy began in an inauspicious manner. A British professor of Anglo-Saxon, very tired of grading school Certificate papers, discovered a blank page and decided to write on it. The sentence that he produced—"In a hole in the ground there lived a hobbit"—intrigued him, and he set out to find out what exactly a hobbit might be. He decided these small furry creatures possessed great courage—the kind of courage the English had shown fighting in the trenches in World War I. At night J. R. R. Tolkien told his sons stories about one hobbit, Bilbo Baggins. Before he had even turned these tales into a finished manuscript for *The Hobbit*, which Tolkien also illustrated, he had already attracted a publisher. Because the book was both a literary and commercial success in England and America, the public and his publishers clamored to learn more about Middle Earth, but anyone interested had to wait almost twenty years before Tolkien completed, to his satisfaction, the Lord of the Rings trilogy. It opens, appropriately, with a chapter entitled, "A Long-Expected Party."

Bilbo Baggins joins a band of dwarfs gathered by the wizard Gandalf, and they set out from his home in the shire to seek the treasure hidden in the lair of the dragon Smaug. Along the way, Bilbo takes a magic ring from the Gollum, a creature of the swamps; it makes him invisible but also bestows greater powers than he even understands. At the end of the story, Gandalf says, "You are a very fine person, Mr. Baggins, and I am very fond of you; but you are only quite a little fellow in a wide world after all." However small in physical stature, Bilbo has exerted tremendous influence over the years, drawing millions and millions of readers into his quest. Kyle Zimmer, director of the literacy organization First Book, delighted in Bilbo's quest when she found him as a child; he still causes her to think about the role of reading in shaping the leaders of society.

Kyle Zimmer

The key to cultivating our next generation of leaders is many books, well chosen.

Science has finally confirmed what anyone who has ever attended a high school reunion already knew: By the time we stumble out of adolescence, we are, fundamentally, who we are going to be. In fact, researchers tell us that by the time we hit "the first grade, we have acquired most of the neurological pathways that will serve us through the rest of our lives." Given that fact, we should never doubt that the stories we share with our children during these critical early years have a profound impact on the adults they become. The heroes we applaud, the jokes we share, and the messages that pour off the pages of children's books form their characters and inform their personalities.

When I was a child, I fell in love with J. R. R. Tolkien's *The Hobbit*. It is a great adventure tale about friendship, bravery, selflessness, and perseverance. The power of the diminutive hero facing down grave peril was not lost on me in those early years when I topped out at about 4 feet 6 inches. I have recently had the joy of introducing this treasure to my own son. He lights up just as I did when it is time to read another chapter and recounts his favorite parts to his friends. There is no superhero fueling this interest—just Bilbo Baggins, a furry-footed character who would really rather be home eating breakfast—but my son can't get enough of him.

When we read great books with our children, we teach them to turn to great books throughout their lives for comfort, humor, and for illumination of the human experience. The most influential leaders and thinkers in the world have consistently relied on literature for inspiration at their most difficult moments. Nelson Mandela turned to Steinbeck during his imprisonment and says it changed his life. Lincoln was criticized for reading novels in the middle of the Civil War; he defended himself by saying that it kept him sane.

Whether we are called upon to govern a nation or organize a birthday party for too many children, the key to both surviving our days and cultivating our next generation of leaders is many books, well chosen.

A woman in an ugly black dress stood before them.

"I am your new teacher, Miss Viola Swamp."

And she rapped the desk with her ruler.

"Where is Miss Nelson?" asked the kids.

"Never mind that!" snapped Miss Swamp. "Open those arithmetic books!"

Miss Nelson's kids did as they were told.

They could see that Miss Swamp was a real witch.

She meant business.

Right away she put them to work.

And she loaded them down with homework.

"We'll have no story hour today," said Miss Swamp.

"Keep your mouths shut," said Miss Swamp.

"Sit perfectly still," said Miss Swamp.

"And if you misbehave, you'll be sorry," said Miss Swamp.

MISS NELSON IS MISSING! by Harry Allard, illustrated by James Marshall

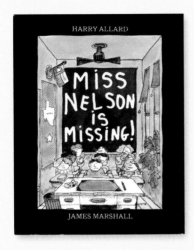

MISS NELSON IS MISSING!

by Harry Allard,
illustrated by James Marshall

The highly inventive James Marshall, who grew up in San Antonio, Texas, created dozens of funny and memorable books. Many of these, such as the George and Martha friendship chronicles, came solely from his own mind. But for a few books, he teamed up with his friend Harry Allard, and they had a highly unconventional means of working together.

One night, around three in the morning, Marshall received a phone call from Allard who said, "Jim, Miss Nelson is missing," and then hung up the phone. Marshall began to think about the mysterious Miss Nelson and the children in Room 207, the worst-behaved class in school. Miss Nelson decides that something needs to be done—and the something turns out to be the most frightening substitute teacher in the canon of children's books, Miss Viola Swamp. In Marshall's sketchbooks, Viola grows meaner and meaner in each rendition, inspired by his least favorite teacher who once told him that he could not draw. She eventually looked, according to Marshall, like "Maria Callas with a fake nose." He also incorporated a lot of personal jokes in the illustrations: the flag of Texas hangs in the classroom; as the children stagger under their homework, one of the books, *Pyramid*, had just been published by one of Marshall's colleagues, David Macaulay.

In this picture book with a perfect ending, the sweet Miss Nelson proves more resourceful than anyone imagined. Lynda Johnson Robb, Chairman Emerita of Reading Is Fundamental, first learned about the books of James Marshall from her mother, First Lady Lady Bird Johnson.

Lynda Johnson Robb
Children's books tie together the stages of life.

Children's books tie together the stages of life. You read them when you are eight or ten or twelve, and then they stay with you. I still have many books that I loved as a child and have kept; I read books to my own children; and now we will share books with my grandchildren.

As a child I loved *Winnie-the-Pooh*. However, when I read that book and other Milne titles to my children, they would roll their eyes and act as if they were bored. But even though I didn't think they were listening to me, after they became adults they spontaneously would recite Milne's poetry—"James James Morrison Morrison"—to tell me that now I needed someone to watch after me.

The books of James Marshall link my mother, me, my children, and my grandchildren together. Jim's mother Cecile roomed with my mother in college and served as her attendant when she married my father. Many years later, my mother said to me, "Oh my friend Cecile's little boy, Jim, creates children's books." By that point Jim was probably in his forties. As a young girl, my daughter Jennifer got to know Cecile when we all took a trip together on the *Delta Queen*. Jennifer fell in love with Viola Swamp—that fabulous character in *Miss Nelson Is Missing!*

When Jennifer went to college, I called her the night before her first set of exams. I wanted to tell her that I knew she would do well. Then she said, "You wouldn't believe the pressure. But you would approve of the way I handled it. I went to the library and read *Miss Nelson Is Missing!* and some of my other favorite children's books. I feel much better now." Eventually she became a high school math teacher and field hockey coach. She has even dressed up as Coach Viola Swamp and does a very fine impersonation, wearing red-laced high top shoes.

For me, celebrities and stars are not the ones in Hollywood. The writers and illustrators of great children's books are my stars—people like Ernest Shepard, the illustrator of *Winnie-the-Pooh*, and Jim Marshall, and so many others that I have been blessed to meet and talk to over the years.

Children's books stabilize me; they are my roots; they help me in times of stress. They help me connect to happy memories, to those I love, to the generations in my family. They provide comfort. Even though at this point my grandchildren are very young, I have been gathering a library for years to share with them. At the right moment they, too, will get to know those great books by Jim Marshall and so many others.

I shook my head and opened my eyes again. There was a man kneeling over me. As I sat up he stood up. He was handing me some clothes, and he was dressed in a most unusual manner. This man wasn't a native, and didn't suggest an explorer or a traveler. He looked like an over-dressed aristocrat, sort of a misplaced boulevardier, lost on this seemingly desolate volcanic island. He was wearing a correctly tailored white morning suit—if you can imagine such a suit—with pin-stripe pants, white ascot tie, and a white cork bowler. The suit he was urging me to put on was just the same as the one he had on, only in my size.

"Am I dead?" I asked. "Is this Heaven?"

"No, my good man," he answered, "this isn't Heaven. This is the Pacific Island of Krakatoa."

(When Professor Sherman mentioned the word "Krakatoa," a shudder of excitement ran through the audience. Only recently there had been news stories telling that half of Krakatoa had blown up in the greatest volcanic eruption of all times.)

"But I always thought Krakatoa was uninhabited," I told the gentleman in the white morning suit as I started painfully to put on the clothes he was handing me. "I always heard that the volcanic mountain made living on the Island impossible."

"This is Krakatoa, all right," he said. "And we who live here are most pleased that the rest of the world is still convinced Krakatoa is uninhabitable. Hurry up, put on your clothes."

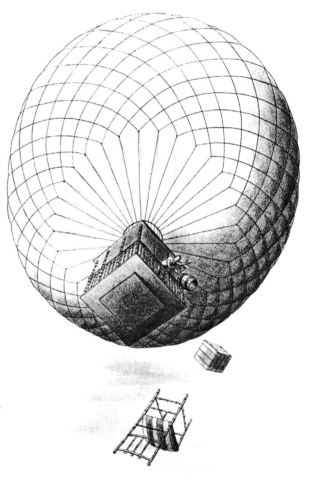

THE TWENTY-ONE BALLOONS by William Pène du Bois

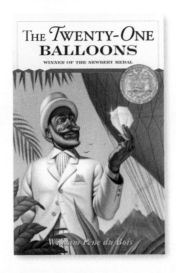

THE TWENTY-ONE BALLOONS

by William Pène du Bois

Although Professor William Waterman Sherman travels around the world in forty days, he began his expedition in 1883 as a leisurely balloon flight, a way to distance himself from all the students who had plagued him over the years. He experiences a week of idyllic ballooning, until a sea gull destroys his conveyance and sends him plummeting to earth. Upon awakening, the Professor asks, "Is this Heaven," only to be told "this isn't Heaven. This is the Pacific Island of Krakatoa." Three days before its historic eruption, the island might be mistaken for paradise. The professor marvels at the amazing community built there, funded by a diamond mine on the island. But eventually all of the inhabitants must flee, on a well-constructed balloon-propelled platform.

Science, invention, fantasy, humor, and fast-paced storytelling distinguish this 1948 Newbery Award winner. William Pène du Bois was one of those unusually gifted individuals who could both draw and write with equal facility; another of his books, *Lion*, received a Caldecott Honor. Fascinated with the work of Jules Verne, Pène du Bois invented some wonderful contraptions for the island of Krakatoa, including a bed with continuous sheets that get mechanically washed, dried, and pressed every day.

When Dr. Jerry J. Mallett, curator of the Mazza Museum of International Art from Picture Books, first read the book, he found another kind of paradise—the art that exists in books for children.

Jerry J. Mallett
It is never too late to have your life changed by a children's book.

My childhood was devoid of books, with the exception of comic books and the Hardy Boys. It wasn't until after I became a teacher and was taking my first course in children's literature that I read my first quality children's book, *The Twenty-One Balloons* by William Pène du Bois. I can remember thinking, *Why didn't someone tell me about this wonderful book? I wonder if there are more?* I was, of course, intrigued by the action-packed story as well as the fact that much of the story is based on scientific truths. But it was the illustrations that totally won me over. Pène du Bois' pen-and-ink meticulous drawings and his amazing use of perspective left me breathless. I kept going back to many of them, particularly the one of Professor Sherman lightening the load in his balloon by throwing the items out of the gondola. They appear to be coming directly at the reader.

From there I discovered picture books and had a reawakening. Imagine seeing *The Biggest Bear, Madeline, Drummer Hoff, Millions of Cats, Once a Mouse, The Snowy Day, Make Way for Ducklings,* and *Where the Wild Things Are* all within a two-week summer workshop. My head was spinning and has yet to stop.

It seemed to me that there was no difference in quality between the art I loved hanging in the Toledo (Ohio) Museum of Art and this wonderful book art in picture books. With this belief I began my crusade. I started to collect, compile, acquire every piece of original art from children's book artists that I could. The first four pieces I collected were a Peter Spier watercolor from *Rain;* a Steven Kellogg watercolor and pen and ink from *Tallyho, Pinkerton!;* an Ezra Jack Keats gouache from *Apt. 3;* and an Eric Carle collage from *The Mixed-Up Chameleon.* Recently, that process culminated in the building of the Mazza Museum of International Art from Picture Books.

What a wonderful life I have had being surrounded by the most marvelous art and literature imaginable. It all started with *The Twenty-One Balloons.* From it I learned that it is never too late to have your life changed by a children's book.

Notes on Contributors

Spokane/Coeur d'Alene Indian **SHERMAN ALEXIE** has overcome numerous personal challenges to become a leading poet and novelist. He has won several awards for his writing including the National Book Award for *The Absolutely True Diary of a Part-Time Indian*. Alexie has explored other artistic venues such as comedy, screenplays, and filmmaking.

Middlebury College professor **JULIA ALVAREZ** has been honored for her work to support the Dominican culture and Dominican-Americans. Her book *In The Time of Butterflies* won numerous awards including finalist for the National Book Critics Circle Award in 1995. In addition to teaching creative writing and English, Ms. Alvarez has addressed social concerns through her novels.

A children's literature consultant and book buyer for twenty-five years, **BECKY ANDERSON** is the co-owner of Anderson's Bookshops and Anderson's Bookfair Company in Naperville, Downers Grove, and Aurora, Illinois. Her business was given the Family Business of the Year award by Loyola University, and she received the Panell award for the best bookseller for children.

ROBERT BALLARD designed an automated submarine, the Argo, and used this device to locate the wreck of the *Titanic*. He has worked with the National Geographic Society and serves as president of the Sea Research Foundation's Institute for Exploration.

His name, Attiim Kiambu, means fiery-tempered king, but everybody calls this famous football player **TIKI BARBER**. After playing college ball at Virginia and pro

ball for the New York Giants, Barber has taken up a broadcasting career and writes children's books with his twin brother.

Actress **KATHY BATES** was nominated for an Academy Award as Best Actress for her role in *Misery*. She was also nominated for an Academy Award for Best Supporting Actress for her role in *Primary Colors*. In addition to acting, Bates directs television shows and movies.

EMILY BAZELON is senior editor of *Slate* and also has written pieces for the *New York Times Magazine, Atlantic Monthly, O, The Oprah Magazine*, and *Mother Jones*. Bazelon studied at Yale College and Yale Law School.

NED BERUBE began working at Digital Equipment Corporation in 1977 and has spent a significant portion of his career in Marketing Communications for the computer industry. He also founded Evergreen Collaborative Enterprises and uses his expertise to help businesses improve revenue streams.

JUDY BLUME has devoted her life to writing and championing intellectual freedom by working with the National Coalition Against Censorship. Author of many ground-breaking books for young readers, including *Are You There God? It's Me, Margaret*, Blume received the 2004 National Book Foundation's Medal for Distinguished Contribution to American Letters.

MARC BROWN is the creator of the PBS television series *Arthur*, which follows the adventures of the aardvark character

he originally developed in books. An author-illustrator, Brown typically bases his characters on family members and friends. He studied at the Cleveland Institute of Art and held a variety of jobs ranging from short-order cook to chicken farmer before his creative efforts began to pay the bills.

In 1971 **BETSY BYARS** won the Newbery Medal for *The Summer of the Swans*. She began her career writing magazine articles and became interested in writing children's stories after she read books to her children. When Byars isn't writing, she is flying her private airplane.

JOHN CECH serves as director of the Center of Children's Literature & Culture at the University of Florida. He produced the public radio program *Recess!* and serves as a National Public Radio commentator on *All Things Considered*. He is author of *Imagination and Innovation: The Story of Weston Woods*.

LOUIS CLARK heads the Government Accountability Project, an organization that came to life following the 1970s Watergate scandal. An attorney, Clark worked for the organization before taking on the role of president. Clark studied law at American University and holds a master of divinity degree from the Pacific School of Religion in Berkeley.

NICK CLARK was the founding director of the Eric Carle Museum of Picturebook Art. Clark has had a long career as museum curator at institutions such as the Chrysler Museum of Art and the National Gallery in Washington, D.C.

BEVERLY CLEARY knew from an early age that she wanted to write humorous books for children because she could never find those books in the library when she was a girl. Trained as a librarian, Cleary found time to write and won the 1984 Newbery Medal for *Dear Mr. Henshaw*.

The common thread of **J. DAVID COOPER**'s teaching career at the elementary, high school, and college levels is reading. In addition to teaching reading and training teachers, Cooper writes extensively on literacy. To recognize his contribution to the field of literacy, the Indiana Reading Professors gave Cooper the 1990 Outstanding Service Award.

Sculptor **ARIS DEMETRIOS** studied sculpture at his father's institution, the George Demetrios School, after he finished his formal education at Harvard University. His large-scale works have been commissioned by public foundations, private residences, and corporate offices.

Heart surgeon **WILLIAM C. DEVRIES** contributed to the development of the world's first artificial heart, the Jarvis 7. He performed the first surgery to implant the device as well. In his mid-fifties DeVries joined the U.S. Army Reserve and went through basic training. He works as a civilian contractor at Walter Reed Army Medical Center.

ANITA DIAMANT started her career as a freelance journalist and then shifted her focus to writing handbooks on Jewish life as well as novels. Diamant founded the Mayyim Hayyim: Living Waters Community Mikveh and Education Center in Newton, MA. Her work in this area reflects her deep regard for Jewish cultural life.

Fulbright Scholar **MICHAEL DIRDA** has been a longtime contributor and editor for the *Washington Post Book World*. He was awarded the Pulitzer Prize for Literary Criticism in 1993. Dirda reviews both adult and children's novels and teaches and lectures around the country.

KIRK DOUGLAS's long acting career has earned him multiple Academy Award nominations, including for his role as Vincent Van Gogh in *Lust for Life*. In 1996, the industry recognized his half century of work with a special Oscar. Douglas has also received a Presidential Medal of Freedom and a National Medal of the Arts.

In 1994, **GERALD EARLY** won the National Book Critics Circle Award for his collection of essays titled *The Culture of Bruising: Essays on Prizefighting, Literature, and Modern American Culture*. Early, the Merle Kling professor of modern letters at Washington University, is particularly interested in African American culture and has written about musicians such as Sammy Davis Jr. and Miles Davis.

When longtime TV film critic **ROGER EBERT** encountered speech difficulties as a result of health problems, he continued writing weekly film reviews. This Pulitzer Prize–winning film critic worked for many years at the *Chicago Sun Times*. Ebert trademarked the phrase "Two Thumbs Up."

DAVE EGGERS has been praised for his innovative writing techniques, and his book *A Heartbreaking Work of Staggering Genius* was nominated for a Pulitzer Prize. His writing genres range from comic strips to memoir. Eggers founded McSweeney's, a publishing firm, which also prints a namesake quarterly literary journal.

An extensive career in school libraries led **BARBARA ELLEMAN** to review and later write books. She has served as editor of *Booklist* magazine and created and edited *Book Links: Connecting Books, Libraries, and Classrooms*. Her work in the field of children's literature was recognized with the Jeremiah Ludington and Hope S. Dean awards.

England-based author **KEN FOLLETT** won a Best Novel Edgar Award for *The Eye of the Needle* in 1979. Follett has served on numerous committees and organizations dedicated to improving literacy. He's also a fellow of England's Royal Society of the Arts.

Editor-in-chief of *Forbes* **STEVE FORBES** has advised numerous political candidates and has twice run for president on platforms that supported simplified tax codes and school choice. Forbes also chaired the Board for International Broadcasting (BIB) as the organization spread radio free broadcasting and contributed to the fight against Eastern-European communism.

RUSSELL FREEDMAN believes every nonfiction book he writes deserves at least four drafts to bring the subject to life. He won the 1988 Newberry Medal for *Lincoln: A Photobiography*. In addition to biographies, animal behavior is another favorite topic for Freedman.

FRED FRIEDMAN hosts the Minnesota Public Radio program *Fool Fred*. Friedman is a longtime Minnesota Public Defender. His work as a professor in the Sociology Department and School of Medicine, University of Minnesota Duluth has won him numerous awards.

JEAN CRAIGHEAD GEORGE's love of nature led her to study science in college. She also studied literature and wrote for the *Washington Post* early in her career. Her novel *Julie of the Wolves* won the Newbery Award in 1973.

MORDICAI GERSTEIN uses his talents to write and illustrate children's books, direct animated films, and create sculpture. Gerstein received the Caldecott Medal in 2004 for *The Man Who Walked Between the Towers*.

ALISON GOPNIK has spent her career studying developmental psychology. Her scientific research in this field has led her to publish dozens of papers and books on the subject. In addition to teaching psychology at the University of California at Berkeley, Gopnik writes for the *New York Review of Books*.

WGBH producer **CAROL GREENWALD** has brought many children's book classics to life on television—Marc Brown's Arthur books, the Reys' Curious George titles, and Susan Meddaugh's Martha the Dog books. Greenwald serves on the board of the National Children's Book and Literacy Alliance.

MICHAEL PATRICK HEARN, the editor of *The Annotated Wizard of Oz*, is an authority on L. F. Baum and *The Wizard of Oz*. Hearn organizes exhibits, teaches graduate level classes on the history of illustration in children's literature, and writes extensively on the topic.

The author of many distinguished children's books, **KAREN HESSE** combined history and poetic form in *Out of the Dust*, winner of the 1998 Newbery Medal. Hesse is also the recipient of a MacArthur Fellowship.

Singer-songwriter **TYLER HILTON** made his professional debut at age sixteen. He has also acted in several TV shows and movies. Hilton is such a strong

advocate of reading that on his twenty-first birthday a literacy organization was established in his name, T.H. Books for Kids, because he believes in "a book in the hand of every child."

ADAM HOCHSCHILD's list of literary credits includes the J. Anthony Lukas Prize in the United States, the Duff Cooper Prize in England, Canada's Lionel Gelber Prize, and the Lannan Literary Award for Nonfiction. In addition to teaching at the Graduate School of Journalism at the University of California at Berkeley, Hochschild, who cofounded *Mother Jones*, writes magazine and newspaper articles.

THACHER HURD studied illustration at the college level in California. As the child of Clement Hurd, illustrator of *Goodnight Moon*, and Edith Hurd, children's book author, Hurd was introduced to children's books at an early age. Hurd cofounded Peaceable Kingdom Press with his wife Olivia.

After meeting Cynthia Rylant, creator of the Henry and Mudge series, **ANGELA JOHNSON** became interested in writing for children. She won the Coretta Scott King Award for her novel *Heaven* and also received a MacArthur Fellowship.

Bookstore owner **MITCHELL KAPLAN** has served as president of the American Booksellers Association. Though he worked in law, Kaplan has spent most of his career owning and operating community bookstores. He also founded The Miami Book Fair International and champions literacy and First Amendment rights.

ROBERT F. KENNEDY JR.'s interest in the environment led him to help those in Latin America and Canada to preserve

their homelands. Kennedy has been instrumental in protecting the water supply for New York City. President of Waterkeeper Alliance, he was named a Hero of the Planet by *Time* magazine.

PERRI KLASS is the medical director of Reach Out and Read, a program designed to help pediatricians improve the literacy rate. A pediatrician, Dr. Klass also teaches journalism and pediatrics at New York University. She often focuses on the connection between medicine and parenting in her writing.

STAN LEE's association with Marvel Comics began just after he graduated from high school. He created action figures such as the Hulk and Spiderman, which were illustrated by Jack Kirby. Most recently, Lee established POW, a public entertainment company that produces DVDs and video games.

URSULA K. LE GUIN has been a finalist for both the Pulitzer Prize and American Book Award. She has won the National Book Award and Hugo Award and is known for adult titles, *The Left Hand of Darkness*, and children's books, *The Wizard of Earthsea*.

JAY LENO has been a comedian, an actor, and host of *The Tonight Show* for more than fifteen years. This Emmy Award–winning television star has appeared in movies, advertisements, and TV shows.

GAIL CARSON LEVINE won a Newbery Honor Award for her first book, *Ella Enchanted*. Though she originally studied illustration, Levine now prefers writing. In telling her stories, Levine often gives traditional fairy tales a new twist.

ANTHONY LEWIS has won two Pulitzer Prizes, one for his coverage of the United States Supreme Court, and he frequently writes on the Supreme Court and matters of constitutional law. He holds a chair at Columbia University's Graduate School of Journalism and contributes frequent op ed pieces for the *New York Times*.

DAVID LINDEN is the chief editor of the *Journal of Neurophysiology*. He is a professor of Neuroscience at Johns Hopkins University School of Medicine. His book, *The Accidental Mind*, attempts to explain the effects of evolution on brain development.

EDEN ROSS LIPSON served as the children's book editor for the *New York Times*. She also worked as a journalist and book editor. While she gave talks on radio and television, she chiefly enjoyed her personal conversations with children.

STEPHANIE LOER has worked as the children's book critic for the *Boston Globe* and reviews books on radio and television. She serves on the board of the National Children's Book and Literacy Alliance.

LOIS LOWRY was able to finish her education and start writing seriously after the birth of her children. She won Newbery Medals for *The Giver* and *Number the Stars*. Lowry maintains that her books cover many aspects of the same topic: "the importance of human connections."

Under **PETER LYNCH**'s guidance, Fidelity Investments' Magellan Fund achieved outstanding portfolio performance. He credits his success to a commitment to research and focus on the fundamentals. Author of *One Up on Wall Street*, Lynch sits on the board of the Fidelity Group of funds and engages in nonprofit works.

Author and illustrator **DAVID MACAULAY** studied at and then joined the faculty at Rhode Island School of Design. His work has won numerous awards including a Caldecott Medal for *Black and White*.

As the longtime children's book reviewer for Scripps Howard News Service, **KAREN MACPHERSON** writes a weekly column on works ranging from picture book to young adult. MacPherson has also written on education, nuclear weapons labs, and Native Americans in her journalism career.

In addition to writing for adults and children, **GREGORY MAGUIRE** works as a consultant in creative writing for children. He cofounded and codirects the nonprofit educational charity Children's Literature New England, Inc.

Founder of the Finlay, Ohio-based Mazza Museum and education professor, **JERRY J. MALLETT** has devoted his career to the study of children's literature. Mallett built the museum, which aims to preserve children's book art, from four pieces of picture-book art originally donated by Dr. August Mazza.

RONALD MALLETT is a professor of physics at the University of Connecticut. He has written articles and published a book on the topic of time travel. Penn State awarded Mallett the Alumni Fellow Award in 2007.

Guardian columnist **LUCY MANGAN** studied at the University of Cambridge. Author of *Hopscotch & Handbags*, a discussion of all things female, Mangan qualified to be a solicitor but prefers to write.

LEONARD MARCUS has written about the history of children's books in titles such as *Dear Genius* and *Minders of Make Believe*. Marcus also critiques children's

books and lectures across the United States and Canada.

Before she began editing and writing children's books, **ANN M. MARTIN** worked as an educator. Author of The Baby-sitters Club series, she established the Ann M. Martin foundation to benefit children, education, and literacy.

BOBBIE ANN MASON's writing ranges from critical essays to magazine articles to novels and short stories. She has won an Ernest Hemingway Award for her writing; her novel *In Country*, adapted for a movie, drew fresh attention to the Vietnam War.

Naturalist **PETER MATTHIESSEN** was one of the founders of the *Paris Review*. He won the National Book Award for *The Snow Leopard*. Matthiessen is a member of the American Academy of Arts and Letters.

DAVID MCCULLOUGH has won Pulitzer Prizes and National Book Awards. A narrator of film documentaries such as *Brooklyn Bridge* and host of the PBS television series *Smithsonian World*, he has also won the Presidential Medal of Freedom.

LAURA MILLER cofounded Salon.com. She writes frequently for Salon and her articles also appear in the *New Yorker*, *Time*, and the *New York Times Book Review*. Miller is the author of *The Magician's Book: A Skeptic's Adventures in Narnia*.

WENDELL MINOR is the award-winning illustrator of more than forty books for children. He has created book jackets for David McCullough and Harper Lee and has illustrated books by Jack London, Jack Schaefer, Jean Craighead George, and Buzz Aldrin. Minor serves on the board of the Norman Rockwell Museum.

LESLIE MOONVES joined CBS in July of 1995 and is president and CEO of CBS Corporation. Moonves has also held senior management positions at Viacom and Time Warner. He briefly worked as an actor before turning to the business side of the entertainment industry.

JULIANNE MOORE is an Academy Award-nominated actress for her roles in *Far from Heaven* and *The Hours*. Moore worked off-Broadway and appeared on several TV soap operas before breaking into film.

AZAR NAFISI, who grew up in Iran, is the author of *Reading Lolita in Tehran*. She is a professor at Johns Hopkins University's School of Advanced International Studies and an activist for the human rights of Iranian women and girls.

LYNN NEARY's award-winning correspondent work at National Public Radio has covered topics ranging from breast cancer to Sing Sing Prison. Neary has hosted several programs including *All Things Considered*.

PHILIP NEL is an English professor and the director of Kansas State University's program in children's literature. A member of the Children's Literature Association and American Studies Association, Nel frequently writes and lectures on topics related to children's literature.

After **PETER NEUMEYER** fled Nazi Germany, he located in the United States and started a career in teaching. He then founded the children's literature center at San Diego State University. Neumeyer has written extensively in the field and has authored children's books.

Country music star **BRAD PAISLEY** is a guitarist, singer, and songwriter. In 2007 he won Male Vocalist of the Year from the Country Music Association. This Grammy Award–winner produces music considered to be a blend of country and pop-rock.

LINDA SUE PARK won the Newbery Medal for her novel *A Single Shard*. Park's stories often connect to Korean history and culture. She continues to write novels, picture books, poems, and short stories.

KATHERINE PATERSON has received every accolade the book community can confer, including two Newbery Awards and the Hans Christian Andersen Award. She initially planned a life as a missionary; after writing curriculum material for the Presbyterian Church, she grew more interested in writing books for children.

In November of 2006 **DEVAL PATRICK** became the first African-American Governor of Massachusetts. A graduate of both Harvard College and Harvard Law School, Patrick brought a range of experience in business, government, and nonprofits, including the NAACP Legal Defense and Education Fund, to his position.

A member of the Reading Hall of Fame, **JACK PIKULSKI** has dedicated his professional career to education. He has written textbooks, articles for professional journals, and parts of the Houghton Mifflin Reading Program.

Harvard researcher, experimental psychologist, and professor **STEVEN PINKER** studies language and the mind. Pinker's research includes a focus on children and language acquisition. He

serves as the chair of the Usage Panel of the American Heritage Dictionary.

Attorney **ROBERT S. PIRIE** has served as CEO of Rothschild North America and as a senior manager at Bear Stearns and SG Cowan Securities Corporation. An astute negotiator in the world of mergers and acquisitions, Pirie also collects works of Elizabethan literature.

JACK PRELUTSKY, the first United States Children's Poet Laureate, has written many collections of children's poetry. Prelutsky originally studied music and did not discover his interest in writing poetry until he was in his mid-twenties.

PHILIP PULLMAN, winner of the Carnegie Medal and Whitbread Prize, is best known for his trilogy His Dark Materials. Pullman worked for many years as a teacher and frequently speaks out against educational systems that do not allow students sufficient freedom to explore their personal strengths.

ANNA QUINDLEN won the Pulitzer Prize for her *New York Times* column, "Public and Private." She held several positions with the *New York Times* before she left to write full time as a novelist and nonfiction writer.

RICK REILLY, long known for "The Life of Reilly," the back-page column of *Sports Illustrated*, has won the national Sportswriter of the Year award eleven times. He has also written films and at ESPN works on the magazine, website, and *SportsCenter*.

LYNDA JOHNSON ROBB served for several years as chairman of the board of Reading Is Fundamental. The daughter of President Lyndon Johnson, she has also served as first lady of the Commonwealth of Virginia.

ERIC ROHMANN writes and illustrates children's books. He won a Caldecott Honor Award for *Times Flies* and the 2003 Caldecott Medal for *My Friend Rabbit*.

LOUIS SACHAR supported himself as an attorney until he could make enough money writing children's books. He won both the Newbery Medal and the National Book Award for *Holes*. When he's not writing, he enjoys playing and competing in bridge tournaments.

MARIA SALVADORE teaches at the University of Maryland, reviews books for the *School Library Journal*, and has served on the American Library Association's Notable Children's Book Committee. As a consultant for Reading Rockets, Salvadore works to improve literacy rates of children.

To introduce families to important messages found in books, **PAT SCALES** started the Communicating Through Literature program. A champion of First Amendment rights, Scales often celebrates Banned Books Week by encouraging young people to read banned books. She is the recipient of a Grolier Award.

JON SCIESZKA excels at telling traditional fairy tales in new ways and writing humorous stories. After college he opted out of medical school and studied for an MFA in writing. Scieszka established the nonprofit organization Guys Read to boost male literacy rates. He also serves as the first National Ambassador for Young People's Literature for the Children's Book Council.

PETE SEEGER has enjoyed a long career as a songwriter and folk singer. He has been associated with The Weavers and Woody and Arlo Guthrie. For writing songs such as *Where Have all the Flowers Gone* and *If I had a Hammer*, Seeger received a Grammy Lifetime Achievement Award in 1993.

Before creating his own picture books, **MAURICE SENDAK** illustrated stories for other authors. His controversial *Where the Wild Things Are* won the Caldecott Medal in 1964; in this book and his other picture books this talented creator expanded the scope and possibilities of the picture-book format.

DONNA E. SHALALA, president of the University of Miami, also served as secretary of Health and Human Services (HHS) for President Bill Clinton. In addition to the many honors and awards she has received for her leadership and service to education, Shalala received the Presidential Medal of Freedom in 2008.

ANITA SILVEY's career includes stints as a publisher of children's books for Houghton Mifflin Company, editor-in-chief of the *Horn Book Magazine*, and president of the Children's Book Council. Winner of several honors including The Ludington Award from EPA, Silvey works tirelessly to promote the best books for children.

SCOTT SIMON is well known as the host of National Public Radio's *Saturday Weekend Edition*. Simon has also appeared on numerous television shows and won an Emmy in 1982 for a public television documentary. He has also written nonfiction books, novels, and magazine and newspaper articles.

PETER SÍS writes and illustrates children's books; in 2003 he was awarded a

MacArthur Fellowship. Sís has also worked as a filmmaker and commercial artist.

LESLEY STAHL's work as a TV journalist has included assignments such as moderator of *Face the Nation*, anchor of *America Tonight*, and correspondent for *60 Minutes*. She has also served as a White House correspondent during numerous presidencies.

Photography expert **MAUREEN TAYLOR** has combined her skills with history to focus on connecting photos and genealogy. Taylor, author of numerous books and articles, shares her expertise with others through workshops and seminars.

A lifelong interest in reading led **JIM TRELEASE** to publish the *Read Aloud Handbook*. Trelease also has enjoyed a career as a journalist and artist. He remains ardent about the importance of parents reading to their children on a daily basis.

Novelist **ANNE TYLER** often uses Baltimore, Maryland, as the setting for her novels. She has been a finalist for the Pulitzer Prize and received a National Book Critics Circle Award. In addition to writing, Tyler has edited short story anthologies.

Beginning his artistic career as a sculptor, **CHRIS VAN ALLSBURG** was awarded the Caldecott Medal for both *The Polar Express* and *Jumanji* and has worked on movie adaptations for several of his books.

Highlights of **EDWARD VILLELLA**'s long career include being the first American dancer to perform with the Royal Danish Ballet and performing at John

F. Kennedy's inauguration. Villella continues to serve on the board of the American School of Ballet and is CEO of the Miami City Ballet.

Cancer researcher **BERT VOGELSTEIN** has spent his career studying the genetic basis for cancer. Dr. Vogelstein is a professor of oncology at the Johns Hopkins School of Medicine. He has won numerous awards and prizes for his research and has sat on the board of the *New England Journal of Medicine*.

ANDREW WEAVER is a climate scientist and faculty member at British Columbia's University of Vancouver. Weaver serves as the Canada Research Chair in Climate Modelling and Analysis and has also developed curriculums on climate, which are used at the elementary and secondary level in Canadian schools.

West Virginia native **BILLY EDD WHEELER** studied playwriting at Yale and authored several outdoor dramas including *Johnny Appleseed*. An award-winning songwriter, Wheeler penned favorites such as *Jackson* and *Coward of the County*.

Children's book author and illustrator **DAVID WIESNER** is well known for his rich paintings and stories that are frequently told in picture form. Wiesner's unique and effective style has earned him three Caldecott Medals for *Tuesday*, *The Three Pigs*, and *Flotsam*.

Two of **MEG WOLITZER**'s novels have been adapted for film: *Surrender, Dorothy*, and *This is My Life*. Wolitzer, a Brown University graduate, has taught writing at Skidmore College and Columbia University. Wolitzer's work often touches on the intersection of women, work, and motherhood.

PETER WOOD teaches anthropology and humanities at King's College in New York. Dr. Wood studies and writes about cultural shifts in the Unites States. He won the Caldwell Award for his book *Diversity: The Invention of a Concept*.

JUDY WOODRUFF has worked as a broadcast journalist for several major networks including PBS. She serves on the board of the Freedom Forum and was a cofounder of the International Women's Media Foundation.

STEVE WOZNIAK helped revolutionize the world of personal computing with engineering wizardry at Apple Inc., the firm he cofounded. To encourage computer literacy for children he has given away computers, servers, and Internet laptops. His expertise and vision was formally recognized with his induction into the Inventors Hall of Fame.

ANDREW WYETH, America's best-known and most celebrated artist, received the National Medal of Arts in 2007. Creator of "Christina's World" Wyeth crafted realistic paintings that often portray the landscapes and people of Maine and Pennsylvania.

First Book founder **KYLE ZIMMER** was called the Social Entrepreneur of the Year in the United States by the Schwab Foundation for Social Entrepreneurship. The goal of Zimmer's enterprise is to distribute new books to low-income families in order to improve literacy.

Selected List of Books by Contributors

Sherman Alexie
Indian Killer
Reservation Blues
*The Lone Ranger and Tonto Fistfight in
    Heaven*
Ten Little Indians
Flight
Smoke Signals
Dangerous Astronomy
*The Abslutely True Diary of a Part-Time
    Indian*

Julia Alvarez
*Once Upon a Quinceañera: Coming of Age in
    the USA*
In the Time of the Butterflies
A Cafecito Story
Saving the World
The Women I Kept to Myself
Before We Were Free
How Tia Lola Came to Stay
How the Garcia Girls Lost Their Accents

Robert Ballard
*Collision with History: The Search for John F.
    Kennedy's PT 109*
Adventures in Ocean Exploration
Ghost Liners
Return to Midway
Lost Liners
Finding the Titanic
Exploring the Titanic

Tiki Barber
Tiki
My Life in the Game and Beyond
By My Brother's Side
Game Day
Teammates
Kickoff!

Judy Blume
Summer Sisters
Smart Women
Wifey
Forever
Are You There God? It's Me, Margaret.
Blubber
Just as Long as We're Together
Tales of a Fourth Grade Nothing

Marc Brown
Arthur's Neighborhood
Arthur Goes to School
Arthur's Reading Race

Glasses for D.W.
Kiss Hello, Kiss Good-bye
Say the Magic Word
What's the Big Secret?
Arthur's Homework

Betsy Byars
The Summer of the Swans
The Night Swimmers
The Moon and I
The Blossom Family books
After the Goat Man
The Glory Girl
The Computer Nut
Coast to Coast

John Cech
A Rush of Dreamers
My Grandmother's Journey
First Snow, Magic Snow
Django
The Southernmost Cat
Jack and the Beanstalk

Nick Clark
Myth, Magic, and Mystery

Beverly Cleary
Dear Mr. Henshaw
Ramona Quimby, Age 8
Ramona and Her Father
Henry Huggins
Henry and the Paper Route
Henry and the Clubhouse
Ribsy
Ellen Tebbits

J. David Cooper
The Struggling Reader: Interventions That Work
Literacy: Helping Students Construct Meaning
*Literacy Assessment: Helping Teachers Plan
    Instruction*

Anita Diamant
The Last Days of Dogtown
The Red Tent
Good Harbor
*Pitching My Tent: On Marriage,
    Motherhood, Friendship, and Other
    Leaps of Faith*

Michael Dirda
Classics for Pleasure
*Bound to Please: Essays on Great Writers and
    Their Books*

Readings: Essays and Literary Entertainments
An Open Book

Kirk Douglas
*Climbing the Mountain: My Search for
    Meaning*
The Ragman's Son: An Autobiography
*Let's Face It: 90 Years of Living, Loving, and
    Learning*
Last Tango in Brooklyn
My Stroke of Luck
Dance with the Devil
The Broken Mirror

Gerald Early
Tuxedo Junction: Essays on American Culture
*Life with Daughters: Watching the Miss
    America Pageant*
*The Culture of Bruising: Essays on Prizefighting,
    Literature, and Modern American Culture*
Daughters: On Family and Fatherhood
*One Nation Under a Groove: Motown &
    American Culture*
*How the War in the Streets Is Won: Poems
    on the Quest of Love and Faith*

Roger Ebert
Your Movie Sucks
Roger Ebert's Four-Star Reviews 1967-2007
Awake in the Dark: The Best of Roger Ebert
The Great Movies
I Hate, Hate, Hated This Movie
Roger Ebert's Movie Yearbook 2009

Dave Eggers
What is the What
A Heartbreaking Work of Staggering Genius
How We Are Hungry: Stories
You Shall Know Our Velocity
Giraffes? Giraffes!
Your Disgusting Head
*Animals of the Ocean, in Particular the
    Giant Squid*

Barbara Elleman
Tomie dePaola, His Art and His Stories
Holiday House: Its First 65 Years
Virginia Lee Burton: A Life in Art

Ken Follett
The Eye of the Needle
Pillars of the Earth
The Key to Rebecca
The Man from St. Petersburg
Lie Down with Lions

The Third Twin
Jackdaws
Whiteout

Steve Forbes
A New Birth of Freedom: A Vision for America
*Flat Tax Revolution: Using a Postcard to
    Abolish the IRS*

Russell Freedman
Lincoln: A Photobiography
Franklin Delano Roosevelt
Eleanor Roosevelt: A Life of Discovery
The Life and Death of Crazy Horse
Buffalo Hunt
Who Was First?: Discovering America
Adventures of Marco Polo
Children of the Wild West

Jean Craighead George
LUCK: The Story of a Sandhill Crane
My Side of the Mountain
Charlie's Raven
Snowboard Twist
Julie of the Wolves
Water Sky
One Day in the Desert
There's an Owl in the Shower

Mordicai Gerstein
Leaving the Nest
The White Ram
The Old Country
The Man Who Walked Between the Towers
Sparrow Jack
What Charlie Heard
Fox Eyes
Noah and the Great Flood

Alison Gopnik
The Scientist in the Crib
How Babies Think
*Causal Learning: Psychology, Philosophy, and
    Computation*

Michael Patrick Hearn
The Annotated Wizard of Oz
The Victorian Fairy Tale Book
The Wonderful Art of Oz
*From the Silver Age to Stalin: Russian
    Children's Book Illustration*
*Seeking a State of Grace: The Art of Arnold
    Lobel*
The Annotated Huckleberry Finn
Myth, Magic, and Mystery
The Porcelain Cat

Karen Hesse
Out of the Dust
The Music of Dolphins
Letters from Rifka

Come On, Rain
Spuds
Stowaway
Witness
Aleutian Sparrow

Adam Hochschild
*Half the Way Home: A Memoir of Father
    and Son*
*The Mirror at Midnight: A South African
    Journey*
*The Unquiet Ghost: Russians Remember
    Stalin*
*King Leopold's Ghost: A Story of Greed,
    Terror, and Heroism in Colonial Africa*
*Finding the Trapdoor: Essays, Portraits,
    Travels*

Thacher Hurd
Mama Don't Allow
Mystery on the Docks
Art Dog
Moo Cow Kaboom
Little Mouse's Big Valentine
Zoom City
Sleepy Cadillac: A Bedtime Drive
Cat's Pajamas

Angela Johnson
The Other Side
Bird
A Cool Moonlight
The Aunt in Our House
Toning the Sweep
The First Part Last
Julius
Looking for Red

Robert F. Kennedy Jr.
The Riverkeepers
Crimes Against Nature
St. Francis of Assisi
*Robert F. Kennedy Jr.'s American Heroes:
    Robert Smalls, the Boat Thief*
*Robert F. Kennedy Jr.'s American
    Heroes: Joshua Chamberlain and
    the American Civil War*

Perri Klass
*Quirky Kids: Understanding and Helping
    Your Child Who Doesn't Fit In*
The Mercy Rule
The Mystery of Breathing
Baby Doctor
Other Women's Children
Two Sweaters for My Father
Love and Modern Medicine
Every Mother is a Daughter

Stan Lee
X-Men

The Incredible Hulk
Spider-Man
Dr. Strange
The Fantastic Four
Captain America

Ursula K. Le Guin
Lavinia
The Left Hand of Darkness
The Dispossessed
The Lathe of Heaven
Changing Planes
Catwings series
A Wizard of Earthsea
Powers: Annals of the Western Shore

Jay Leno
Jay Leno's Police Blotter
Jay Leno's Headlines
If Roast Beef Could Fly
How to be the Funniest Kid in the Whole World

Gail Carson Levine
Ella Enchanted
Fairest
Dave at Night
The Fairy's Mistake
The Princess Test
Princess Sonora and the Long Sleep
The Wish
The Two Princesses of Bamarre

Anthony Lewis
Make No Law
Freedom for the Thought that We Hate
Gideon's Trumpet

David Linden
*The Accidental Mind: How Brain Evolution
    Has Given Us Love, Memory, Dreams,
    and God*

Eden Ross Lipson
*The New York Times Parent's Guide to the
    Best Books for Children*
Applesauce Season

Lois Lowry
The Giver
Anastasia Krupnik
Looking Back
Gossamer
Gooney the Fabulous
All About Sam
Number the Stars
A Summer to Die

Peter Lynch
One Up on Wall Street
Learn to Earn
Beating the Street

David Macaulay

The New Way Things Work
Black and White
The Way We Work
Building the Book Cathedral
City
Castle
Pyramid
Shortcut

Gregory Maguire

Confessions of an Ugly Stepsister
Lost
Wicked
Mirror, Mirror
Leaping Beauty
Five Alien Elves
The Good Liar
Seven Spiders Spinning

Jerry J. Mallett

Reading Bulletin Boards & Display Kits
World Folktales: A Multicultural Approach to
*   Whole Language Grades K-2*
101 Make and Play Reading Games for the
*   Intermediate Grades*
Fold and Cut Stories

Ronald L. Mallett

Time Traveler: A Scientist's Personal
*   Mission to Make Time Travel a Reality*

Lucy Mangan

Hopscotch and Handbags: The Essential
*   Guide to Being a Girl*

Leonard Marcus

Minders of Make Believe: Idealists,
*   Entrepreneurs, and the Shaping of*
*   American Children's Literature*
Golden Legacy: How Golden Books Won
*   Children's Hearts*
Awakened by the Moon: Margaret Wise
*   Brown*
The Wand in the Word: Conversations
*   with Writers of Fantasy*
Ways of Telling: Conversations on the Art
*   of the Picture Book*
Side by Side: Five Picture-Book Teams Go
*   to Work*
Author Talk
Storied City: A Children's Book Walking-
*   Tour Guide to New York City*

Ann M. Martin

Secret Book Club, Main Street series
Baby-sitters Club series
The Runaway Dolls
Snail Mail, No More
Here Today
Belle Teal

A Corner of the Universe
A Dog's Life

Bobbie Ann Mason

In Country
Love Life: Stories
Shiloh and Other Stories
Nancy Culpepper: Stories
Spence & Lila

Peter Matthiessen

The Snow Leopard
Tigers in the Snow
Shadow Country
Cloud Forest
The Birds of Heaven: Travels with Cranes

David McCullough

The Great Bridge
The Path Between the Seas
The Johnstown Flood
1776
Mornings on Horseback
Brave Companions
Truman
John Adams

Laura Miller

The Salon.com Reader's Guide to
*   Contemporary Authors*
The Magician's Book: A Skeptic's Adventures
*   in Narnia*

Wendell Minor

America the Beautiful
Reaching for the Moon
Look to the Stars
Pumpkin Heads
Christmas Tree!
Abraham Lincoln Comes Home
Into the Woods: John James Audubon Lives
*   His Dream*

Julianne Moore

Freckleface Strawberry
Freckleface Strawberry and the Dodgeball Bully

Azar Nafisi

Reading Lolita in Tehran
Things I've Been Silent About
My Uncle Napoleon: A Novel

Philip Nel

Tales for Little Rebels
J. K. Rowling's Harry Potter Novels
Dr. Seuss: An American Icon
The Avant-Garde and American
*   Postmodernity: Small Incisive*
*   Shocks*
The Annotated Cat: Under the Hats of Seuss
*   and his Cats*

Peter Neumeyer

Donald Has a Difficulty
Donald and the Picture...
Sleep Well, Little Bear
The Collector of Moments
Dancing Line and Merry Color

Linda Sue Park

A Single Shard
Seesaw Girl
When My Name Was Keoko
Archer's Quest
Tap Dancing on the Roof
The Kite Fighters
Keeping Score
Project Mulberry

Katherine Paterson

The Invisible Child
Bridge to Terabithia
Jacob Have I Loved
The Great Gilly Hopkins
Come Sing, Jimmy Jo
Lyddie
Preacher's Boy
Bread and Roses, Too

Steven Pinker

The Language Instinct: How the Mind Creates
*   Language*
The Blank Slate: The Modern Denial of Human
*   Nature*
How the Mind Works
Words and Rules: The Ingredients of Language
The Stuff of Thought: Language as a Window
*   Into Human Nature*

Jack Prelutsky

My Dog May Be a Genius
Pizza, Pigs, and Poetry: How to Write a Poem
The New Kid on the Block
Awful Ogre's Awful Day
It's Halloween
Something Big Has Been Here
It's Raining Pigs and Noodles
My Parents Think I'm Sleeping

Philip Pullman

The Golden Compass
The Amber Spyglass
The Subtle Knife
Lyra's Oxford
The White Mercedes
The Ruby in the Smoke
Shadow in the North
Clockwork: Or All Wound Up

Anna Quindlen

Good Dog. Stay.
A Short Guide to a Happy Life
How Reading Changed My Life

Black and Blue
Blessings
Loud and Clear
Happily Ever After
One True Thing

Rick Reilly
Missing Links
Shanks for Nothing
Who's Your Caddy?
Slo Mo!

Eric Rohmann
My Friend Rabbit
Time Flies
Pumpkinhead
The Cinder-Eyed Cats
A Kitten Tale
Clara and Asha

Louis Sachar
Small Steps
Holes
Sixth Grade Secrets
Sideways Stories from Wayside School
Someday Angeline
Dogs Don't Tell Jokes
Wayside School is Falling Down
There's a Boy in the Girl's Bathroom

Maria Salvadore
Books Kids Will Talk About

Pat Scales
Teaching Banned Books: 12 Guides for
    Young Readers

Jon Scieszka
The Stinky Cheese Man and Other Fairly
    Stupid Tales
The True Story of the 3 Little Pigs
Math Curse
Time Warp Trio
Cowboy and Octopus
The Book that Jack Wrote
The Frog Prince, Continued
Squids Will Be Squids

Pete Seeger
How to Play the 5-String Banjo
American Favorite Ballads
Carry It On
Turn! Turn! Turn!
Some Friends to Feed: The Story of Stone Soup
Pete Seeger's Storytelling Book

Maurice Sendak
Where the Wild Things Are
In the Night Kitchen
Higglety Pigglety Pop!
Outside Over There

Alligators All Around
Very Far Away
Pierre
The Nutshell Library

Donna E. Shalala
Medicare and You
Your Guide to Choosing Quality Health Care
Mental Health: A Report of the Surgeon
    General

Anita Silvey
100 Best Books for Children: A Parent's Guide
    to Making the Right Choices for Your
    Young Reader, Toddler to Preteen
The Essential Guide to Children's Books and
    Their Creators
500 Great Books for Teens
I'll Pass for Your Comrade: Women Soldiers in
    the Civil War

Scott Simon
Windy City: A Novel of Politics
Home and Away: Memoir of a Fan
Jackie Robinson and the Integration of Baseball
Pretty Birds

Peter Sís
The Wall: Growing Up Behind the Iron Curtain
Tibet Through the Red Box
The Three Golden Keys
The Tree of Life: Charles Darwin
Starry Messenger: Galileo Galileo
Madlenka
Fire Truck
A Small Tall Tale From the Far Far North

Lesley Stahl
Reporting Live

Maureen Taylor
Uncovering Your Ancestry Through Family
    Photographs
Preserving Your Family Photographs
Through the Eyes of Your Ancestors

Jim Trelease
The Read-Aloud Handbook
Hey! Listen to This: Stories to Read Aloud
Read All About It: Great Read-Aloud Stories

Anne Tyler
The Accidental Tourist
Breathing Lessons
Saint Maybe
Ladder of Years
A Patchwork Planet
Back When We Were Grownups
The Amateur Marriage
Digging to America

Chris Van Allsburg
The Polar Express
Jumanji
Two Bad Ants
The Mysteries of Harris Burdick
The Garden of Abdul Gasazi
The Wreck of the Zephyr
The Widow's Broom
The Z Was Zapped

Edward Villella
Prodigal Son

Bert Vogelstein
The Genetic Basis of Human Cancer
Learning from Patients: The Science of
    Medicine
The Molecular and Metabolic Bases of
    Human Disease

Billy Edd Wheeler
Laughter in Appalachia: A Festival of
    Southern Mountain Humor
Kudzu Covers Manhattan
Star of Appalachia
Curing the Cross-Eyed Mule: Appalachian
    Mountain Humor

David Wiesner
Flotsam
Sector 7
The Three Pigs
June 29, 1999
Tuesday
Free Fall
Hurricane
The Loathsome Dragon

Meg Wolitzer
The Ten Year Nap
The Wife
The Position
Surrender, Dorothy
This is Your Life

Peter Wood
Diversity: The Invention of a Concept
A Bee in the Mouth: Anger in America Now

Judy Woodruff
This is Judy Woodruff at the White House

Steve Wozniak
iWoz: Computer Geek to Cult Icon

Andrew Wyeth
Andrew Wyeth: Master Drawings from the
    Artist's Collection
Andrew Wyeth: Close Friends
Andrew Wyeth: Autobiography

Recommended Booklist

This list includes books mentioned in *Everything I Need to Know I Learned from a Children's Book* as well as other recommended titles. Ages are suggestions only.

PRESCHOOL (0–2)

Black on White by Tana Hoban
Brown Bear, Brown Bear, What Do You See? by Bill Martin Jr.
The Carrot Seed by Ruth Kraus
Don't Let the Pigeon Drive the Bus by Mo Willems
Freight Train by Donald Crews
Goodnight Moon by Margaret Wise Brown
Have You Seen My Ducklings? by Nancy Tafuri
Max's First Words by Rosemary Wells
"More More More," Said the Baby by Vera B. Williams
Mr. Gumpy's Outing by John Burningham
My Friend Rabbit by Eric Rohmann
Rosie's Walk by Pat Hutchins
Sheila Rae's Peppermint Stick by Kevin Henkes
Tickle, Tickle by Helen Oxenbury
The Very Hungry Caterpillar by Eric Carle
We're Going on a Bear Hunt by Michael Rosen
Where's Spot? by Eric Hill
Whose Mouse Are You? by Robert Kraus

ALPHABET BOOKS

Aardvarks, Disembark! by Ann Jonas
Anno's Alphabet by Mitsumasa Anno
Brian Wildsmith's ABC by Brian Wildsmith
Chicka Chicka Boom Boom by Bill Martin Jr. and John Archambault
Jambo Means Hello by Tom Feelings
Pigs from A to Z by Arthur Geisert

COUNTING BOOKS

Anno's Counting Book by Mitsumasa Anno
Mojo Means One: A Swahili Counting Book by Muriel and Tom Feelings
One Hunter by Pat Hutchins
1, 2, 3 by Tana Hoban
Pigs from 1 to 10 by Arthur Geisert
Ten Black Dots by Donald Crews
Ten, Nine, Eight by Molly Bang
Who's Counting? by Nancy Tafuri

NURSERY RHYMES

Father Fox's Pennyrhymes by Clyde Watson
London Bridge Is Falling Down by Peter Spier
The Mother Goose Treasury by Raymond Briggs
My Very First Mother Goose by Iona Opie
The Real Mother Goose by Blanche Fisher Wright
The Random House Book of Mother Goose by Arnold Lobel
The Tall Book of Mother Goose by Feodor Rojankovsky

PICTURE BOOKS (2–8)

Alexander and the Terrible, Horrible, No Good, Very Bad Day by Judith Viorst
And to Think That I Saw It on Mulberry Street by Dr. Seuss
Angelina Ballerina by Katherine Holabird
Andy and the Lion by James Daugherty

The Animal Book by Alice and Martin Provensen
Arthur the Aardvark series by Marc Brown
Babar series by Jean de Brunhoff
Bark, George by Jules Feiffer
Bread and Jam for Frances by Russell Hoban
Caps for Sale by Esphyr Slobodkina
A Chair for My Mother by Vera Williams
Choo Choo by Virginia Lee Burton
Click Clack Moo by Doreen Cronen
The Color Kittens by Margaret Wise Brown
Corduroy by Don Freeman
Crictor by Tomi Ungerer
Crow Boy by Taro Yashima
Curious George by H. A. Rey
Do Not Open by Brinton Turkle
Donald Has a Difficulty by Peter Neumeyer
Dr. De Soto by William Steig
Flat Stanley by Jeff Brown
Flotsam by David Wiesner
Freckleface Strawberry books by Julianne Moore
The Gardener by Sara Stewart
George and Martha by James Marshall
Gorilla by Anthony Browne
Harold and the Purple Crayon by Crockett Johnson
Harry the Dirty Dog by Gene Zion
A Hole Is to Dig by Ruth Krauss
Horton Hatches the Egg by Dr. Seuss
If Roast Beef Could Fly by Jay Leno
Ira Sleeps Over by Bernard Waber
It Could Always Be Worse by Margot Zemach
The Judge by Harve Zemach
Leo the Late Bloomer by Robert Krauss
Lilly's Purple Plastic Purse by Kevin Henkes
The Little Engine That Could retold by Watty Piper
The Little House by Virginia Lee Burton
Liza Lou and the Yeller Belly Swamp by Mercer Mayer
Lunch by Denise Fleming
Madeline by Ludwig Bemelmans
Make Way for Ducklings by Robert McCloskey
Mama Don't Allow by Thacher Hurd
The Man Who Walked Between the Towers by Mordicai Gerstein
Many Moons by James Thurber
Martha Speaks by Susan Meddaugh
Mike Mulligan and His Steam Shovel by Virginia Lee Burton
Millions of Cats by Wanda Gág
Miss Nelson Is Missing! by Harry Allard
Miss Rumphius by Barbara Cooney
No, David! By David Shannon
Officer Buckle and Gloria by Peggy Rathman
Ox-Cart Man by Donald Hall
Pink Ice Cream by Launa Latham
The Polar Express by Chris Van Allsburg
The Porcelain Cat by Michael Patrick Hearn
The Red Balloon by Albert Lamorisse
The Relatives Came by Cynthia Rylant
The Shrinking of Treehorn by Florence Parry Heide
The Snowman by Raymond Briggs

The Snowy Day by Ezra Jack Keats
The Story About Ping by Marjorie Flack
The Story of a Fierce Bad Rabbit by Beatrix Potter
The Story of Babar by Jean de Brunhoff
The Story of Ferdinand by Munro Leaf
Swamp Angel by Anne Isaacs
Swimmy by Leo Lionni
Sylvester and the Magic Pebble by William Steig
The Tailor of Gloucester by Beatrix Potter
The Tale of Peter Rabbit by Beatrix Potter
The Tale of Squirrel Nutkin by Beatrix Potter
The Three Pigs by David Wiesner
The Three Robbers by Tomi Ungerer
The True Story of the 3 Little Pigs by Jon Scieszka
Tuesday by David Wiesner
Where the Wild Things Are by Maurice Sendak
William's Doll by Charlotte Zolotow
Yo! Yes? by Chris Raschka

BEGINNING READERS (5–7)
Amelia Bedelia series by Peggy Parish
Bedtime for Francis by Russell Hoban
The Cat in the Hat by Dr. Seuss
Frog and Toad Are Friends by Arnold Lobel
Go, Dog. Go! by P. D. Eastman
Henry and Mudge by Cynthia Rylant
Little Bear by Else Holmelund Minarik
Nate the Great series by Marjorie Sharmat
Small Wolf by Nathaniel Benchley
The King, the Mice and the Cheese by Nancy and Eric Gurney

FLUENT READERS/CHAPTER BOOKS (7–9)
Betsy-Tacy by Maud Hart Lovelace
Centerburg Tales by Robert McCloskey
The Courage of Sarah Noble by Alice Dalgliesh
Encyclopedia Brown series by Donald J. Sobol
The Enormous Egg by Oliver Butterworth
Great Brain series by John Fitzgerald
Happily Ever After by Anna Quindlen
Henry Huggins series by Beverly Cleary
The Hundred Dresses by Eleanor Estes
Impunity Jane by Rumer Godden
Little House in the Big Woods by Laura Ingalls Wilder
The Mouse on the Motorcycle by Beverly Cleary
Miss Pickerell Goes to Mars by Ellen MacGregor
Mr. Popper's Penguins by Richard and Florence Atwater
Mrs. Piggle-Wiggle by Betty MacDonald
My Father's Dragon by Ruth Stiles Gannett
Ramona the Pest by Beverly Cleary
Sarah, Plain and Tall by Patricia MacLachlan
Stone Fox by John Gardiner
Tales of a Fourth Grade Nothing by Judy Blume

MIDDLE-GRADE FICTION (8–11)
Anastasia Krupnik series by Lois Lowry
Anne of Green Gables by L. M. Montgomery
Ballet Shoes by Noel Streatfeild
The Best Christmas Pageant Ever by Barbara Robinson
Bridge to Terabithia by Katherine Paterson
Emil books by Erich Kästner
Freaky Friday by Mary Rodgers

From the Mixed-up Files of Mrs. Basil E. Frankweiler
  by E. L. Konigsburg
Gone-Away Lake by Elizabeth Enright
The Great Gilly Hopkins by Katherine Paterson
Harriet the Spy by Louise Fitzhugh
Henry Reed series by Keith Robertson
Holes by Louis Sachar
Homer Price by Robert McCloskey
The House with a Clock in Its Walls by John Bellairs
Humbug Mountain by Sid Fleischman
Joey Pigza series by Jack Gantos
On My Honor by Marion Dane Bauer
Ordinary Jack by Helen Cresswell
Pippi Longstocking by Astrid Lindgren
Roller Skates by Ruth Sawyer
The Pushcart War by Jean Merrill
The Saturdays by Elizabeth Enright
Summer of the Swans by Betsy Byars
Swallows and Amazons series by Arthur Ransome
The Westing Game by Ellen Raskin

ANIMAL/HORSE STORIES
Black Stallion series by Walter Farley
King of the Wind by Marguerite Henry
Misty of Chincoteague by Marguerite Henry
My Friend Flicka by Mary O'Hara
Owls in the Family by Farley Mowat
Rascal by Sterling North
Smoky, the Cowhorse by Will James
The Wolfling by Sterling North
The Yearling by Marjorie Kinnan Rawlings

DOG STORIES
Because of Winn-Dixie by Kate DiCamillo
The Call of the Wild by Jack London
The Incredible Journey by Sheila Burnford
Lassie Come-Home by Eric Knight
Old Yeller by Fred Gipson
Sounder by William Armstrong
Where the Red Fern Grows by Wilson Rawls

FANTASY
The Animal Family by Randall Jarrell
Behind the Attic Wall by Sylvia Cassedy
The BFG by Roald Dahl
The Borrowers series by Mary Norton
Chronicles of Prydain series by Lloyd Alexander
The Children of Green Knowe by L. M. Boston
The Dark Is Rising by Susan Cooper
David and the Phoenix by Edward Ormondroyd
The Diamond in the Window by Jane Langton
Ella Enchanted by Gail Carson Levine
Finn Family Moomintroll by Tove Jansson
Freaky Friday by Mary Rodgers
The Gammage Cup by Carol Kendall
Half Magic by Edward Eager
The Hamlet Chronicles by Gregory Maguire
Harry Potter series by J. K. Rowling
The Hobbit by J. R. R. Tolkien
The Lion, the Witch and the Wardrobe by C. S. Lewis
The Little Prince by Antone de Saint-Exupéry

Mary Poppins by P. L. Travers
The Mouse and His Child by Russell Hoban
The Perilous Gard by Elizabeth Marie Pope
The Phantom Tollbooth by Norton Juster
The Secret Garden by Frances Hodgson Burnett
The Story of Dr. Dolittle by Hugh Lofting
The Sword in the Stone by T. H. White
Tom's Midnight Garden by Philippa Pearce
Tuck Everlasting by Natalie Babbittt
The Twenty-One Balloons by William Pène du Bois
The Wind in the Willows by Kenneth Grahame
Winnie-the-Pooh by A. A. Milne
The Wolves of Willoughby Chase by Joan Aiken
The Wizard of Earthsea by Ursula K. Le Guin

FANTASY — ANIMAL

Babe: The Gallant Pig by Dick King-Smith
A Bear Called Paddington by Michael Bond
The Book of the Dun Cow by Walter Wangerin Jr.
Charlotte's Web by E. B. White
Freddy the Pig series by Walter R. Brooks
Redwall by Brian Jacques
Rabbit Hill by Robert Lawson
The Cricket in Times Square by George Selden

HISTORICAL FICTION

Across Five Aprils by Irene Hunt
All-of-a-Kind Family series by Sydney Taylor
Ben and Me by Robert Lawson
The Broken Mirror by Kirk Douglas
Caddie Woodlawn by Carol Ryrie Brink
Catherine, Called Birdy by Karen Cushman
Jeremy Visick by David Wiseman
Johnny Tremain by Esther Forbes
A Long Way from Chicago by Richard Peck
My Brother Sam Is Dead by James and Christopher Collier
Out of the Dust by Karen Hesse
A Single Shard by Linda Sue Park
The True Confessions of Charlotte Doyle by Avi
The Witch of Blackbird Pond by Elizabeth George Speare

SCIENCE FICTION

Devil on My Back by Monica Hughes
The Ear, the Eye, and the Arm by Nancy Farmer
Enchantress from the Stars by Sylvia Louise Engdahl
Eva by Peter Dickinson
The Giver by Lois Lowry
Interstellar Pig by William Sleator
Mrs. Frisby and the Rats of NIMH by Robert C. O'Brien
A Wrinkle in Time by Madeleine L'Engle

SURVIVAL STORIES

Call It Courage by Armstrong Sperry
Hatchet by Gary Paulsen
Julie of the Wolves by Jean Craighead George
Island of the Blue Dolphins by Scott O'Dell
My Side of the Mountain by Jean Craighead George
Z for Zachariah by Robert C. O'Brien

OLDER READERS (11–16)

The Absolutely True Diary of a Part-Time Indian by Sherman Alexie
Beauty by Robin McKinley
The Chocolate War by Robert Cormier
A Corner of the Universe by Ann M. Martin
His Dark Materials series by Philip Pullman
Fallen Angels by Walter Dean Myers
First Part Last by Angela Johnson
The Friendly Persuasion by Jessamyn West
The Ghost Belonged to Me by Richard Peck
The Goats by Brock Cole
Hero and the Crown by Robin McKinley
Homecoming by Cynthia Voigt
In the Time of the Butterflies by Julia Alvarez
Maniac Magee by Jerry Spinelli
The Moves Make the Man by Bruce Brooks
One-Eyed Cat by Paula Fox
One Fat Summer by Robert Lipsyte
The Outsiders by S. E. Hinton
Shane by Jack Schaefer
Skellig by David Almond
Stotan! by Chris Crutcher
To Kill a Mockingbird by Harper Lee
Zel by Donna Jo Napoli

CLASSICS

The Adventures of Huckleberry Finn by Mark Twain
The Adventures of Pinocchio by Carlo Collodi
Alice's Adventures in Wonderland by Lewis Carroll
The Adventures of Tom Sawyer by Mark Twain
The Bad Child's Book of Beasts by Hilaire H. Belloc
The Boy's King Arthur edited by Sidney Lanier
The Call of the Wild by Jack London
The Fairy Tales of Hans Christian Andersen by Hans Christian Andersen
Five Children and It by E. Nesbit
The Golden Bible: The New Testament by Else Jane Werner
Heidi by Johanna Spyri
The Jungle Book by Rudyard Kipling
Just So Stories by Rudyard Kipling
Kidnapped by Robert Louis Stevenson
Kim by Rudyard Kipling
Little Women by Louisa May Alcott
The Merry Adventures of Robin Hood by Howard Pyle
Peter Pan by J. M. Barrie
Pinocchio by Carlo Collodi
The Railway Children by E. Nesbit
Rolf in the Woods by Ernest Thompson Seton
The Time Machine by H. G. Wells
Treasure Island by Robert Louis Stevenson
Twenty Thousand Leagues under the Sea by Jules Verne
The Wonderful Wizard of Oz by L. Frank Baum

CLASSIC SERIES (6–10)

Bobbsey Twins series by Laura Lee Hope
Hardy Boys series by Frank W. Dixon
Nancy Drew series by Carolyn Keene
Poppy Ott series by Leo Edwards
Tom Swift series by Victor Appleton II

INFORMATION BOOKS

America the Beautiful by Katharine Bates and Wendell Minor
And Then What Happened, Paul Revere? by Jean Fritz
Astronomy books by Isaac Asimov
Bard of Avon: The Story of William Shakespeare by Diane Stanley
Boy Scout Handbook
The Boys' War by Jim Murphy
Cathedral by David Macaulay
The Diary of a Young Girl by Anne Frank
The Endless Steppe by Esther Hautzig
Exploring the Titanic by Robert Ballard
Giraffes? Giraffes! by Haggis-on-Whey
The Golden Book of Science by Bertha Morris Parker
From Hand to Mouth by James Giblin
The Great Fire by Jim Murphy
Harriet and the Promised Land by Jacob Lawrence
How Much Is a Million? by David Schwartz
I'll Pass for Your Comrade by Anita Silvey
Lincoln: A Photobiography by Russell Freedman
The Magic School Bus at the Waterworks by Joanna Cole
The New Way Things Work by David Macaulay
Paddle-to-the-Sea by Holling C. Holling
Profiles in Courage by John Fitzgerald Kennedy
Reaching for the Moon by Buzz Aldrin
Robert F. Kennedy Jr.'s American Heroes: Joshua Chamberlain and the American Civil War by Robert F. Kennedy Jr.
Sir Walter Ralegh and the Quest for El Dorado by Marc Aronson
Snowflake Bentley by Jacqueline Briggs Martin
The Story of Mankind by Hendrik Willem Van Loon
The Wall by Peter Sis
Wild Animals I Have Known by Ernest Thompson Seton
Wilma Unlimited by Kathleen Krull
The Wright Brothers by Russell Freedman

MULTICULTURAL BOOKS

Abuela by Arthur Dorres
Baseball in April and Other Stories by Gary Soto
Baseball Saved Us by Ken Mochizuki
Breaking Through by Francisco Jimenez
Chato's Kitchen by Gary Soto
The Circuit by Francisco Jimenez
Dragonwings by Laurence Yep
Flossie and the Fox by Patricia McKissack
Grandfather's Journey by Allen Say
Hershel and the Hanukkah Goblins by Eric Kimmel
Honey, I Love by Eloise Greenfield
In the Hollow of Your Hand by Alice McGill
In the Year of the Boar and Jackie Robinson by Bette Bao Lord
John Henry by Julius Lester
Julius by Angela Johnson
Martin's Big Words by Doreen Rappaport
Mirandy and Brother Wind by Patricia McKissack
Molly Bannaky by Alice McGill
Morning Girl by Michael Dorris
Mufaro's Beautiful Daughters by John Steptoe
By My Brother's Side by Tiki Barber
The People Could Fly by Virginia Hamilton

Roll of Thunder, Hear My Cry by Mildred D. Taylor
Sadako and the Thousand Paper Cranes by Eleanor Coerr
Stevie by John Steptoe
The Star Fisher by Laurence Yep
Tales from the Gold Mountain by Paul Yee
To Be a Slave by Julius Lester
The Watsons Go to Birmingham—1963 by Christopher Paul Curtis
The Winter People by Joseph Bruchac
Zeely by Virginia Hamilton

MYTHS, LEGENDS, AND FOLKLORE

Aesop's Fables illustrated by Jerry Pinkney
Arabian Nights by Kate D. Wiggin
D'Aulaires' Book of Greek Myths by Ingri and Edgar D'Aulaire
Jack and the Beanstalk by John Cech
Jack Tales by Richard Chase
Keepers of the Earth by Joseph Bruchac and Michael Caduto
Little Red Riding Hood by Paul Galdone
The Mitten by Jan Brett
The Naked Bear: Folktales of the Iroquois by John Bierhorst
Nursery Tales Around the World by Judy Sierra
Paul Bunyan by Steven Kellogg
The People Could Fly by Virginia Hamilton
Pete Seeger's Storytelling Book by Pete Seeger
The Rainbow People by Laurence Yep
Seven Blind Mice by Ed Young
Snow White and the Seven Dwarfs by The Grimm Brothers
Strega Nona by Tomie dePaola
The Stinky Cheese Man and Other Fairly Stupid Tales by Jon Scieszka
Tales from Grimm by Wanda Gág
Uncle Remus by Julius Lester
Why Mosquitoes Buzz in People's Ears by Verna Aardema
Zlateh the Goat and Other Stories by Isaac Bashevis Singer

POETRY

A Visit to William Blake's Inn by Nancy Willard
All Small: Poems by David McCord
All the Small Poems by Valerie Worth
Alligator Pie by Dennis Lee
Bronzeville Boys and Girls by Gwendolyn Brooks
The Child's Garden of Verses by Robert Louis Stevenson
Come Hither by Walter de la Mare
The Complete Nonsense of Edward Lear by Edward Lear
Dream Keeper and Other Poems by Langston Hughes
I Met a Man by John Ciardi
Joyful Noise: Poems for Two Voices by Paul Fleischman
My Dog May Be a Genius by Jack Prelutsky
Now We Are Six by A. A. Milne
Peacock Pie by Walter de la Mare
The Dragons Are Singing Tonight by Jack Prelutsky
The New Kid on the Block by Jack Prelutsky
The Place My Words Are Looking For by Paul Janeczko
The Random House Book of Poetry for Children by Jack Prelutsky
This Same Sky by Naomi Shihab Nye
Waiting to Waltz by Cynthia Rylant
Where the Sidewalk Ends by Shel Silverstein

Contributor Index

Excerpt Index

Acknowledgments

This project began as the brainchild of Lauren Wohl of Roaring Brook Press; one cold February day she called to entice me with the idea. I am so grateful to Lauren, to Simon Boughton for his brilliant editorial direction, and to Katherine Jacobs, handmaiden for this book, for her attention to the details.

A book of this complexity would not have been possible without the help of so many people. Peter Sieruta, researcher extraordinaire, led me to many of the existing quotes. Kathy Crosett served as my assistant for a semester at Simmons College, helping pull the final manuscript together. Others assisted in making connections to the contributors in the volume. Peter Rollins, President of the Chief Executives' Club of Boston, provided links to the business community. Eden Ross Lipson of the *New York Times* gave me access to her friends. Thanks also go to my agent Doe Coover, Wendell and Florence Minor, Alison Morris, Allyn Johnston, David Gale, Paula Wiseman, Melanie Cecka, Barbara Lalicki, Betsy Groban, Julie Roach, and Sheryl de Paola. As always, my mentor and friend, Hal Miller, former CEO of Houghton Mifflin, provided encouragement and advice when I most needed it.

From the first editorial meeting on a beautiful July day in the Berkshires to the proofreading of the final pages, my beloved Bernese Mountain dog Merlin lay at my feet while I worked on the book. I only hope he can obtain a copy in dog heaven.

Julia Alvarez's essay was given as a gift to the Children's Book Council Foundation. Excerpted and adapted from "How the Alvarez Girl Found Her Magic" by Julia Alvarez. Copyright © 1999 by Julia Alvarez. First published in "Mothers Who Think," Salon.com. May 10, 1999. Reprinted by permission of Susan Bergholz Literary Services, New York, NY, and Lamy, NM. All rights reserved.

Betsy Byars and Eden Ross Lipson adapted their pieces from essays that first appeared in *The Horn Book Magazine*.

Dave Eggar's essay on *The Book of the Dun Cow* was adapted from an essay that appeared on the First Book website.

Adam Hochschild's essay on *Freddy the Pig* first appeared in *Finding the Trapdoor: Essays, Portraits, Travels* (Syracuse University Press, 1997).

Bobbie Ann Mason's essay was reprinted by permission of International Creative Management, Inc.

Laura Miller's essay on *The Lion, the Witch and the Wardrobe* was adapted from *The Magician's Book: A Skeptic's Adventures in Narnia*. Little Brown 2008.

Peter Wood's essay on *Goodnight Moon* was adapted from a piece that originally appeared in *National Review* online.

Essays by Michael Patrick Hearn, Bobbie Ann Mason, Leonard Marcus, and Philip Pullman are copyrighted in their name.

Grateful acknowledgment is made to the following for permission to reprint excerpts from previously published material:

The Adventures of Huckleberry Finn by Mark Twain. First published in the United States of America by Charles L. Webster and Company in 1885.

The Adventures of Tom Sawyer by Mark Twain. First published in the United States of America by American Publishing Company in 1876.

Alice's Adventures in Wonderland by Lewis Carroll. First published in the United States of America by D. Appleton and Company in 1866. Cover art used by permission of HarperCollins Publishers.

All-of-a-Kind Family by Sydney Taylor. First published in the United States of America by Wilcox and Follett in 1951. Cover art used by permission of Yearling, an imprint of Random House Children's Books, a division of Random House, Inc.

The Animal Book by Alice and Martin Provensen. Copyright © 1952 by Golden Press, Inc. Used by permission of Alice Provensen.

The Arabian Nights edited by Kate Douglas Wiggin and Nora A. Smith, illustrated by Maxfield Parrish. Copyright © 1909 by Charles Scribner's Sons. Copyright © renewed 1937 by Maxfield Parrish. Reprinted by permission of Atheneum Books for Young Readers, an imprint of Simon & Schuster Children's Publishing Division.

Ben and Me by Robert Lawson. Copyright © 1939 by Robert Lawson. Copyright © renewed 1967 by John W. Boyd. Reprinted by permission of Little, Brown & Company.

The Bobbsey Twins, Or Merry Days Indoors and Out by Laura Lee Hope. Copyright © 1904. Reprinted with the permission of Simon & Schuster, Inc. The Bobbsey Twins ® is a registered trademark of Simon & Schuster, Inc. The classic editions are published by Grosset & Dunlap Inc., an imprint of Penguin Books for Young Readers. All rights reserved.

The Book of the Dun Cow by Walter Wangerin, Jr. Text copyright © 1978 by Walter Wangerin, Jr. Used by permission of HarperCollins Publishers.

The Boy's King Arthur by Sidney Lanier, illustrated by N. C. Wyeth. Copyright © 1917 by Charles Scribner's Sons. Copyright © renewed 1945 by N. C. Wyeth. Reprinted by permission of Atheneum Books for Young Readers, an imprint of Simon & Schuster Children's Publishing Division.

Boy Scout Handbook, 1941 edition, excerpt and images used by permission of the Boy Scouts of America.

The Call of the Wild by Jack London, illustrated by Wendell Minor. First published in the United States of America by The Macmillan Company in 1903. Illustrations copyright © 1999 by Wendell Minor. Reprinted by permission of Atheneum Books for Young Readers, an imprint of Simon & Schuster Children's Publishing Division.

"The Case of the Civil War Sword" from *Encyclopedia Brown: Boy Detective* by Donald J. Sobol, illustrated by Leonard Shortall. Copyright © 1963 by Donald J. Sobol. Copyright © renewed 1991 by Donald J. Sobol. Used by permission of Lodestar Books, an affiliate of Dutton Children's Books, A Division of Penguin Young Readers Group, A Member of Penguin Group (USA) Inc., 345 Hudson Street, New York, NY 10014. All rights reserved.

The Cat in the Hat Comes Back by Dr. Seuss. TM and copyright © 1958 and renewed 1986 by Dr. Seuss Enterprises, L.P. "Book Cover" copyright © 1958, 1986. Used by permission of Random House Children's Books, a division of Random House, Inc.

Cautionary Tales for Children by H. Belloc, illustrated by B.T.B. First published in the United States by Alfred A. Knopf, 1922.

The Centerburg Tales by Robert McCloskey. Copyright © 1951 and renewed 1979 by Robert McCloskey. Used by permission of Viking Penguin, A Division of Penguin Young Readers Group, A Member of Penguin Group, (USA) Inc., 345 Hudson Street, New York, NY 10014. All rights reserved.

Charlotte's Web by E. B. White, illustrated by Garth Williams. Copyright © 1952 by E. B. White. Text copyright © renewed 1980 by E. B. White. Illustrations copyright © renewed by the Estate of Garth Williams. Cover art copyright © renewed 1980 by the Estate of Garth Williams. Used by permission of HarperCollins publishers.

Choo Choo by Virginia Lee Burton. Copyright © 1937 by Virginia Lee Burton. Copyright © renewed 1964 by Aristides Burton Demetrios and Michael Burton Demetrios. Reprinted by permission of Houghton Mifflin Harcourt Publishing Company. All rights reserved.

David and the Phoenix by Edward Ormondroyd. Copyright © 1957, 2000 by Edward Ormondroyd. Excerpt and image used by permission of Purple House Press. www.purplehousepress.com.

The Diamond in the Window by Jane Langton. Text copyright © 1962 by Jane Gillson Langton. Illustrations copyright © 1962 by Eric Blegvad. Used by permission of HarperCollins Publishers.

The Diary of a Young Girl: The Definitive Edition by Anne Frank, edited by Otto H. Frank and Mirjam Pressler, translated by Susan Massotty. Translation copyright © 1995 by Doubleday, a Division of Random House, Inc. Used by permission of Doubleday, a division of Random House, Inc.

Do Not Open by Brinton Turkle. Copyright © 1981 by Briton Turkle. Used by permission of Dutton Children's Books, A Division of Penguin Young Readers Group, A Member of Penguin Group (USA) Inc., 345 Hudson Street, New York, NY 10014. All rights reserved.

Emil and the Three Twins by Erich Kästner. First published in the United States of America by Franklin Watts in 1961.

"The Case of the Civil War Sword" from *Encyclopedia Brown, Boy Detective* by Donald J. Sobol, illustrated by Leonard Shortall. Copyright © 1963 by Donald J. Sobol. Copyright © renewed 1991 by Donald J. Sobol. Used by permission of Lodestar Books, an affiliate of Dutton Children's Books, A Division of Penguin Young Readers Group, A Member of Penguin Group (USA) Inc., 345 Hudson Street, New York, NY 10014. All rights reserved.

Flat Stanley by Jeff Brown. Text copyright © 1964 by Jeff Brown. Used by permission of HarperCollins Publishers.

Freddy the Detective by Walter R. Brooks, illustrated by Kurt Wiese. Copyright © 1932 by Walter R. Brooks. Copyright © renewed 1960 by Dorothy R. Brooks. All rights reserved. Published by The Overlook Press, New York, NY. www.overlookpress.com

Excerpt from "First Day Finish" from *The Friendly Persuasion* by Jessamyn West. Copyright © 1944 and renewed 1971 by Jessamyn West. Reprinted by permission of Houghton Mifflin Harcourt Publishing Company.

Go, Dog. Go! by P. D. Eastman. Copyright © 1961 by P. D. Eastman. Copyright © renewed 1989 by Mary L. Eastman. "Book Cover" copyright © 1961 and renewed 1989. Used by permission of Random House Children's Books, a division of Random House, Inc.

The Golden Bible for Children edited by Elsa Jane Werner, illustrated by Alice and Martin Provensen. Copyright © 1953 by Random House, Inc. "Book Cover" and "Illustrations" by Alice and Martin Provensen. Used by permission of Golden Books, an imprint of Random House Children's Books, a division of Random House, Inc.

The Golden Book of Science by Bertha Morris Parker. First published in the United States of America by Golden Press, Inc. in 1956.

Goodnight Moon by Margaret Wise Brown, illustrated by Clement Hurd. Copyright © 1947 by Harper & Row. Text copyright © renewed by Roberta Brown Rauch. Illustrations copyright © renewed by Edith T. Hurd, Clement Hurd, John Thacher Hurd, and George Hellyer, as trustees of the Edith and Clement Hurd 1982 Trust. Used by permission of HarperCollins Publishers.

The Hardy Boys: The Shore Road Mystery by Franklin W. Dixon. Copyright © 1928, 1956, 1964, 1992 by Simon & Schuster, Inc. Reprinted with the permission of Simon & Schuster, Inc. Hardy Boys ® is a registered trademark of Simon & Schuster. All rights reserved. The classic editions are published by Grosset & Dunlap Inc., an imprint of Penguin Books for Young Readers.

Harold and the Purple Crayon by Crockett Johnson. Text copyright © 1955 by Crocket Johnson. Copyright © renewed 1983 by Ruth Krauss. Used by permission of HarperCollins Publishers.

Harriet the Spy by Louise Fitzhugh. Copyright © 1964 by Lois Anne Moorehead. Used by permission of Delacorte Press, an imprint of Random House Children's Books, a division of Random House, Inc.

Henry Huggins by Beverly Cleary. Copyright © 1950 and renewed 1978 by Beverly Cleary. Used by permission of HarperCollins Publishers.

The Hobbit by J. R. R. Tolkien. Copyright © 1937 by George Allen & Unwin Ltd. Copyright © 1966 by J. R. R. Tolkien. Copyright © renewed 1994 by Christopher R. Tolkien and Priscilla M. A. R. Tolkien. Copyright © restored 1996 by the Estate of J. R. R. Tolkien; assigned 1997 to the J. R. R. Tolkien Copyright Trust. Reprinted by permission of Houghton Mifflin Harcourt Publishing Company. All rights reserved.

Horton Hatches the Egg by Dr. Seuss. TM and copyright © 1940 and renewed 1968 by Dr. Seuss Enterprises, L. P. Used by permission of Random House Children's Books, a division of Random House, Inc.

Impunity Jane by Rumer Godden. Copyright © 1954 by Rumer Godden. First appeared in *Impunity Jane*, published by Viking Press. Used by permission of Curtis Brown, Ltd.

Johnny Tremain by Esther Forbes. Copyright © 1943 by Esther Forbes Hoskins. Copyright © renewed 1971 by Linwood M. Erskine, Jr., Executor of Estate. Reprinted by permission of Houghton Mifflin Harcourt Publishing Company. All rights reserved.

Just So Stories for Little Children by Rudyard Kipling, first published in the United States of America by Doubleday, Page & Company in 1902.

Kidnapped by Robert Louis Stevenson, illustrated by N. C. Wyeth. First published in the United States of America by Harper & Brothers in 1887. Illustrations copyright © 1913 by Charles Scribner's Sons. Copyright © renewed 1941 by N. C. Wyeth. Reprinted by permission of Atheneum Books for Young Readers, an imprint of Simon & Schuster Children's Publishing Division.

The King, the Mice and the Cheese by Nancy and Eric Gurney. Copyright © 1965 by Nancy Gurney and Eric Gurney. Copyright © renewed 1993 by Charles Lance Gurney, Lassie Anne Gurney-Bauli, and Catherine Lorna Gurney Engler. "Book Cover" copyright © 1965, 1993. Used by permission of Random House Children's Books, a division of Random House, Inc.

The Lion, the Witch and the Wardrobe by C. S. Lewis. Copyright © 1950 by C. S. Lewis Pte. Ltd. Extract reprinted by permission.

The Little Engine That Could by Watty Piper, with new art by Loren Long. Regristration ® and Copyright © 2005 by Penguin Group (USA) Inc. The Little Engine That Could, I Think I Can, and all related titles, logos, and characters are trademarks of Penguin Group (USA) Inc. Used by permission. All rights reserved.

The Little House by Virginia Lee Burton. Copyright © 1942 by Virginia Lee Burton. Copyright © renewed 1969 by Aristides Burton Demetrios and Michael Burton Demetrios. Reprinted by permission of Houghton Mifflin Harcourt Publishing Company. All rights reserved.

Little House in the Big Woods by Laura Ingalls Wilder, illustrated by Garth Williams. Text copyright © 1932, 1960 Little House Heritage Trust. Illustrations copyright © 1953, 1981 by Garth Williams. Cover art by Garth Williams. Cover design copyright © HarperCollins Publishers. Used by permission of HarperCollins Publishers. "Little House"® is a registered trademark of HarperCollins Publishers, Inc.

Little House on the Prairie by Laura Ingalls Wilder, illustrated by Garth Williams. Text copyright © 1935, 1963 Little House Heritage Trust. Pictures copyright © 1953 by Garth Williams. Copyright © renewed 1981 by Garth Williams. Cover art by Garth Williams. Cover design copyright © HarperCollins Publishers. Used by permission of HarperCollins Publishers. "Little House"® is a registered trademark of HarperCollins Publishers, Inc.

The Little Prince by Antoine de Saint-Exupéry. Copyright © 1943 by Harcourt, Inc. Copyright © renewed 1971 by Consuelo de Saint-Exupery. English translation copyright © 2000 by Richard Howard. Illustrations from *Le Petit Prince* by Antoine de Saint-Exupery, copyright © 1943 by Houghton Mifflin Harcourt Publishing Company; copyright © renewed 1971 by Consuelo de Saint-Exupery. Reprinted by permission of Houghton Mifflin Harcourt Publishing Company.

Little Women by Louisa May Alcott. First published in the United States of America by Roberts Brothers in 1868.

Liza Lou and the Yeller Belly Swamp by Mercer Mayer. Copyright © 1976 by Mercer Mayer. Reprinted by permission of Simon & Schuster Books for Young Readers, an imprint of Simon & Schuster Children's Publishing Division.

Madeline by Ludwig Bemelmans. Copyright © 1939 by Ludwig Bemelmans. Copyright © renewed 1967 by Madeleine Bemelmans and Barbara Bemelmans Marciano. Used by permission of Viking Penguin, A Division of Penguin Young Readers Group, A Member of Penguin Group (USA) Inc., 345 Hudson Street, New York, NY 10014.

Maniac Magee by Jerry Spinelli. Copyright © 1990 by Jerry Spinelli. Reprinted by permission of Little, Brown & Company.

Mary Poppins by P. L. Travers, illustrated by Mary Shepard. Text copyright © 1934 and renewed 1962 by P. L. Travers. Illustrations copyright © 1934 and renewed 1962 by Mary Shepard. Reprinted and reproduced by permission of Houghton Mifflin Harcourt Publishing Company.

Mike Mulligan and His Steam Shovel by Virginia Lee Burton. Copyright © 1939 by Virginia Lee Burton. Copyright © renewed 1967 by Aristides Burton Demetrios and Michael Burton Demetrios. Reprinted by permission of Houghton Mifflin Harcourt Publishing Company. All rights reserved.

Miss Nelson is Missing! by Harry Allard, illustrated by James Marshall. Text copyright © 1977 by Harry Allard. Illustrations copyright © 1977 by James Marshall. Reprinted by permission of Houghton Mifflin Company. All rights reserved.

Miss Pickerell Goes to Mars by Ellen MacGregor, illustrated by Paul Galdone. First published in the United States of America by Whittlesey House in 1951.

Mrs. Frisby and the Rats of NIMH by Robert C. O'Brien, illustrated by Zena Bernstein. Text copyright © 1971 by Robert C. O'Brien. Copyright © renewed 1999 by Chistopher Conly, Jame Leslie Conly, Kate Conly, and Sarah Conly. Reprinted by permission of Atheneum Books for Young Readers, an imprint of Simon & Schuster Children's Publishing Division.

My Father's Dragon by Ruth Stiles Gannett. Copyright © 1948 by Random House Inc. "Book Cover" copyright © 1948 by Random House, Inc. Used by permission of Random House Children's Books, a division of Random House, Inc.

My Side of the Mountain by Jean Craighead George. Copyright © 1959. Copyright © renewed 1987 by Jean Craighead George. Used by permission of Dutton Children's Books, A Division of Penguin Young Readers Group, A Member of Penguin Group (USA) Inc., 345 Hudson Street, New York, NY 10014. All rights reserved.

Ox-Cart Man by Donald Hall, illustrated by Barbara Cooney. Text copyright © 1979 by Donald Hall. Illustrations copyright © 1979 by Barbara Cooney Porter. Used by permission of Viking Penguin, A Division of Penguin Young Readers Group, A Member of Penguin Group (USA) Inc., 345 Hudson Street, New York, NY 10014. All rights reserved.

Peter and Wendy by J. M. Barrie, illustrated by F. D. Bedford. First published in the United States of America by Charles Scribner's Sons in 1911. First published in the UK by Hodder & Stoughton, 388 Euston Road, London NW1 3BH.

Pink Ice Cream by Launa Latham. Copyright © 1951 by Launa Latham.

Poppy Ott by Leo Edwards. First published in the United States of America by Grosset & Dunlap in 1927.

Profiles in Courage by John F. Kennedy. Copyright © 1955, 1956, 1961 by John F. Kennedy. Copyright renewed © 1983, 1984, 1989 by Jacqueline Kennedy Onassis. Foreword copyright © 1964 by Robert F. Kennedy. Reprinted by permission of HarperCollins Publishers.

Rabbit Hill by Robert Lawson. Copyright © 1944 by Robert Lawson. Copyright © renewed 1971 by John W. Boyd. Used by permission of Viking Penguin, A Division of Penguin Young Readers Group, A Member of Penguin Group (USA) Inc., 345 Hudson Street, New York, NY 10014. All rights reserved.

The Red Balloon by Albert Lamorisse. Copyright © 1956 by Albert Lamorisse. Used by permission of Doubleday, a division of Random House, Inc. Photos used by permission of the Lamorisse estate.

Rolf in the Woods by Ernest Thompson Seton. First published in the United States of America by Grosset & Dunlap in 1911.

Roller Skates by Ruth Sawyer, illustrated by Valenti Angelo. Copyright © 1936 and renewed 1964 by Ruth Sawyer Durand. Used by permission of Viking Penguin, A Division of Penguin Young Readers Group, A Member of Penguin Group (USA) Inc., 345 Hudson Street, New York, NY 10014. All rights reserved.

Roll of Thunder, Hear My Cry by Mildred D. Taylor. Copyright © 1976 by Mildred D. Taylor. Used by permission of Dial Books for Young Readers, A Division of Penguin Young Readers Group, A Member of Penguin Group (USA) Inc., 345 Hudson Street, New York, NY 10014. All rights reserved.

"Mona went on reading . . ." from *The Saturdays* by Elizabeth Enright. Copyright © 1941 by Elizabeth Enright Gillham. Copyright © 1969 by Robert M. Gillham. Reprinted by arrangement with Henry Holt and Company, LLC.

The Secret Garden by Francis Hodgson Burnett. First published in the United States of America by F. A. Stokes in 1911. Illustrations copyright © 1962 by J. B. Lippincott Company. Illustrations copyright © renewed 1990 by HarperCollins Publishers. Used by permission of HarperCollins Publishers.

Shane by Jack Schaefer, illustrated by John McCormack. Text copyright © 1949 by Jack Schaefer. Copyright © renewed 1976 by Jack Schaefer. Illustrations copyright © 1954 and renewed 1982 by John McCormack. Reprinted by permission of Houghton Mifflin Harcourt Publishing Company. All rights reserved.

The Snowy Day by Erza Jack Keats. Copyright © 1962 by Ezra Jack Keats. Copyright renewed © 1990 by Martin Pope, Executor. Used by permission of Viking Penguin, A Division of Penguin Young Readers Group, A Member of Penguin Group (USA) Inc., 345 Hudson Street, New York, NY 10014. All rights reserved.

The Story of a Fierce Bad Rabbit by Beatrix Potter. Copyright © 1906, 2002 by Frederick Warne & Co. Reproduced by permission of Frederick Warne & Co.

The Story of Mankind by Hendrik Willem Van Loon. First published in the United States of America by Boni and Liveright in 1921.

Strega Nona by Tomie dePaola. Copyright © 1975 by Tomie dePaola. Reprinted by permission of Simon & Schuster Books for Young Readers, an imprint of Simon & Schuster Children's Publishing Division.

Swallows and Amazons by Arthur Ransome. First published in the United States of America by J. B. Lippincott Co. in 1931. Published in the UK by Jonathan Cape. Reprinted by permission of The Random House Group Ltd.

The Tailor of Gloucester by Beatrix Potter. Copyright © 1903, 2002 by Frederick Warne & Co. Reproduced by permission of Frederick Warne & Co.

The Tale of Squirrel Nutkin by Beatrix Potter. Copyright © 1903, 2002 by Frederick Warne & Co. Reproduced by permission of Frederick Warne & Co.

Tales from Grimm by Wanda Gág. Used by permission of University of Minnesota Press.

The Time Machine by H.G. Wells. First published in the United States of America by H. Holt and Company in 1895.

To Kill a Mockingbird by Harper Lee. Copyright © 1960 and renewed 1988 by Harper Lee. Foreword copyright © 1993 by Harper Lee. Reprinted by permission of HarperCollins Publishers.

Tom Swift and His Giant Robot by Victor Appleton II. Copyright © 1954 by Simon and Schuster, Inc. Reprinted with permission of Simon & Schuster. Tom Swift ® is a registered trademark of Simon & Schuster, Inc. All rights reserved. The classic editions are published by Grosset & Dunlap Inc., an imprint of Penguin Books for Young Readers.

The Travels of Babar by Jean de Brunhoff. Copyright © 1934 by Random House, Inc. Copyright renewed © 1962 by Random House, Inc. Reprinted by permission of Hachette Jeunesse.

Treasure Island by Robert Louis Stevenson, illustrated by N. C. Wyeth. First published in the United States of America by Cassell in 1883. Copyright © 1911 by Simon & Schuster, Inc. Copyright © renewed 1939 by N. C. Wyeth. Reprinted by permission of Atheneum Books for Young Readers, an imprint of Simon & Schuster Children's Publishing Division.

The Twenty-One Balloons by William Pène du Bois. Copyright © 1947 and renewed 1975 by William Pène du Bois. Used by permission of Viking Penguin, A Division of Penguin Young Readers Group, A Member of Penguin Group (USA) Inc., 345 Hudson Street, New York, NY 10014. All rights reserved.

Twenty Thousand Leagues Under the Sea by Jules Verne. First published in English by Douglas & Meyers in 1874.

Waiting to Waltz by Cynthia Rylant, illustrated by Stephen Gammell. Text copyright © 1984 by Cynthia Rylant. Illustrations copyright © 1984 by Stephen Gammell. Reprinted by permission of Atheneum Books for Young Readers, an imprint of Simon & Schuster Children's Publishing Division.

Where the Wild Things Are by Maurice Sendak. Copyright © 1963 by Maurice Sendak. Used by permission of Maurice Sendak and HarperCollins Publishers.

Wild Animals I Have Known by Ernest Thompson Seton. First published in the United States of America by Charles Scribner's Sons in 1898.

The Wind in the Willows by Kenneth Grahame, illustrated by Ernest H. Shepard. Copyright © 1933 by Charles Scribner's Sons. Copyright © renewed 1961 by Ernest H. Shepard. Jacket illustration copyright © 1960 by Ernest H. Shepard. Reprinted by permission of Atheneum Books for Young Readers, an imprint of Simon & Schuster Children's Publishing Division.

The Wonderful Wizard of Oz by L. Frank Baum, illustrated by W. W. Denslow. First published in the United States of America by the George M. Hill Company in 1900.

The Wolfling by Sterling North, illustrated by John Schoenherr. Illustrations copyright © 1969 by E. P. Dutton & Co., Inc. Used by permission of Dutton Children's Books, A Division of Penguin Young Readers Group, A Member of Penguin Group (USA) Inc., 345 Hudson Street, New York, NY 10014.

Excerpt from "Mrs. Who" from *A Wrinkle in Time* by Madeleine L'Engle. Jacket design copyright © by Ellen Raskin. Text copyright © 1962, renewed 1990 by Madeleine L'Engle Franklin. Reprinted by permission of Farrar, Straus and Giroux, LLC.

The Yearling by Marjorie Kinnan Rawlings, illustrated by N. C. Wyeth. Text copyright © 1928 by Marjorie Kinnan Rawlings; copyright © renewed 1966 by Nora Baskin. Illustrations © copyright 1939 by Charles Scribner's Sons; copyright © renewed 1967 by Charles Scribner's Sons.